AFTER NATURE'S REVOLT

Eco-Justice and Theology

Dieter T. Hessel, Editor

Wipf and Stock Publishers
EUGENE, OREGON

Wipf and Stock Publishers
199 West 8th Avenue, Suite 3
Eugene, Oregon 97401

After Nature's Revolt
Eco-Justice and Theology
By Hessel, Dieter T.
Copyright© January, 1992 Augsburg Fortress
ISBN: 1-59244-205-6
Publication date: March, 2003 .
Previously published by Augsburg Fortress, January, 1992 .

To people throughout society who have been doing eco-
justice despite the church, and to theological forerunners
who have led the church to confess:
  In sovereign love God created the world good
    and makes everyone equally in God's image . . .
  But we violate the image of God in others and ourselves,
    accept lies as truth,
    exploit neighbor and nature,
    and threaten death to the planet entrusted to our
    care. . . .
Yet God acts with justice and mercy to redeem creation.

From "A Brief Statement of Faith,"
Book of Confessions,
Presbyterian Church (U.S.A.), 1991.

CONTENTS

PART TWO: Issues for an Eco-Justice Ethic

CONTRIBUTORS

John B. Cobb, Jr. is Director of the Center for Process Studies in Claremont, CA. Recently he retired as Ingraham Professor of Theology at the School of Theology at Claremont and as Avery Professor of Religion at the Claremont Graduate School. His books include *Is It Too Late? A Theology of Ecology* (Bruce Books, 1972), (with Charles Birch) *The Liberation of Life* (Cambridge Univ. Press, 1981), and (with Herman Daly) *For the Common Good: Redirecting the Economy toward Community, the Environment, and a Sustainable Future* (Beacon, 1989).

William E. Gibson founded and is now a consultant to the Eco-Justice Project, Center for Religion, Ethics and Social Policy, Cornell University, and is Senior Editor of the quarterly journal *The Egg*. He has written extensively about eco-justice ethics and life-style change.

Heidi Hadsell is Associate Professor of Social Ethics at McCormick Theological Seminary. One of her major areas of interest is the complex set of ethical issues embedded between North and South. Dr. Hadsell has spent a number of years living and working in Brazil and France.

Dieter T. Hessel is a social ethicist and educator who served for twenty-five years on the national staff of the Presbyterian Church (U.S.A.), most recently as Director of Social Witness Policy. Currently Dr. Hessel is a resident member of the Center of Theological Inquiry, Princeton, N.J. His earlier books pertaining to environmental concerns include *For

Creation's Sake: Preaching, Ecology, and Justice (Westminster, 1985) and *Energy Ethics: A Christian Response* (Friendship Press, 1979). He is also Editor of *The Egg: An Eco-Justice Quarterly.*

Philip Hefner is Professor of Systematic Theology at Lutheran School of Theology at Chicago. He also serves as Director of the Chicago Center for Religion and Science and Editor-in-Chief of *Zygon: Journal of Religion and Science.*

Carol Johnston is a Presbyterian minister and Evaluation Coordinator for the Lilly Endowment, Religion Division. Having served as a Visiting Scholar with the Presbyterian Committee on Social Witness Policy, she is completing a Ph.D. dissertation in theology at Claremont Graduate School.

George H. Kehm is James Henry Snowden Professor of Systematic Theology, Pittsburgh Theological Seminary. An interpreter of Wolfhart Pannenberg's work to American audiences, Kehm translated the two volumes of Pannenberg's *Basic Questions in Theology* (Fortress Press, 1970–72). Following many years of personal involvement in environmental organizations, he served on the drafting committee for "A Brief Statement of Faith" (PCUSA) and recently helped form an interdisciplinary study team on the Bible and environmental theology.

Larry Rasmussen is Reinhold Niebuhr Professor of Social Ethics, Union Theological Seminary, N.Y., and has written numerous articles on environmental ethics. He is author of *Dietrich Bonhoeffer: His Significance for North Americans* (Fortress Press, 1990) and coauthor of *Bible and Ethics in the Christian Life* (Augsburg, rev. ed., 1989).

Holmes Rolston III is Professor of Philosophy at Colorado State University, Fort Collins. He is author of *Environmental Ethics: Duties to and Values in the Natural World* (Temple University Press, 1988) and *Philosophy Gone Wild* (Prometheus, 1986). He is also Associate Editor of the journal *Environmental Ethics.*

H. Paul Santmire is pastor at Grace Lutheran Church, Hartford, Conn. He is author of *The Travail of Nature: The Ambiguous Ecological Promise of Christian Theology* (Fortress, 1985) and *Brother Earth: Nature, God and Ecology in a Time of Crisis* (Thomas Nelson, 1970).

George E. Tinker, an Osage/Cherokee, is Assistant Professor of Cross-Cultural Ministries, Iliff School of Theology, Denver. He is completing a volume offering a critical perspective on Native American missions.

Introduction

ECO-JUSTICE THEOLOGY AFTER NATURE'S REVOLT

Dieter T. Hessel

> *If human beings insist upon pressing nature beyond its capacities to produce; if human societies value standards of living more grandiose than their natural habitat can consistently sustain; if for the sake of its own (short-term) survival the human species is ready to 'sacrifice' other species and ecological systems on which its (long-range) survival is dependent, then, surely, one can expect nature to respond to these inordinate demands in a manner suggestive of a rebellion.*
>
> Douglas John Hall,
> *Thinking the Faith*

> *The immediate danger is not* possible *nuclear war, but* actual *industrial plundering. . . . Our real threat is from the retaliatory powers of the abused earth, not from other nations.*
>
> Thomas Berry,
> "Economics: Effect on the Life Systems of the World"

*M*odern humanity almost forgot that nature has limits; the natural world is not infinitely resilient. Human activity in just a half century has altered vital functions of the global biosphere. Today, there is growing scientific and social awareness of the real danger that the life-supporting capacities of our planet will be crippled in the near future, unless industrial, technocratic civilization changes behavior to get along with nature. Inappropriate human enterprise has destabilized or degraded natural systems at an increasing rate, resulting in destruction of ecosystems and a startling loss of species—already one plant or animal species is lost daily. By the year 2000, scores of species could disappear daily.[1]

1

In reaction to extreme stress, nature has begun a silent but effective revolt—withdrawing its awesome, vital diversity while lashing back to protest human insults. Humanity now has the power to defeat God's rainbow covenant intention to preserve "you and every living creature that is with you, for all further generations" (Gen. 9:12). A rapidly growing "earth deficit"[2] leaves twenty-first-century humanity with no guarantees that "While the earth remains, seedtime and harvest, cold and heat, summer and winter, day and night, shall not cease" (Gen. 8:22). The earth, increasingly damaged by human abuse, may fail to deliver needed sustenance through natural processes that until recently seemed ever renewable, never spent.

> The most elementary of givens, taken for granted as the background of all acting and never requiring action itself—that there are [humans], that there is life, that there is a world for both—this suddenly stands forth, as if lit up by lightening, in its stark peril through human deed. In this very light the new responsibility appears. Born of danger, its first urging is necessarily an ethics of preservation and prevention, not of progress and perfection.[3]

In this very light it is evident that the earth community urgently requires eco-responsible human activity.

This book focuses on the response of Christian faith to the environmental challenges that confront people in every locale and the planet as a whole. What are the claims of the Creator-Deliverer, and of other creatures, on human society? What are the implications of emerging ecological-social peril for Christian theology, church life and mission, public policy, and economic practice? Recognizing the seriousness of nature's plight under human assault and the ominous signs of ecosystem rebellion against massive abuse, human beings and organizations are called to think and act in ways that make peace with the earth.

The contributors to this book share three assumptions. First, the world faces unprecedented environmental peril that will have profound ecological and social effects. Second, this situation exposes major problems in the (Western) Christian tradition and stimulates theological-ethical rethinking to meet the future. Third, the church has a special mission and responsibility for eco-justice in these times.

The second of these three assumptions was the focus of the papers that became chapters in this book. Regarding the first assumption, the contributors to *After Nature's Revolt* were asked not to repeat information already widely available about the contemporary environmental peril. Rather, this editor's introduction summarizes the environmental situation, with special attention to root causes.

This introduction also indicates the rich biblical resources for theological reflection on the perennial problem of eco-injustice. Several of the following chapters—particularly those by George Kehm, Holmes Rolston, George Tinker, and Carol Johnston—dig deeply into selected biblical texts to articulate a fresh theology of creation and redemption that is responsive to nature's plight, quite in contrast to a nature-negating Protestant tradition.

Recognizing the distinctly modern shape of the eco-justice crisis, this introduction also notes some of the problems in Christian theological tradition and modern philosophy that require careful attention in a serious theological-ethical response. Chapters in this book by John Cobb, Larry Rasmussen, H. Paul Santmire, Heidi Hadsell, Bill Gibson, and Philip Hefner explore facets of a positive correction to modern Christianity's tolerance of poverty and its indifference toward nature. The introduction closes by identifying emphases needed in church life and mission to restore creation for ecology and justice.

PROFILE OF ENVIRONMENTAL PERIL

In recent years, the world has been alerted to such environmental dangers as a thinning layer of ozone, global warming due to a greenhouse effect in the upper atmosphere, and population growth rapidly approaching 5.5 billion persons—a quarter of whom live in abject poverty.[4] We have learned about acid rain ruining forests and lakes, massive pollution of land and water from toxic technologies including weapons of war, and ominous radiation fallout from nuclear power plant accidents. Technological prowess at the service of economic enterprise and nationalist ambition has advanced to the point that environmentally degrading human activity can cripple any region's capacity for life support and intensify various kinds of natural calamities. Some of the more tragic consequences include species extinction, ruined fisheries and wild places, devastating floods, altered climate, and rapid erosion and desertification.

Regarding the latter consequence, take a good look at the vast areas of human-induced desertification that appear on current maps of the five most-inhabited continents (for example, in the *National Geographic Atlas of the World,* sixth edition). And consider what may lie ahead for areas that have been inappropriately developed. In its early stages, "desertification can be *un*recognized by most people. For instance, overgrazing has ruined much of the grasslands of the Western United States.

Nonetheless the average citizen of, say Albuquerque, New Mexico, does not realize that he or she lives in an area desertified by human action—that the upper Rio Grande Valley was once a rich grassland."[5]

1. An especially ominous aspect of environmental peril world-wide is the rapid degradation of *renewable resources*—particularly croplands and grazing lands, forests and fisheries. These provide sustenance and have regenerative power when cared for with ecological wisdom. But inappropriate use can destroy their renewable character.

Consider the startling pattern of deforestation on every continent to obtain "cheap" lumber. This is due in part to greater demand for housing and fuel as population grows. Thus Nepal is deforested, and Bangladesh experiences worse floods. To take a Western hemisphere example, the state of Rondonia in western Brazil doubled its population in the 1980s while destroying a fifth of its rain forest. A national development program invited corporate logging and then encouraged poor Brazilians to settle and farm the deforested land, which is now exhausted.

The illustration shows that population growth is *not* the primary but a reinforcing cause of ecosystem degradation. Most of the world's tree loss and related land devastation can be traced to unnecessary consumption by affluent people and "efficient" but unecological techniques used by economically powerful entities to extract (rapidly deplete) both renewable and nonrenewable resources. Ordinary folks, including many desperate poor people, certainly do participate in denuding forest land or over-grazing grassland near settlements, but rich corporations and government allies are the far-reaching, large-scale destroyers of rain forests (in the Amazon, Indonesia, or in the United States' Northwest). Preservation of these forests is crucial to reducing the threat of a disastrous greenhouse effect.

A similar mixture of demand and greed combined with inappropriate technology undermines land stewardship, as soil erosion and toxic pesticide runoff result from industrialized, "green revolution" agriculture that depends on heavy machinery and dangerous chemicals. Soil eroding at a faster rate than can be replaced by natural processes affects one-third of U.S. cropland. Other continents are experiencing similar difficulties. Thus, denuded hills and inappropriate farming methods have diminished the ability of African societies to feed themselves.

I recall a walking tour with Wes Jackson at the Land Institute, Salina, Kansas, where the objective is to run agriculture and culture on sunlight with due respect for the local ecosystem. The "Land" experiments with the development of herbaceous perennial seed-producing polycultures to displace annual monocultures that depend on expensive, oil-powered machines, nitrogen fertilizer, and chemical pesticides. After passing experimental plots of land we came to a desolate section where, Jackson observed, land regeneration is not possible in the near future, due to severe ecological damage before the Land Institute located there. "Beware of romantic vitalism," said Jackson; ecology defines the limits of regenerative agriculture or forestry.

2. Depletion of *nonrenewable resources*, particularly minerals, is one of the most obvious patterns of recent human enterprise. Industry depends on iron, copper, aluminum, tin, and so on. But the higher-quality deposits of these nonfuel minerals have been exhausted. Use of lower quality ores requires more energy for mining and refining. And the preferred energy source is getting scarce too.

Oil was this century's most prominent fuel mineral, shaping what energy analyst Daniel Yergin calls Hydrocarbon Society.[6] Oil has been the energy source of economic power and a major cause of war. Struggles over access to oil and the actual processes of extracting and transporting this nonrenewable resource have done much violence to people and nature. And those who would control and deplete oil tended to seek stability without justice. Similarly, George Bush, representing "Hydrocarbon Man," first as an oil entrepreneur drilling off-shore wells on the coast of Texas and in the Persian Gulf, and years later as president of the United States leading the war against Iraq over Kuwait, has brought the oil century to culmination with a bang.

Seventy percent of the world's oil reserves are in the Persian Gulf. Today there is "no large inventory of diversified, non-OPEC oil waiting to come into the system, as had been the case with Alaska, Mexico, and the North Sea" two decades ago.[7] In the meantime, serious conservation strategies coupled with sustainable, renewable energy systems have been pursued half-heartedly. Approximately 25 percent energy efficiency has been achieved in U.S. industry and transportation over the last twenty years. That figure could have been doubled with relatively little inconvenience. But U.S. government planning favors more domestic fossil fuel output. An early 1991 newspaper headline said it all: "Conservatives Oppose Conservation Plan."

3. Contamination of waterways and groundwater is another focus of environmental concern. *Water quality* declines as rivers, lakes, and ocean zones are contaminated by industrial discharges, municipal sewage, and agricultural and urban runoff. Aquatic life is threatened by estuary pollution. Toxic landfills and pesticide residues leach into groundwater. Drinking water becomes unsafe, affecting the health of human populations. In poorer countries with fewer pollution controls,

millions of people, mostly children, die each year from diseases bred in or spread by water. Preservation of clean water and restoration of water quality depend on education, regulation, and ecologically sensitive environmental incentives.

4. Each year, Americans produce about 230 million tons of garbage— more than five pounds per person per day. This per capita amount of *solid waste* is twice that of France or former West Germany, and more than China produces with four times as many people. There is growing citizen participation in efforts to recycle waste and some initiative by producers and consumers to reduce the quantity of wasteful products and packaging. There is widespread public concern about the toxic effects of leaking landfills and the health risk of incinerator fumes and ash. But there is only modest movement as yet to tackle solid waste at its source by substituting products that are more durable, repairable, less resource-intensive or toxic—by producing and reusing earth-friendly products.[8]

5. Industrial and agricultural uses of chemicals have resulted in phenomenal growth of *hazardous wastes*. The problem has several aspects: "inadequate safety precautions for workers, accidental releases from chemical plants, improper and illegal disposal of wastes, excessive use of toxic products or use without adequate protective gear (as is often the case with farm workers), pesticide residues on fruits and vegetables, and the export to developing countries of pesticides (e.g., DDT) considered too dangerous to use in the U.S."[9]

In the United States and many other "developed" countries there are thousands of active and abandoned disposal sites that demand costly cleanup. When radioactive waste sites are added to the picture of poorly managed chemical wastes, we begin to discern how urgent and extensive is the need to abandon hazardous waste-producing technologies and to "clean up" earlier misdevelopment by careful processing, as well as safer storage and disposition, of hazardous wastes.

6. In one century, the number of people alive on earth has tripled. *Population growth* is an urgent concern, since the earth's population already exceeds five billion and will reach six billion by the year 2000. Ninety percent of the increase is occurring in countries with predominantly poor people. Poor societies lack adequate nutrition, maternal and child health services, fertility-control programs, and economic opportunity. Millions of the world's poor have already become environmental refugees.

The population problem can be clarified by identifying how many people are using how many resources how fast. Affluent people in rich countries use many more nonrenewable resources, eat higher on the food chain, and generate far more solid and hazardous waste. Still, the rapid growth of poor-country populations puts severe pressure on regional habitats and reduces chances for humane survival. There is an urgent need to stabilize population through enhanced access to education, health care, family planning services, and employment.

7. There is another concern besides the number of people using what resources how fast—namely, what other animals require. If human population doubles as projected in the next forty years, what *other creatures, wild and domestic,* will the planet also carry? This question focuses most poignantly on the fate of the more sentient creatures, particularly higher land and marine mammals. But many other species of animal and plant life are also threatened. Failure to preserve the diversity of interdependent beings is ecocidal. The science of ecology studies "organisms 'at home' [the Greek root is *oikos*], with everything that affects them there."[10] Ecologists focus on the healthy functioning of the biotic community in its inorganic setting. From a biocentric point of view, the human species threatens the habitats and existence of other animals as well as many plants. Continuing human destruction of wildlife and wild places drastically impairs the vital diversity of creation itself.

See chapter 7 by Holmes Rolston for a fuller explication of human threats to and responsibility for the well-being of wildlife. His reflections complement John Cobb's emphasis on human responsibility for the well-being of domesticated animals. Both regard other forms of life as having intrinsic value, transcending their instrumental value to humans. Other contributors to this volume, such as H. Paul Santmire, George Tinker, Carol Johnston, and Philip Hefner, are also quite alert to the ecologically disastrous impact of anthropocentrism, that is, the self-centered attitude that only human well-being and interests really matter.

New developments in *biotechnology* expose a sharp contrast between caring for biodiversity within natural constraints on the one hand, and manipulating genetics to further dominate nature on the other. Genetic engineering promises crops that need little water, less toxic control of pests, and genetic therapy to combat some diseases. But a biotechnological ability "to snip, insert, stitch, edit, program and produce new combinations of living things" has ominous implications for biological and chemical weaponry, animal patenting, and human manipulation.[11] Biotechnology applied to agriculture and health care in a "free market" is likely to widen the agricultural gap between rich and poor.

8. Environmentally inappropriate human economic activity has effects that are world-wide, although they are most noticeable in a given

bioregion.[12] Earth's *atmospheric mantle* is being destabilized by the production of heat-trapping greenhouse gases—carbon dioxide, nitrous oxide, and methane—that lead to *global warming;* and by the release of other gases such as chlorofluorocarbons or CFCs ("chemical wonders, atmospheric villains") that destroy the *ozone shield.* The latter came into dramatic focus with the discovery barely a decade ago of an enlarged hole in the ozone over Antarctica. Depletion of the upper-atmosphere ozone shield is occurring at both poles and temperate zones even faster than had been forecast, intensifying ultraviolet radiation with such inevitable consequences as: more skin cancer, immune-system impairment, and degradation of aquatic systems as plankton deteriorates.

If ozone depletion is no longer a matter for speculation, the pace and effects of global warming are still being debated. The issue among thoughtful scientists is not whether it will happen, but how rapidly temperatures will rise and with what results. Climatic warming due to the greenhouse effect could eliminate entire ecosystems as temperate zones migrate poleward, intensifying the desperation of poor countries nearer the tropics. A reasoned projection and faithful response to the ominous challenge of global warming is the subject of William E. Gibson's chapter, which begins Part Two of this volume.

PROSPECTS FOR HUMAN RESPONSE

This brief overview shows that the milieu of life, the natural setting for creaturely existence, is under great stress as a whole. The environment being threatened is more than the sum of numerous degraded places; it is the dynamic community of living and nonliving entities, an eco-social system of diverse bioregions where plants, animals, and humans interact. The above profile reveals that human beings and cultures are inseparable parts of the environment in crisis. The whole community of earth's living and nonliving entities, which Christian theology views as God's creation, is imperiled by the recent and projected activity of human creatures assaulting the environment.

The pattern of environmental peril summarized above is cumulative. It developed over time but with accelerating pace in the later decades of the twentieth century, as human population and resource extraction grew exponentially. Yet, even as the peril grew, so did the science of ecology and biosphere-modeling that enables humans to see the relationships between environmental degradation and social misdevelopment, as well as necessary limits to growth. Today there is more awareness on every continent of global environmental problems as well as severely degraded locales, and there are many grassroots initiatives as well as some corporate policy changes to restore creation for ecology and justice. Try as political leaders may to postpone corrective action, they can no longer ignore the need to preserve ecological health while fostering more appropriate and sustainable economic development.[13]

The twentieth anniversary of Earth Day in spring 1990 stimulated another surge of journalistic attention to environmental problems and coincided with the publication of numerous tracts that specify what can be done by concerned citizens and governments to protect the environment or to "save" the earth. Business quickly got on board with cosmetic and real efforts to reduce pollution and become environmentally "safe." Meanwhile, the ecumenical Christian community, with slow but growing appreciation for the connection between oppressing people and brutalizing nature, covenanted at Seoul, Korea, to seek justice, peace, and the integrity of creation (see chap. 8, n.1).

At the beginning of chapter 3 in this volume, H. Paul Santmire wonders how much difference this new wave of environmental consciousness will make. Common, secular discourse at least reflects a minimal consensus that humans must learn, or relearn, how to get along with nature—if for no other reason than to preserve an ecological base of life-support for teeming humanity. But the faith community has better reasons, since believers are called to do more than worry about species self-preservation. Religion, by definition concerned with binding reality, should foster positive respect for creation and strengthen the links between environmental preservation and social justice. Christians especially ought to discern that the cry of the environment is a crisis of creation, and that the future of all "createds" (see chap. 8) depends on human beings showing love and doing justice to earth and people.

For we confront a dual crisis: degradation of the natural environment and impoverishment of low-power people, particularly in the two-thirds world. The faithful response is to attend to eco-justice—ecological integrity and social equity together. Eco-justice refers to constructive human responses that concentrate on the link between ecological health and economic justice. The common goal of such careful efforts to engage the world crisis of ecology and justice is to restore earth community or to secure "the well-being of all humankind on a thriving earth."[14] *Eco-justice* occurs wherever human beings receive sufficient sustenance and build enough community to live harmoniously with God, each other, and all of nature, while they appreciate the rest of creation for its own sake and not simply as useful to humanity.

Recognizing that all createds share great vulnerability and are now more interdependent than ever, who will help deliver them and us from oppression? So far, the churches have offered social services and advocated economic justice while doing little for ecological integrity. Meanwhile, secular environmental groups have fostered "positive ecology" without attending to social justice.[15] Popular action and social policy to meet the environmental crisis have yet to focus on engendering ecology and justice together.

A social agenda of eco-justice extends the emerging ecumenical ethic of just peace to include making peace with the earth. It seeks both human rights and "rights of nature."[16] Such an earth-community focus for theological reflection and social practice is guaranteed to bring communities of faith into direct, lively encounter with their own and others' traditions while wrestling with crucial problems facing persons and the planet.

This is an urgent responsibility now as humanity, having nearly exhausted the earth by implementing mistaken notions of economic and social progress, must relearn how to respect all createds in each place. If the international community is to experience a genuine "turnaround decade"[17] to meet growing environmental peril and a widening rich-poor gap, the church and other social institutions must (a) repent of nature domination as well as injustice to human creatures, (b) comprehend why and how to do "eco-justice," and (c) engender this way of responding throughout society.

READING THE BIBLE WITH NEW ECO-SENSITIVE EYES

There are both ancient and modern reasons why humanity has failed to do justice to God's creation by caring for ecology and equity together. The ancient barrier to eco-justice is carelessness, greed, ignorance, and oppression. Jewish and Christian Scriptures illumine this perennial aspect of human disregard for environmental health. In the language of Gen. 2:15, human creatures of the earth, though charged with "keeping" the creation, have failed to "till" the planetary garden with care and to distribute fairly the fruits of tilling. This is the major cause of many local environmental disasters, past and present. People in positions of economic and political power had and still have an alarming tendency to abuse the common environment for selfish gain and to consign native or poor people to wasted eco-systems.

In the biblical story, the age-old pattern of carelessness, greed, ignorance, and oppression is juxtaposed with worshipful praise of the

Creator and a covenant ethic of loving justice toward all creatures including people (particularly the poor and dependent). Numerous passages affirm the intrinsic value of all creatures in their natural settings as God's good creation. Biblical theology emphasizes that God loves and cares for the whole creation (Ps. 145:5, 16) and intends harmonious earth community. God breathes spirit into earth (Gen. 1:1-2), signifies covenant with earth in the rainbow (Gen. 9:13), and makes it perennially productive (Mark 4:28).

Despite deep appreciation of nature and reverential descriptions (in Genesis, in Psalm 104, and in Jesus' Sermon on the Mount) of God's loving work as Creator and tender of all earth creatures; despite Job's awe when confronting the tangible, transcendent presence of God in the wild; and despite Isaiah's hopeful vision of shalom, which includes a restored creation, Hebrew history is a long story of land coveting and defilement.

Some examples of biblical eco-injustice are the tale of Naboth's vineyard (1 Kings 21), Solomon's order to cut down the beloved cedars of Lebanon to aggrandize Jerusalem (1 Kings 5:6-11; Ps. 104:16), and the people's lament at being powerless tenant farmers after the return from exile (Neh. 5:3-5). The eighth-century prophets, especially Hosea (4:1-3) and Jeremiah (9:4-11), warn that social injustice produces environmental disaster, with severe effects on human society and on wild animals, birds, and fish.

The alternative, portrayed in Psalm 104, is for the human community to adore God as Creator and tender of all earth creatures and places. In response to this God, humanity has the function of caring deputy, applying to stewardship of nature the standards of just kingship depicted for ancient Israel itself (in Ps. 72:1-3, 16).[18]

Covenant theology and statutes expect eco-justice to be done. Exodus 23, Leviticus 19 and 25, plus Deuteronomy 15 emphasize the religious obligation of faithful people to give animals sabbath rest and to let the land lie fallow at least once every seven years. This *sabbath ethic* reflects the implicit ecological wisdom of herding tribes and the primitive agrarian know-how of social life close to the land.[19] Covenant law fosters an ethic of environmental care with social justice. Moral responsibility toward land and beasts is coupled with social justice toward the poor, through debt relief, provisions for gleaning, and equitable redistribution of land (slaves and women, however, are accorded no rights!).

In sharp contrast to modern church and culture, biblical thought poses no either/or choice between caring for people and caring for the earth. Covenant theology emphasizes that the way people treat the land is as important a sign of faithfulness as is the way they treat each other. The earth is the Lord's. Therefore, land, rather than being a commodity traded for personal gain, becomes a community trust with appropriate landmarks (Deut. 19:14) to be apportioned equitably (Ezek. 47:13— 48:29) and to be restored to productive harmony (Hos. 2:21f.).[20]

Both testaments yearn for a harmonious community of life and affirm the divine intention to redeem all creatures as well as the natural habitat. Poetic Isaiah of the exile envisions a future of shalom in which all nature rejoices and cooperates: ". . . the mountains and hills before you shall break forth into singing and all the trees of the field shall clap their hands" (Isa. 55:12); ". . . they shall plant vineyards and eat their fruit . . . they shall not plant and another eat. . . . The wolf and the lamb shall feed together, and lion shall eat straw like the ox . . ." (Isa. 65:21, 22, 25). Though this idealized picture of the near future describes animal behavior in anthropomorphic terms, it expresses deep eschatological hope for the reconciliation of all beings.

At the end of the New Testament vivid images of apocalypse, which dispensationalist preachers have often interpreted wrongly in world-negating ways, actually include a positive valuation of nature. For example, Rev. 4:11 praises the Creator and 22:2 portrays the new Jerusalem as a magnificent city with restored garden.

These passages speak quite clearly to perennial, ancient patterns of eco-injustice caused by carelessness, greed, ignorance, and oppression. That old problem is also contemporary, requiring that we share in the eco-justice struggle against powerful people, corporations, and governments who use the earth community as a mere mine and sink, abusing ecosystems for short-term gain and exposing low-power groups of people as well as defenseless creatures and places to toxic waste.

My quick tour of Scripture sets the stage for richer interpretations of particular passages in the chapters that follow. It also underscores the need to revise the agenda for theology and mission, to give more coherent emphasis to joyful praise of God's wisdom and glory in creation, coupled with visionary stewardship that is trifocal—attending *to the view from below,* the view from *abroad,* and the view from *nature.* In response to the Creator-Deliverer, we are called to appreciate the goodness and interdependence of all created beings, human and nonhuman, to discern the intricacies of creation known through natural sciences, to appropriate the life-affirming wisdom of cultures that have been or are better at getting along with nature, and to join in the work of protecting and restoring earth's ecosystems while showing loving justice toward all creatures.

In the meantime, however, humans and other creatures experience world disharmony and disrespect. In the face of pervasive environmental challenges, the church must discern and grapple with earth-destroying ideologies, institutions, and ways of living—what the New Testament epistles call "principalities and powers"—that have put the earth community in such peril. Over against these idolatries, an authentic church will reassert the creation-reconciling purpose and work of Jesus Christ. Who is Jesus Christ today for us who face the eco-justice crisis? Several chapters in this book, particularly chapters 2, 3, 5, and 10, explore the question in depth. They give new meanings to Jesus' passion and to familiar passages such as Paul's declaration that "God was in Christ, reconciling the world unto God's self"; and that meanwhile the "creation groans in travail," waiting for redemption (Rom. 8:22). Contributors to this book also help us to think in earthier terms about the resurrection Paul pictures in 1 Cor. 15:28-49. Easter preaching, which coincides seasonally with nature's rebirth, has to do with profound reality—a transformed integration of matter and spirit.

The Fourth Gospel proclaims God's love for the world, asserting that God's son is the earth's logos (John 1:1-10) and savior of the cosmos (John 3:17). In the Deutero-Pauline epistles Jesus the Christ is viewed as the first-born of all creation, the reconciler of all being, in whom all things hold together (Col. 1:15-20). (Regarding the cosmic Christology of Colossians 1, see the chapters by Santmire and Hefner.)

In light of such passages of Scripture, an important theological task of the church today is to recover authentic biblical appreciation of nature as active participant in human community and humans as caring creatures of the earth. It is equally important to rediscover the Bible's prophetic, apostolic yearning to restore ecology while doing justice. Several contributors, particularly Kehm, Rolston, Tinker, and Johnston, demonstrate how positive a resource both testaments can be for a wholistic theology of creation and redemption.

Building on this affirmative and comprehensive understanding of God as Creator-Deliverer, contributors Rasmussen, Hadsell, Cobb, and Gibson go on to explicate a Christian ethic of ecological and social justice. But to interpret Scripture and do theological work with eco-justice eyes—sensitized to both social injustice and ecological peril—has not yet become the church's habit. The church still is preoccupied with individual human salvation that ignores earth community; it has become indifferent to widespread use of disruptive technologies that treat nature mechanistically; and it remains acculturated to market economics that promise "progress" even as they disregard earth keeping.

The contributors to this book do not view the Bible itself as responsible for part of the eco-justice crisis, as Thomas Berry asserts. We view the Bible, read with eco-sensitive eyes, as a promising resource for faith that would meet the future. But we are quite aware of the problematic character of Western Christianity, which has collaborated with modern culture to devalue nature and to ignore environmental responsibility, despite strong biblical mandates to serve ecological integrity while doing social justice. To overcome this problem, Cobb, Rasmussen, Santmire, Rolston, Tinker, Hefner, and Johnston, point to a postmodern, nondualistic way of viewing God's relation to the world—not as spirit apart from matter but as spirit of matter, breath of all life, or presence throughout nature. In so doing they do not rely on Scripture alone. They also rely on aboriginal wisdom and contemporary physical and social sciences to give fresh insight into life processes and world history. They show how a relevant theology of creation and redemption can incorporate new understandings of reality that affirm human creatureliness, instead of repeating a nature-negating gospel. The contributors to this book share some degree of confidence that over time both church and society will get the point.

DEALING WITH MODERN IDOLATRY

Environmental degradation coupled with social injustice is as old as human sin. But human activity in the twentieth century has added some important new dimensions to this old story. Environmental abuse is now occurring in greater quantity on a much larger scale, and violence to ecosystems and created beings who depend on them is increasingly toxic in its potential or actual effects. The Valdez and Gulf War oil spills, Three-Mile Island and Chernobyl, Rocky Flats and Hanover, Love Canal and Times Beach, the Amazon and all those poisoned sites left in Eastern Europe after communism—these represent the twentieth-century emergence of larger scale and increasingly toxic eco-injustices that threaten whole bioregions, human communities, and the earth itself.

Pride of mastery and fascination with technological prowess have become partner with economic greed and ecological carelessness in "peaceful" high-tech activity and military weaponry. This was most noticeable in risky efforts to harness the atom for national defense and development. Capitalist and socialist societies alike were blind to the long-term hazardous effects of using plutonium in nuclear weapons making and were quite stunned by power plant accidents.

This exposes the distinctly *modern* character of the global ecology and justice crisis. Large-scale perils to the earth expose a striking irony, namely, the unexpected ecology-destroying consequences of developing and disseminating convenient, even well-intentioned, technologies. Modern economics values industrial processes and products that reduce labor and move goods without regard for cumulative ecological effects. Now ozone depletion and global warming—accelerated by widespread human use of effective technologies such as gasoline and diesel engines, air conditioning, and convenience packaging that use CFCs—reveal that ecologically destructive human enterprise can threaten earth's health as a whole and human existence itself. We have begun to experience the failure of our technological success, even while continuing to develop a global structure of political economy that increases human poverty.

RESPONSIVE ETHICS AND THEOLOGY

As Bill McKibben pictures our new situation in *The End of Nature*, basic natural processes, once beyond human reach, are now subject to dominating human activity that alters landscapes, waters, and atmosphere, while manipulating or obliterating species.

Science writer McKibben, who is also a Methodist layman, wonders what will happen to religion as nature "ends." He writes, "We as a race turn out to be God's equal—or at least God's rival—able to destroy creation." Three possibilities are: "God thoroughly approves of what we have done, it is our destiny; God doesn't approve, but is powerless to do anything about it, either because God is weak or has created us with free will; or God is uninterested, or absent, or dead."[21] Wondering why God let it happen, McKibben leaves us with a sad theodicy of nature.

There is a fourth alternative: God delights in the creation and suffers wherever it is destroyed. The Creator-Deliverer calls us to join in the work of freeing oppressed nature and people from bondage, loving other creatures as neighbors while tilling with care.[22]

But our society has yet to face the limits nature places on polluting economic growth and material consumption and to adopt an ethic and practice of eco-justice. This ethic comes into sharp focus in terms of four eco-justice norms: ecologically *sustainable* or environmentally fitting enterprise; socially *just participation* in obtaining sustenance and managing community life; *sufficiency* as a standard of organized sharing, requiring basic floors and ceilings of equitable consumption; and *solidarity* with other people and creatures—companions, victims, and allies—in earth community. Observance of each ethical norm reinforces the others, serving the common eco-social good by joining what is socially just with what is ecologically right.[23]

For example, resource-conservation ethics has long argued for "material sufficiency" as an instrumental ethical norm. By only using as much as we need, we have more to share with other human beings. But within the context of an eco-justice ethic, sufficiency is also a primary ecological good. One notion of justice now includes giving the human body its due and the values of other natural things, including their "use values," their due as well. Simply stated, eating "enough" is good for the individual who eats, for other human consumers, and for the natural environment.[24]

Such an ethic no longer views nature as a mere stage for the drama of human redemption or as an expendable resource to be managed for mere human use. Such an ethic reflects new sensitivity to spirited earth along with continuing commitment to healthy social relations, thus affirming the intrinsic value of all creatures and the importance of political and economic justice. It features responsibility toward future generations in linkage with responsibility toward persons who are already alive. With a disposition toward humble stewardship, rather than arrogant nature-manipulation, this ethic emphasizes the need for equitable human relations even as it serves principles of ecology that modern society has ignored, such as the need to protect natural diversity and constraints, plus the importance of proceeding on modest scale in technological undertakings.

As chapter 7 by Holmes Rolston reminds us, authentic human stewardship of earth will enable all creatures, not just humans, to "be fruitful and multiply" (Gen. 1:22, 28). The objective of human stewardship is to care for the well-being of other people and diverse species mostly by letting them be. Wherever human activity endangers other species, extra care should be taken to "Keep them alive with you" (Gen. 6:19).

In that spirit, we must learn quickly to act in ways that get along with nature. Farmer-philosopher Wendell Berry suggests what that would mean: proper human sounds do not obliterate other sounds in nature; appropriately scaled technologies allow other creatures to thrive and do not burden future generations.[25] Such a beautiful definition of the appropriate social future contrasts sharply with what has been going on in modern culture. This down side of modernity is a matter for cogent critique by John Cobb in the opening chapter of Part One of this book.

After Nature's Revolt, of course, is not the first book to ask how it happened that personal salvation could be projected and human convenience pursued apart from planetary well-being. Others have also pondered how this could occur in a civilization with Judeo-Christian roots. Space does not permit a detailed discussion of this cultural failure of Western churches, but we must at least point to patterned habits of dualistic thinking, combined with millennial confidence in unfailing technological and social progress.

The basic dualism, suggests British theologian Grace Jantzen, is a theology of creation that views God as pure spirit apart from the material universe. In this view God exerts all the power over passive matter. "God is all knowing; matter is mindless, irrational. God is goodness itself; matter in itself is without value, mere stuff." A "wholly other" God over-against but in control of material creation was mirrored in and reinforced by a dualistic view of human beings caught in a struggle between mind and body—with the mind being viewed as divinely rational and the body's needs (especially sexual impulses) as quite negative. Historically, male-female dualism has identified the male with mind and God, and the female with body and material universe.

> This male-female dualism identifies women strongly with the material, the earth. The male principle of rationality and mastery, by contrast, is identified with the technological dominance of nature. Just as men by their rationality master their bodies, feelings and women, so technology is the rational mastery of nature by males.[26]

God-world, mind-body, and male-female dualisms that alienate human society from earthy origins are a major factor in the eco-justice crisis. Christian theology that is critically conscious of this pattern and intends to speak to realities of life on an imperiled planet must move beyond these dualisms and related theological rationales for subduing the earth and for subordinating women and dark-skinned people. The chapters in Part One below, "Assessing the Christian Legacy," show how the church must revise the story it would tell and the way it lives in the world. Because religious myths, liturgies, and doctrines shape consciousness (see chap. 10 by Hefner), appreciation of our creature-hood and the threat to other creatures impel us to communicate the full Christian story in environmentally aware words and deeds that undergird human well-being on a thriving earth. Important examples of how to restate Christian theology and ethics in a time of eco-justice crisis are provided below in chapters 2, 3, 5, 7, 8, and 9. These authors find new meanings in God's triune being.

ROLES OF THE CHURCH

Alienating dualisms are a major, but not the only, cause of eco-injustice. I have already referred to our culture's entrancement with earth-destroying technologies. Given the heavy financial investment of modern government and corporations in the development and application of such toxic technologies, one must emphasize that structures of power shaped by vested political and economic interests have also played a large role in precipitating the eco-justice crisis. So, in addition to recovering an authentically biblical appreciation of the creation and revising its theology in light of new understandings of planetary reality, the church has a responsibility to face issues of political and personal responsibility that emerge under ecological challenge.

Besides rethinking the faith and expressing it in a wholistic way that views human history and the natural world as one unified reality with a destiny of shalom, there are several related eco-justice or earth-community responsibilities of the church, namely, to:

• Inform ourselves and explore with others the environmental peril and a theology of eco-justice.

• Inculcate a new ethic of respect for all creatures and careful stewardship of every place.

• Explore urban and rural dimensions of ecology, participating in community organizations seeking eco-justice.

• Foster constructive local responses to global problems (and explore the international, ecumenical connections).

• Advocate changes in social policy and practice that serve the goals of positive ecology and social justice (working with elected and appointed officials along with environmental specialists and corporate managers).

• Build communities of sustainable sufficiency, joining with others to envision and move toward reverential, sustainable development, while fostering corporate responsibility consistent with this goal.

• Encourage appropriate technologies at home and abroad (become informed about some of these—e.g., renewable energy systems—and how to implement them locally).

• Express individual and institutional life-style integrity consistent with a spirituality of creation-justice-peace (avoiding trivial and legalistic responses).[27]

Christians are called to affirm creation in liturgy and life, and to exercise personal and political responsibility that serves planetary well-being. The objective, working with and through various social organizations, is to move "from pollution to solution" through positive ecology and social justice that makes peace with the earth.

Part One
Assessing the Christian Legacy

1

POSTMODERN CHRISTIANITY IN QUEST OF ECO-JUSTICE

John B. Cobb, Jr.

In 1969 I was abruptly awakened to the ecological crisis. It was for me a theological conversion, which changed my sense of theological vocation. Prior to that time I understood theology as an academic discipline whose function was to help Christians understand their faith and how that could be articulated in the contemporary world. Since that time I have understood theology to have two additional tasks. First, it should work toward changing the way faith has led Christians to understand the world. Second, it should bring this changed understanding to bear critically on other disciplines and in the public discussion. I will illustrate these two additional tasks in this chapter.

I wrote a little book, *Is It Too Late?*, in which I argued that we need a *new* Christianity.[1] That is strong language, and it expressed the way I felt. I came to see that a new world view was necessary, and this seemed to me so profoundly different from the theology then dominant that I thought the requirement was not for reform but for a new beginning. I was convinced by the famous paper of Lynn White, Jr., that central Christian teaching had been a major factor in producing the attitudes and practices that were responsible for the ecological crisis.[2] It was now necessary, I thought, explicitly to criticize our own Scriptures. This meant that we had to rethink the whole matter of biblical authority. Yet I was equally convinced that it was a new Christianity that we needed, not the abandonment of Christianity and the adoption of some other religion.

In the two decades since I wrote that little book a great deal has happened. Much work has been done along the lines of the first of the two new tasks of theology I have mentioned: that is, Christian thinkers have been engaged in changing the way faith has led modern Christians to understand the world. Of particular importance was the fresh work of biblical scholars, who studied the texts again. It turned out that much of the destructive effect of the Bible's influence has been the result of misunderstanding rather than accurate interpretation. Many of the ideas that I first thought needed to be affirmed *against* the Bible are in fact affirmed *in* the Bible. It was modern biblical scholarship that had imposed on the Scriptures the dualism of nature and history, derived not from them but from modern philosophy and theology. Such dualism was as alien to ancient Israel as it should become to us.

ASSESSING MODERNITY

As I have gradually learned that an honest return to the Bible can be a positive resource rather than an obstacle to the kind of thinking and acting now required, I have given up the language of a "new Christianity." Today I would say instead that our need is for a postmodern Christianity.[3] Although Lynn White clearly showed that the problems with Christian teaching about nature did not begin with modernity, nevertheless, our most pressing task is to overcome the extreme anthropocentrism, individualism, and dualism that were thematized in the Enlightenment. If we can agree that anthropocentrism, individualism, and dualism are hallmarks of modern thinking, then we can also agree that the theology we need involves a fundamental negation of modern thought.

There are two ways in which the modern can be negated. One is by returning, or attempting to return, to premodern forms of life. Such an effort is not to be ridiculed. The Middle Ages hardly deserve the scorn that modernity accorded them. Medieval thought was theocentric rather than anthropocentric, and it did not separate humanity from the context of the entire creation in the way modernity has. Medieval thought gave a place to the individual, but the individual was understood as a person in community. Although the value of mental and spiritual activity was fully appreciated, it was not separated from its material or physical basis, and although the importance of history was not questioned, nature was also given its due.

In many respects the medieval way of thinking and of relating thought to life was healthier than what followed. The actual relation to nature in the Middle Ages was more nearly sustainable than that of modernity. Of course, many people were poor and wretched, but whether modernity has improved on this situation when viewed in global perspective is hard to say.

Nevertheless, I am not advocating the effort to return to medieval thought and life or to that of any other past period. There are three reasons. First, it is in fact impossible to return to past forms, and the effort to do so is destructive and disillusioning. Second, there has never been a golden age. And third, there is much of modernity that we want to affirm and preserve. With all its failures, the modern world has given political meaning to the dignity of human life that Christians affirm. Human rights and democratic institutions are worth preserving even if they must be separated from the excessively individualistic ways of thinking often connected with them. Gains in medicine and hygiene are worth preserving even if, when accompanied by other features of modernity, they have led to overpopulation, environmental decay, and spreading poverty. And much of the technology is worth preserving, even if in the modern world much of its development and use has been for the sake of war, either among nations or against nature.

In addition to these practical attainments of modernity that the post-modern world should retain, there has been an enormous advance in knowledge. None of us would wish to unlearn all that has been discovered about human beings and the rest of nature. This knowledge has in fact led to fragmentation and the widespread abandonment of the quest for wisdom. But it has also provided priceless tools for understanding and it offers insights into the nature of reality that make possible far richer ways of overcoming anthropocentrism, individualism, and dualism.

THE POSTMODERN THEOLOGICAL TASK

Although postmodern theology joins medieval theology in placing God and not humanity at the center, postmodern thought of God cannot simply return to medieval ideas. Although these were varied, they too often allowed for a rhetoric and spirituality that could lead to a service of God somewhat separated from service of the creatures. Sometimes for the sake of God terrible things could be done to creatures! This was because the thought of God tended to be of an entity separate from the world. Theologically this was expressed in the view that God was not affected by changes taking place in the world, at least not in a direct and straightforward sense. For postmodern thinking such separateness is not meaningful. God is bound up with the world and the world with God. In Paul's language, Christ is in us and we are in Christ. As is stated

in the First Epistle of John, to say that we love God when we do not
love our neighbor is to lie. In Jesus' message, what we do to one of
the least of our neighbors we do to Christ.

Thus the theocentrism with which anthropocentrism is replaced in
postmodern theology will not juxtapose the service of God and the
service of human beings either in principle or in fact. On the contrary,
it will stress that God is served in and through the neighbor, and any
evil inflicted upon the neighbor is inflicted on God as well. It will also
erase the line between concern for human beings and concern for other
creatures. All are in God and God is in all. Not a sparrow falls to the
ground apart from God's participatory knowledge. When we inflict
suffering on a whale, God suffers with it. When we make possible the
healthy functioning of the biosphere, God enjoys the vitality.

In postmodern theology, anthropocentrism gives way to a theocentrism that finds God in the whole of creation and the whole of
creation in God. Certainly human beings have special responsibilities
and special opportunities, and we receive special providential care. Our
lives are worth those of many sparrows. But God and the created order
in their intimate connection constitute the context of all our thought
and life.

Similarly the overcoming of individualism in postmodern theology
is more radical than the medieval balance of the individual in the community. Developments in the sciences, from physics to social psychology,
have shown us that Paul's idea that we are members one of another is
more profound and universal than even he could have recognized. We
are not individuals who are then bound together in community. We are
communal beings constituted by our relations with others. The community is nothing but its members, but the members are who they are
by virtue of their joint participation in the community. It is our social
being that makes possible our profound interiority and personal freedom
as well.

In premodern thought the emphasis on community often expressed
itself in highly authoritarian and hierarchical structures. It was a justification for severe restrictions on individual freedom and narrow can-
alization of the contributions of the members. The postmodern vision
of person in community moves in another direction. It emphasizes
participation by all in shaping the patterns of community life, patterns
that should adjust flexibly to changing circumstances, interests, and
needs. It seeks forms of order that are as liberating as possible to the
members. It emphasizes that the diversity and creativity of the individual
members contribute to the richness of the whole and that the richness

of the whole facilitates the creativity of each. Of course, the realization of such a vision is never perfect, far from it, but a different understanding of order directs experimental energies in new directions.

The avoidance of dualism in postmodern theology is also far more radical than in medieval thought. There, even though the embodiment of spirit was acknowledged, the bias against the body was often strong. Postmodern thought celebrates embodiment. Although the spirit may soar in imagination and prophesy, it joyfully finds its nourishment in the concrete particularity of time and place. Tender care for the body and its needs, and pleasure in sensual experience, are not felt as inferior to intellectual accomplishment. The awareness of the full range of feeling is preferred to the subordination of what has been thought of as lower to what has been thought of as higher.

These practical and attitudinal changes are rooted in the postmodern theological rejection of the dualism of body and mind. That does not mean that there is no distinction between bodily and mental activity. But all experience is both physical and mental. There is no mere matter and there is no mere mind. The extended and thinking substances of Descartes do not exist. This means also that the dualism between human beings and other animals is not real. They, too, are at once physical and mental. And, indeed, we cannot draw sharp lines between animals and the other creatures that make up our world with us.

TOWARD WHOLISTIC HABITS OF THOUGHT

Modernity has been characterized by other features as well. I refer here to its manner of knowing. Without denying that modern methods discovered much, postmodern thinkers are freeing themselves from some features of the modern approach. The three I want to note are its literalness, its objectification of what is known, and its quest for certainty. Indeed, what is most often called postmodern thought today places a stronger emphasis on the manner of modern knowing than on the points I have made above. I reverse the order, since I find one-sided and dangerous the deconstructive tendencies that result from the primacy of the epistemological critique. As my colleague David Griffin argues, the danger is that the primacy of the epistemological focus could lead to a "most modern" nihilism rather than to a constructive postmodern vision. Nevertheless, the constructive postmodern vision shares much with those who place their emphasis on deconstruction just along the lines suggested by these three points.

The Enlightenment sought to cut through the fog of vague and unfounded medieval thinking to attain clear and distinct ideas founded on indisputable first principles. It would be absurd to minimize the achievements based on this program. But now we are more aware of the limitations. The relation between thought, language, and reality is very complex. Thought and language simply cannot mirror, or correspond to, a reality that is not thought or language in the way that modernity hoped. Indeed, thought and language cannot be separated from reality, or, to put the same point in reverse, reality cannot be separated from thought and language. The interconnectedness of all things applies here, too. This also means that there is no place to begin that is not already in the middle.

We no longer seek a system of thought based on secure foundations, expressed in univocal language, and describing with exactness an objective world. Our thinking has to begin wherever we are, recognizing how profoundly it is conditioned in all sorts of ways and that it is only one among many ways of thinking. It proceeds with a language that is inescapably metaphorical even when it rightly strives for conceptual rigor. We see now that thought may be more fruitful and illuminating when it accepts its metaphorical nature without complaint. The whole process is informed by the reality it describes and in turn contributes to that reality.

None of this need lead to extreme relativism. Of course, all thought is relative, but the realization of its relativity can heighten self-criticism. As H. Richard Niebuhr pointed out long ago, the fact that our perspectives are conditioned does not mean that nothing true appears in them. It does mean that we will never claim exhaustiveness for our truth or assume that those who hold to other aspects of the truth are wrong. Postmodern thinking is open to what others see from their equally, but no more, conditioned standpoints. It accepts nothing uncritically, but it seeks to grow toward fullness through having new features of reality pointed out. It is informed by features of reality that have been pointed out by blacks and women, for example, not because these people offer unconditioned truth, but because they have noticed much of the highest importance that had eluded the vision of the moderns. It does not disparage the insights it already has just because they are fragmentary and relative, but it does not cling to them either.

Since I am calling for a rejection of the modern that nevertheless includes and builds on many of the accomplishments of modernity, the term "postmodern" has quite straightforward application. Since I am doing so as a Christian who believes that Christianity is the last, best hope for humankind, I speak quite straightforwardly of "postmodern Christianity." Since I believe that many of the reasons for Christian decline in the modern period arise out of features of modernity that for other reasons as well we now see must be overcome, I am optimistic that the union of postmodernity and Christianity will be easier and healthier than was the union of modernity and Christianity.

Biblical thinking is not anthropocentric, individualistic, or dualistic. It is not literalist, objectifying, or foundationalist. Hence the rejection of all these features of modernity brings postmodern thinking closer to that of the Bible. This makes it easy for postmodern theology to be more authentically biblical than modern theology could be. But it rejects biblicism even more emphatically than did modern theology. Modern theology, in its quest for a fixed foundation, has often emphasized the authority of Scripture or revelation in ways that are authoritarian. For postmodern theology the authority of the Bible is the authority of its felt truth, its power to illumine our lives and our history. The Bible can never be accepted as heteronomously imposed. In this respect I would point to the work of Reinhold Niebuhr as a model for postmodern theology.

Postmodern Christians know that they live from a particular history that has formed them as a community and as individuals. The story line and many of the most important incidents in that history they find in the Bible. To read the Bible is to know who we are. There is much about our identity for which we need to repent. The Bible itself teaches us that as few stories do. There is much also that we can celebrate. In this respect I would point to H. Richard Niebuhr's *The Meaning of Revelation*.[4]

OVERCOMING CHURCH RESISTANCE

Although I rejoice that what is needed is in so much richer continuity with biblical modes of thought than I had first supposed, I have still been impressed by the deep resistance within the church to shedding its modernist commitments. These modernist commitments in their most positive form have been to human rights and to justice for the oppressed. These are not aspects of modernity we want to give up. But the commitment to social justice has been so deeply tied to the dualistic view of history and nature that many of the most committed Christians opposed having the church give any attention to the degradation of the environment for fear that it would remove attention from issues of justice. As a result, the World Council of Churches lagged behind the United Nations on these issues. The church was conspicuous by its absence at the 1972 Stockholm meeting. The establishment of the United Nations environmental agency in Nairobi had no equivalent in the

World Council. In the church, issues of social justice and the environment were still viewed dualistically, and the church's inescapable commitment to justice for human beings blocked attention to the natural
world.

There have, of course, been Christians who *were* concerned. None
of these wanted to reduce attention to issues of justice. To make that
clear, the term "eco-justice" was devised, and eco-justice task forces
emerged all over the world, especially in this country, in the early
seventies. I chaired one for a while for the Southern California Council
of Churches. The term continues to function well. It helps to make
clear that there can be no justice today that is not ecologically informed
and no commitment to improving the environment that is not motivated
by the passion for justice.

At the ecumenical level a different way of introducing these concerns
was employed. At the WCC Nairobi Assembly (1975), it was argued
that to the commitment to a just and participatory society should be
added the concern for a sustainable society. By focusing on the good
of human society, the fears of those who opposed attention to nature
were eased. They could agree that among the conditions for a good
society is the natural environment that is the context and basis of human
life.

My point is that neither "eco-justice" nor "sustainable society" necessarily challenges the anthropocentrism and dualism of modern Christianity. Their acceptance was merely the acknowledgment that the condition of the natural world is important for human well-being. That
even this was strongly resisted indicates how deeply the modern world
has influenced us. Christians have shared in viewing nature as simply
the unchanging stage on which the human drama is enacted or as the
passive matter to be formed by human beings according to their needs.
That nature has limited capacity to survive our onslaughts was a new
and troubling insight that many have still not internalized, despite the
overwhelming evidence.

Commitment to a sustainable society at Nairobi provided a foothold
in the church for attention to the environment. That this foothold was
a precarious one became apparent at the 1983 Vancouver Assembly
eight years later. There the discussion focused on the relation of peace
and justice. Representatives of the North Atlantic nations were intensely
concerned about the threat of a nuclear war. Third World representatives
feared that this concern for rapprochement between the superpowers
could leave their oppression unchanged. These were familiar topics long
at the center of theological discussion. Sustainability disappeared as a

topic. Fortunately, almost as an afterthought it seemed, the assembly added "the integrity of creation" to its charting of direction for the future. This has provided a new opening for advancing the churches' thinking about the relation of human beings and the natural world. Now attention is directed to the whole of creation as such rather than only to human society's dependence on its natural environment for its survival.

I do not mean that under the rubric of a sustainable society the intrinsic reality and value of nature had not been discussed in meetings of various groups within the World Council; they had. Perhaps these discussions paved the way for this next step at Vancouver, but that is not clear. In any case, the first and second drafts of the document prepared for the World Convocation on Justice, Peace, and the Integrity of Creation of the World Council of Churches, despite an overwhelmingly anthropocentric tone, make explicit the doctrine that nature has its own value even apart from its relationship to human beings. This affirmation marks the second great step toward a postmodern theology of nature: the first, that what happens in the natural world requires our attention; the second, that it matters not only because of its effects on us but also in itself. The church has come a long way! It is beginning to catch up with the Bible.

It would be interesting to trace the history of statements in national councils of churches and individual denominations. My expectation is that, with important exceptions, they have lagged behind the World Council. Certainly the Presbyterian Eco-Justice Task Force Resource Paper, *Keeping and Healing the Creation,* is one of the happy exceptions.[5]

I have suggested that there has been resistance to this advance in the churches. I hope I am not understood as implying that academia in general, or theological faculties in particular, have been in the vanguard. Anthropocentric, individualistic, and dualistic habits of mind, as well as literalistic, objectifying, and foundationalist styles of thought, still shape our academic disciplines. Furthermore, the separation of theology and ethics into distinct disciplines has inhibited both theologians and ethicists from giving sustained attention to these issues. At the meetings of the American Academy of Religion there was for several years a section devoted to this topic, but it was tiny and marginal. One can expect references and occasional (very occasional) papers in other sections. But the great majority of the most vigorous discussion proceeds as if there were no environmental crisis, sometimes as if there were no natural world. It is noteworthy that some of the most important scholarship dealing with Christian views of the environment has come from pastors. I refer especially to the work of H. Paul Santmire. I doubt that he would have done as much to advance this discussion if he had been in academia! The church may lag behind the United Nations, but it is ahead of the university.

At least the leadership of the churches now understands that concern for the whole of creation is not a departure from biblical teaching, and that it is certainly not antithetical to concern for the poor and the oppressed. I trust we have gotten past those debates. I trust we recognize that the victims of global warming will be all of us, but especially the human poor and the animals. I trust we realize that the loss of forest cover causes suffering for all, but especially for the poor and for animals. I trust we see that chemical poisoning of water and land lowers living standards for all, but that it is the poor and the animals that suffer most. I trust we understand that the loss of protection by the ozone layer will lower the quality of life for all of us, but that it is the poor and the animals that will be least able to substitute artificial protections.

The church is ready to affirm a solidarity of human beings and other creatures as together making up one interdependent creation. It is willing to assert that the other creatures exist, not only for our sake, but also for their own sake and for God. But we have hardly begun to discuss the new issues that these affirmations raise.

HUMAN OBLIGATIONS TO ANIMALS

One particularly obvious topic is our treatment of other animals. As long as the church's doctrine was completely anthropocentric, this issue did not arise. Some Christians, it is true, have argued that mistreating animals leads to mistreatment of human beings, but most ignored the topic altogether, and it was absent from official consideration. As long as animals are thought to exist only for the sake of human beings, no moral issue arises in their abuse. Concern about cruelty to them is viewed as sentimentality. Because the church has viewed matters in this way, it has given no support to the humane societies by which secular people have expressed their greater sensitivity.

But once we recognize that animals do not exist only for our use and benefit, once we see that they are part of a creation that has value in itself and for God, then treatment of animals would seem to become an issue in theological ethics as it has already become one in philosophical ethics. Again, we must anticipate resistance. Indeed, the resistance is already manifest. The deeply anthropocentric commitments of so many Christians oppose any serious attention to animal welfare. Even those who do not, in principle, oppose considering this matter are likely to drag their feet. As long as there are any human beings whose rights are denied them, they will regard concern for other animals as misplaced.

Fortunately, many of the oppressed people themselves do not share these anthropocentric attitudes. Where the cultural values of Africans, Native Americans, and South Asians have not been uprooted by Western modernity, feelings of kinship with other creatures are vivid and effective. Alice Walker commends a powerful little book, *The Dreaded Comparison: Human and Animal Slavery*, with these words: "The animals of the world exist for their own reasons. They were not made for humans any more than black people were made for whites or women for men."[6] But for many modern Westerners, and especially for many Christians, the issue is still viewed dualistically, as if concern for animals reduced concern for human beings. It is doubtful that any progress on this topic can be made within the church until this dualistic thinking is overcome.

One might suppose that what I have called resistance to consideration of animal welfare is, in fact, just a matter of ignorance and neglect. But my personal experience with this matter suggests otherwise. In September 1988 I took part in a WCC Church and Society meeting at Annecy, near Geneva. Our task was to produce a statement on the integrity of creation. I think it was reasonably good on the general topic. But it also introduced the issue of moral responsibility in relation to other animals, and because this topic was new to the World Council, the statement gave disproportionate attention to it. Our report has received more than its share of media attention, and, according to the national office of the WCC, it has been in greater demand than any other WCC document. In view of all this, the fact that this report has been shelved, and that no mention of this topic is made in the new WCC statement, is not likely to be an accident or oversight.

Those who hope to prevent this issue from getting onto the agenda of the churches would like to do so without fanfare. But they are likely to be disappointed. Because of their interest in the topic, the organizers of the Annecy conference invited Tom Regan to participate. He did so, and he had a large effect on the outcome. Tom Regan is a very dedicated, as well as a very attractive and effective, man. He cares about animal suffering intensely. He is a philosopher, and it was his work, more than that of anyone else, at least in the United States, that led to the introduction of the topic of animal rights into textbooks in philosophical ethics during the past decade. Having accomplished this, he is now determined to introduce the topic into the churches as well. Those who oppose this introduction have a formidable opponent! In this project

Regan also has some committed allies strategically located within the church. The topic may yet come before the next assembly of the World Council even if efforts to ignore it continue.

My thesis is that each step the church takes confronts it with the need to take another. I have argued that once we assign intrinsic value to other creatures besides human beings, the logical implication is that our dealings with these creatures are ethically significant. But that simply opens up a new discussion. It in no way predetermines the outcome. To illustrate, I strongly support Regan in his effort to introduce this topic into the churches. I equally strongly disagree with his own arguments and some of his conclusions.

Regan's arguments are philosophically formulated. I do not think Christians can avoid philosophical debate on this issue, but this is not the time or place to engage in it. Nevertheless, to give substance to my point that once we acknowledge the question we are only in position to begin to discuss the answer, I will identify a figure familiar to us as a theologian, Albert Schweitzer. Regan's conclusions resemble those of Schweitzer. In Schweitzer's terms, once we see that it is to life as such that we owe reverence, rather than only to its human form, our duties to all living things are much like those to other human beings. All killing is wrong.

Despite my respect for both Schweitzer and Regan, and for others who argue in this way, I do not find it justified either biblically or philosophically. Here I will limit myself to biblical considerations. I focus on the first chapter of Genesis, believing that other biblical statements on this topic are generally consistent with the vision presented there.

In this chapter we read that at various stages of creation God saw that what had come into being was good. Later anthropocentric exegetes interpreted this as meaning that it was good as a context for the yet-to-be-created human beings, but this is not in the text. If the text is translated straightforwardly into philosophical language, it asserts that the other creatures, quite independently of human beings, have intrinsic value. The implication is that they should not be treated *merely* as means. This point, taken by itself, may seem to support the position I am criticizing.

But the text makes a second point just as clearly as this one. God gives some creatures to others for food, specifically, plants to animals. Contemporary ecologists may emphasize, correctly, that there is in fact a reciprocal relation between plants and animals such that the excretion of animals and their carcasses become food for plants. No doubt the

Hebrews knew this rather obvious fact, but they did not focus on it. A nonsymmetrical relation is described. The text clearly implies that in the divine order of things, the intrinsic value of animal life is greater than that of plant life, so that the sacrifice of the lesser value for the sake of the greater value is justified.

The text implies that the relation of human beings to plants is not different from that of other animals. However, it unequivocally assigns a special value and role to human beings. We are made in the image of God and given dominion over all other creatures. That dominion is surely misunderstood when it is viewed as reducing all its subjects to mere means to human enjoyment or need. No study of rule or kingship in the Bible gives any support to this misreading. But just as there is a major differentiation between animals and plants, so also there is a major differentiation between human beings and other animals.

DIFFERENTIATED RESPONSIBILITY

The implication I draw is that human beings have obligations to all other creatures for their own sake, but that these obligations are differentiated. The obligations we owe to inanimate things, to plants, to other animals, and to human beings differ, and the differentiation involves an ascending scale. The fact that we should not kill other human beings does not necessarily entail that we should not kill other animals. In fact, in the ninth chapter of Genesis, when, after the flood, God makes a covenant with all living things, God specifically authorizes human beings to eat other animals.

My point is that both these stories affirm the intrinsic value of all creatures, but neither affirms that possession of intrinsic value entails the unqualified right to live. *My interpretation is that there are grades of value and diversities of rights.* I believe that empirical and philosophical grounds can also be given for this position, but, as I indicated, I will not do so here. I mention this only to suggest that the biblical view can be shown to be plausible and realistic as an alternative to the more absolutist one of Schweitzer and Regan.

In sum, the basic biblical view accords a differentiated human responsibility under God toward other creatures, each of which has intrinsic value. I believe this provides better direction for ethical reflection today than any of its competitors. But this vision will not become effective in the current debate unless the church owns it, develops its implications, and vigorously seeks its implementation in relation to the many issues now being discussed: the raising of animals for food and fur; the use of animals in scientific experimentation and education; the treatment of animals in zoos; the use of animals for entertainment in rodeos and bullfights; methods of trapping; and so forth.

Once one has acknowledged that members of other animal species do not exist only for the sake of human beings, the issues I have just identified cease to be insignificant. Even if we affirm the legitimacy of killing animals for meat, there remain questions as to the justification of inflicting enormous suffering upon them simply to make their meat more tender or cheaper. Even if we see as legitimate the killing of some animals for the purpose of learning how to cure human diseases, we must still raise questions about the annual torture and slaughter of five hundred million animals that is supposedly justified for culinary, educational, and scientific purposes. If the well-being of other animals matters at all, the long silence of the church cannot be continued.

A second set of issues arises when we relate our biblically warranted concern for individual fellow creatures to our concern for creation as a whole. The distinction can be found even in the biblical passage I have chiefly followed. When God has completed the creation, God sees that the whole is very good.

The contemporary ecological vision suggests that what is most important is not the lives of individuals or their freedom from suffering, but rather the total system of interactions. The concern is for the health and vitality of the whole biosphere rather than for its individual members. It is this vision that the church has incorporated through concern for eco-justice, the just, participatory, and sustainable society, and the integrity of creation. Whereas on the side of human beings, the balance and synthesis of concern for individuals and for social systems has been richly developed, on the side of other creatures, the concern has thus far been limited to systems.

My argument is that Christians should be concerned both with the health of the whole biosphere and for the suffering of the individual creatures. Of course, a great deal of suffering is involved in the natural and healthy functioning of the biosphere. Most of the young of most species die, and death is not always quick. It would certainly be harmful for human beings to exercise their dominion by interfering in the often bloody and cruel processes that jointly contribute to a rich biosphere. But this does not justify the unlimited infliction of additional suffering by humans for human purposes.

There is also a tension between the intrinsic value of individual creatures and their importance for the whole. Whales, I believe, have far more intrinsic value than plankton, but the extinction of plankton would have far worse consequences for the oceanic ecosystem. We have reason to be concerned for both, but in different ways. Clarifying the dual concern, and thereby developing an adequate ethic of relations to the natural world, are important agenda for the church. Thus far they have not been acknowledged, much less carried out. When the church does accept its responsibilities, its biblical sources should enable it to give badly needed leadership in a confused discussion.

Concern for individual creatures and for the biosphere must be systematically integrated with commitment to the oppressed. It is at this point that the church has already given leadership. Whereas outside the church ecological concerns are sometimes formulated in ways that are insensitive to the poor, this does not occur in church pronouncements. Furthermore, the church has structures through which the oppressed can participate in shaping the church's reflection about the integrity of creation. Here lies the church's greatest opportunity for leadership.

TOWARD ALTERNATIVE ECONOMICS

The major emphasis in the preceding has been on the first of the two additional tasks of theology that I identified at the beginning. I have been talking about changing the way Christians understand the world. I have argued that in general these changes involve recovery of the biblical vision and thinking through its implications for contemporary issues. The collaboration of biblical scholars, theologians, and ethicists is particularly needed. I have already suggested that the results will bring the church helpfully into aspects of the public discussion in which its voice is not now heard.

I turn now, in conclusion, to illustrate the second additional task that I identified at the outset. That is to bring this changed understanding to bear on other disciplines. This is a type of reflection that has grown rare in the church. Here, too, the best model I can propose is Reinhold Niebuhr. My own efforts in this direction have been in economics. There is certainly nothing new about Christians addressing economic issues. But I am calling for a new way of doing this.

In general the church, in this century, at least, has allowed the issues and alternative solutions to be defined in terms of the best economic thinking available, namely, that of professional economists. This thinking has been shaped by the same modern beliefs that have so deeply influenced modern theology: anthropocentrism, individualism, and dualism. It has sought knowledge in typical modern fashion: objectifying, literal, and certain. As long as theology shared these assumptions, it had no choice but to accept the formulations of the academic discipline of economics as definitive.

But that division of labor changes when postmodern theology is born. A theology that recovers and develops the biblical alternatives to anthropocentrism, individualism, and dualism can critique both modern theology and modern economics. It can press for, and help to give birth to, a postmodern economics in which the issues and alternatives will be posed quite differently. If the church is truly concerned with eco-justice, or with peace, justice, and the integrity of creation, it cannot continue to leave unchallenged economic thinking based on assumptions it rejects.

My own efforts motivated by these concerns have led to writing a book with Herman Daly, *For the Common Good.*[7] We have shown that indeed modern economics is based on anthropocentric, individualist, and dualist assumptions. And we have tried to spell out what follows from thinking about the economy with different assumptions. The practical consequences are quite different.

When the economy is viewed with anthropocentric assumptions, the nonhuman world has value only as it is valued by human beings. This value is measured by the price someone will pay. This means that wilderness, with all its living species, is worth only what someone will pay for it, normally in order to "develop" it. Similarly, whatever is abundant, such as the air, is valueless.

The accompanying dualism has additional consequences for the understanding and use of the natural world. The one way that world appears in economic thought is as "land." This includes the soil, the whole biosphere, and any minerals or other subsoil resources. Originally, land, with farmland chiefly in view, was treated as one of the three factors of production, along with capital and labor. This implied a certain activity on the part of land, along with labor, but rather quickly the dualistic habit of mind prevailed. Land came to be viewed as mere matter and, therefore, as purely passive. For all practical purposes it ceased to function in economic theory as a factor of production and became, instead, one of the commodities to be bought and sold in the marketplace. It is not seen as making an independent contribution.

This depreciation of land has a very specific effect in today's economic thinking about natural resources. Whereas those who examine the world physically in terms of available resources often find these disturbingly limited in relation to projected demand, those whose thinking is shaped by the discipline of economics do not. Indeed, they often vehemently declare, on the basis of their mathematical models and formulae, that resources are inexhaustible. Capital, they say, is a substitute for land or natural resources. Our task is to increase artificial capital. The economy will then take care of itself. Since there are no limits to resources, there are no limits to growth.

The individualistic assumptions of economics are equally fateful. They lead to the view that the goal of economics is to increase the total value of goods consumed with value determined by price. Success is measured by growth in per capita gross product. This growth is attained by efficient employment of labor and capital, which in turn requires that capital flow freely to whatever place it can be most profitably employed, with labor following. The result, of course, is a highly mobile labor force. The casualty is any form of stable community.

These economic principles have been applied vigorously to American agriculture since World War II. The results have been an immense success from the point of view of economists. If one is concerned about the land, and about human community, on the other hand, the results appear disastrous.

ECONOMICS FOR COMMUNITY

Herman Daly and I view the land as having intrinsic value, human persons as being fundamentally social or communal in nature, and their community as extending to the wider, natural environment. We work out the implications for economics that follow. We call this an economics for community. That means that the economy should be ordered for the well-being of human communities understood to be immersed in larger natural communities whose well-being is also important.

The effort is then no longer to increase per capita consumption in general. It is, instead, to develop healthier communities. Because we are social beings, participation in healthy community contributes as much to our enjoyment of life as does the consumption of the goods that are priced in the marketplace. But of course in a healthy community sufficient goods are available, and they are so distributed that the basic needs of all are met. Further, the community extends into the future, so that consumption now must be compatible with continued consumption in the future. And since the community extends beyond the boundaries of the human, human consumption must be compatible with continuing health of the biosphere and the relative freedom of its individual members from unnecessary suffering.

With this as a goal the principles of good economics change. Capital should be used efficiently, but locally, so as not to disrupt community.

Equally, resources should be used efficiently so as to meet as many human needs as possible with minimum disruption of the natural system or exhaustion of resources. This thinking leads to support for economic decentralization into relatively self-sufficient communities—a profound reversal of the present goal of a single global market with the free flow of capital and goods everywhere. Note that no one seriously proposes the free flow of labor everywhere, which in pure theory would be required, and the lack of which will inevitably lower wages in industrial nations and widen the gap between those who live by labor and those who live from capital. The global market will intensify regional specialization, the dependence on trade, and hence also on those who determine the terms of trade.

PARTICIPATING IN PUBLIC DISCOURSE

I would be pleased if I could persuade you to support the very different policies that would follow from an economics for community. But my purpose here is more modest. I want to persuade you that it is worthwhile for Christians, once they have adopted a postmodern and more biblical theology, to examine the secular thought of our time and to engage it critically. I have been using economics as my example, both because the church has long recognized its importance and because I have been working in this field. But there is a similar need to engage political theory, sociology, psychology, and even the natural sciences. All continue to work with modern assumptions that no longer carry conviction. Further, once we reject the deeper assumption that these are all separable bodies of knowledge dealing with separate aspects of reality, thinking must flow across all such boundaries. The opportunity of the church is now to guide the thinking of a new generation in a wholistic direction based on a view of God, humanity, and the rest of creation that it can affirm with conviction. I find that exciting.

One obstacle to getting a hearing for such a project is the widespread anti-intellectualism in the church. This is also a part of the modernity we need to leave behind. Once the life of the modern mind was divided up into academic disciplines, the work of these disciplines became largely irrelevant to life. Where it was relevant, the implications were announced by experts. The public was offered no participation. "Lay" thinking has been treated with contempt. All of this is as true of theology as of other academic disciplines. This situation as such is anti-intellectual.

One reason for the ferment of thinking generated by the ecological movement and by feminism is that, as new movements, they have invited participation by thoughtful people regardless of their expertise. Many of these people have read avidly and studied intensively. The level of critical inquiry in these movements is not lower than in established disciplines in universities. But it is open and participatory. Ecological and feminist thinking has not yet been channeled into academic disciplines requiring special socialization. They cut across all the disciplinary boundaries, throwing a fresh light on all they touch. This is what the church's thinking should be like, whether we call it theology or not. It should be an open discussion of how Christian faith illumines the whole of reality. The end of the modern era frees us for this.

2
RETURNING TO OUR SENSES
The Theology of the Cross as a Theology for Eco-Justice
Larry Rasmussen

*I*n the twelfth century parts of Europe faced serious deforestation. Apart from water and the soil itself, woodlands were the most important resource for the population. Trees provided food, fuel, and building materials for shelter, furnishings, and tools. In 1338 the Bishop of Bamberg took a pledge, as did his successor. The bishops vowed not only to place the people, but also the forests, under the protection of Christian faith and the church.[1]

But does Christian faith, in its manifold traditions to date, truly offer protection for an endangered ecosystem? If the churches throughout the world were suddenly to pledge the security of both people and the rest of nature, would something salvatory happen thereby? What would change? What theological perspectives would themselves be altered? What "faith-full" views would come to expression in such a pledge? In the end, is "The Ambiguous Ecological Promise of Christian Theology"[2] genuine promise or only genuine ambiguity?

This chapter explores one of those theological possibilities, a Lutheran recasting of catholic themes. I will trace a few impulses from Luther's theology of the cross in order to explore its potential as a theological ethic for eco-justice.

Theological/ethical reflection is always the second partner in a two-step dance. It doesn't lead; rather, it responds to events and conditions that hit us where we live. It does so in order to help us shape our actions. This means that we do not seriously entertain faith reflection that fails to resonate with the reality we experience.

Yet we experience more reality than we can address. We cannot respond in careful thought to all of it any more than we can act upon all of it. So I must be clear about what, in my judgment, Christian faith must address in our time if it is to be a viable public faith. *What must be addressed is massive public suffering, both human and extrahuman.* And Christian faith must show, in deed, that an available power exists for addressing and overcoming creation's travail.

I am far from certain that Lutheran cross theology can yield decisive substance for this viable, powerful theological ethic. But I do know that I immediately understood Kosuke Koyama's testimony about his own experience: "The slow assimilation of the traumatic events of 1945, which only gradually yielded their theological implications, has moved me towards the emotive region of the cross of Christ."[3] Creation's conditions today move me instinctively "towards the emotive region of the cross of Christ." A powerful resonance is there.

This chapter is also a delayed response to a challenge lodged a half-dozen years ago by James Cone, who faults Lutherans like me for failing "to extend Luther's theology of the cross to society."[4] I offer the beginnings of an extension here.

Situated, then, in the "emotive region of the cross," and with cross theology at hand, what might we say in a Lutheran way about present and prospective massive public suffering, human and extrahuman? It should be theologically direct, simple, and clear in its moral implications. Three affirmations guide us.[5]

1. Being with the gracious God means loving the earth.
2. Being with the gracious God means loving Jesus.
3. Being with the gracious God means going home.

BEING WITH THE GRACIOUS GOD MEANS LOVING THE EARTH
(FINITUM CAPAX INFINITI)

For Europe, World War I meant massive public suffering and shattered cultural confidence. How do we do post-liberal theology for this battered and beaten age? became the question for a generation of theologians. The answer for many was to reassert the majesty, glory, and power of God. Fascinating in all this was the theological divergence of two young German minds. The young Karl Barth, desiring to proclaim God's majesty, began by placing God at a remote and awesome distance. The even younger Dietrich Bonhoeffer, desiring to proclaim the same majesty, began by bringing God into the closest possible, but also awesome, proximity. Barth drew from the Calvinist insistence, *finitum non capax infiniti* (the finite cannot hold the infinite) while Bonhoeffer insisted, with Luther, upon *finitum capax infiniti*—the finite bears the infinite, the transcendent is utterly immanent. "God is in the facts themselves," said Bonhoeffer, asserting not only his conviction that God is discerned amid the living events of history but drawing out as well his favorite quotation from F. C. Oetinger: "the end of the ways of God is bodiliness."[6]

The meaning of *finitum capax infiniti* is simple enough: God is pegged to the earth. So if you would experience God, you must love the earth. The infinite and transcendent are always dimensions of what is intensely at hand. Don't look up for God, look around. The finite is all there is, because all that is, is there.

This is earthbound theology, and with it Luther is boldly pan*en*-theistic. H. Paul Santmire cites a nice passage in which Luther asserts this, despite the offense it gives medieval reason:

> For how can reason tolerate it that the Divine majesty is so small that it can be substantially present in a grain, on a grain, over a grain, through a grain, within and without, and that, although it is a single Majesty, it nevertheless is entirely in each grain separately, no matter how immeasurably numerous these grains may be?[7]

It is true that at least until the Enlightenment, the common catholic conviction was that God is revealed in two books, Scripture and the book of nature. But to recognize only this in Luther's discourse on God-in-a-grain is to miss the radical character of his panentheism. His is a massive protest against a Christian world with Greek philosophical genes and against the kind of idolatry this Christianity fostered, an idolatry that took the form of the speculative theology of glory. It was the serious mistake of Christianity to think, from the Apologists onward, that the way to God was via the contemplative mind ascending the ladder stretched from earth to heaven, progressively abandoning material reality in a preference for pure spirit. It was a disastrous mistake to Platonize Christianity and affirm the split and dual realities of a corruptible body and a transcendent, immortal soul, thereby progressively falling out of love with the earth in the course of nurturing soul (and mind and reason). Rather, one should image God and thus, like God, love the earth itself. In the course of this imaging of God we would simultaneously be falling in love with ourselves as creatures.

Luther utterly rejects any flight from the creaturely and finite as the path to communion with God. His earthy sacramentalism says God is *wholly* in the grain, and the grain is *holy* in God. True, Luther is an Augustinian and, true, he is a mystic of sorts. But Luther emphatically turns back Augustine's contention that Christ descended to help us ascend. He counters that Christ descended precisely to keep us from trying! This is a repudiation of the most pervasive medieval metaphor of all, the metaphor of ascetic ascent. It is rejected as spirituality and as metaphysics. Luther rejects the great chain of being as the way heaven and earth are composed in neoplatonic Christianity and as the way they sing together.

But why does Luther reject a reigning Christian construct with this much seniority and tenure? He rejects it because it subtly refuses to accept finitude as good and proper. And our finitude is where none less than, and none other than, God is! God is with us as utter *sarx*. At least so far as humans can know, God is never disembodied. God is always in the facts themselves.

The very essence of sin, for Luther, is precisely to try to rise above nature. To repent of our sin is always to "return to our senses"[8] and live in celebration of, and accord with, our fleshy humanity—and in celebration of, and accord with, the rest of nature. Luther rejects the gradual, graded severance of heaven and earth because it means that in our thirst for God, we abandon our purpose for being. We are created, and we are saved, to rejoice in being who we are, utter creatures of God's *adamah*. The particular kind of self-denial that rejects our finitude invariably leads to idolatry or to religion, which is the same thing, as we shall soon note.

Luther's panentheism as whole-earth theology is nicely illustrated in Santmire's discussion. He points out that for Luther, the nakedness of Adam and Eve was their "greatest adornment before God and all creatures" and that Luther pictured their "common table" as one that included the animal kingdom as part of God's kingdom.[9] This echoes the ancient Jewish belief that before the playing out of the evil impulse all creatures were vegetarians (Gen. 1:29) and will be so again when Messiah's work is done. It is more than an aside, then, to note that in the second creation account, after Yahweh concludes that "It is not good that the earth creature [*Adam*] should be alone, I will make [earth creature] a helpmate," (2:18) the creation of Eve does not immediately ensue. Rather, "From the soil [*adamah*] all the wild beasts and all the birds of heaven" were created (2:19). They were candidates for a fitting helpmate because, like *Adam*, they were also *adamah*. The fit is not wholly sufficient, however. (God makes his/her first mistake here!) So Yahweh creates another from earth creature's very own flesh, and the match takes. But the point is *the companion character of all creatures*, and, indeed, their essential commonality precisely as *adamah*, as creatures of the same vibrant combination of dust and spirit. (God's mistake is the kind God can be forgiven and the kind we ought to commit!)

Another aside may also be permitted as we learn to reread the Bible ecologically. Like the human earth creatures, fish and birds are also blessed with God's command to be fruitful and multiply (1:22), and the sun and moon are told to govern, one light by day, the other by night (1:18). Moreover, the "crown of creation" is not so much *Adam* (the collective noun for human earth creatures) as it is the sabbath itself. With sabbath, rather than with humanity, creation is complete. Here the day is hallowed in the full rest of God amid creation's total goodness (2:2-3).

The intuitive correctness of Luther's "common table" of beast and human alike is thus very striking. English, and not only Hebrew, happily retains a whisper of this. Humans, like all things of the earth, are of humus. We ought, then, to be humble. Humility means never trying to outgrow our humanity and escape or transcend our earthiness. It means accepting ourselves for what we are, spirit-animated nature. To sin is to overstep finitude and reject creatureliness. This is the basic meaning for the kind of pride that corrupts and destroys rather than enhances. Its corrective is humility/humus/humanity. Not by coincidence the humble are precisely those who are rightly related to God. They, in faith, gladly accept the freely given grace by which they are content to be God's creatures, nothing else and nothing more. They are "faith-full" when, as fragile, vulnerable creatures, they freely trust in God in a way something akin to the way sparrows and lilies and other creatures do. We do not *have* bodies but we *are* "our bodies, ourselves," and should treat our bodies "as the earth we carry" (to borrow Augustine's lovely image). This mobile humus, erect on its own two legs, ought trustfully to accept its own mortal character as the place God is, among us.

Luther is rarely cautious, so it is noteworthy that he is sometimes cautious in his panentheism. He is cautious because of our idolatrous propensities. We try to capture God in the finite, just as we try to manage an end run around our finitude (the theology of glory). Luther thus insists that to experience the transcendent immanently (the only place we can) is *not* to circumscribe the divine presence itself, despite all the valiant and not-so-valiant efforts of religion to do so. For Luther religion is the best thing idolatry has going for it, even better than politics, the next best thing. Indeed, all efforts to either capture God in our terms, or to be like God by denying our death and finitude, including political and economic efforts, eventually turn religious or quasi-religious. We seek power, including cosmic power, to escape the insecure and mortal character of our finitude. Religion ratifies this mad effort.

Why can we not circumscribe God? In part because we cannot, as creatures, know the fullness of God. We can only know how God is *with us*, on the terms of our particular brand of humus. We cannot know how rocks experience God, or how sparrows do. We cannot know how baobab trees know God's power or graciousness, or how tulips and lilies do. We might well surmise that "fields and floods, rocks, hills, and plains, repeat the sounding joy" all in their own way. And we might understand, reflecting Luther's common table of all *adamah's* kin, that all things are indeed creationally connected and share a collective doxology that divinity itself experiences.[10] We might well nurture Shug's sensibility that "I knew that if I cut the tree, my arm would bleed," or wholeheartedly affirm Celie's conjecture that God must certainly get "pissed off" if you walk by the color purple in a field and don't even notice![11] But we cannot, as the finite creatures we are, know the full majesty of God. In the end we must be content to let God be God and let ourselves be the glorious, but partial, refracted image of divinity. The lines following the God-in-a-grain passage are these:

> And that the same Majesty is so large that neither this world nor a thousand worlds can encompass it and say: "Behold, there it is!" . . . [God's] own divine essence can be in all creatures collectively and in each one individually more profoundly, more intimately, more present than the creature is in itself; yet it can be encompassed nowhere and by no one. It encompasses all things and dwells in all, but not one thing encompasses it and dwells in it.[12]

There remains the crucial matter of saying what *imago Dei* would mean. It would not mean to possess some substantive faculty or quality that at the same time makes us like God and "above" other creatures— reason or will or freedom, to cite three historical contenders. It would mean that precisely as the creatures we are, situated in a threefold relatedness to God, other human creatures, and extrahuman ones, we would be turned toward God. In this stance we would image, or mirror, God's way in our own way.[13] This might be thought of in the manner of the priestly vocation, that is, "to stand before the Creator on behalf of all creation (intercession), and, in turn, to interpret the good intention of the Creator to and for all."[14] *Imago Dei* might then be thought of in moral terms, that is, imaging God is acting in a godly way toward one another and other creatures. Imaging God is loving the earth as fiercely as God does. Understood christologically, as Luther would and as the classic creeds do, this means exercising dominion in the manner of Jesus, who is *dominus*. The manner of Jesus' lordship will be noted in the next discussion; here the point is that *imago Dei* is understood relationally and dynamically, as human imaging of God's way and as humans turning toward God on behalf of creation as priest, trustee, and servant.

To summarize, *finitum capax infiniti* is grassroots, whole-earth theology. It is earthbound. That is God's way, among us. The body, nature, is the end of God's path. The universe itself is God's body. God is not totally encompassed by the creaturely, but the creaturely is the one and only place we know the divine fullness in the manner appropriate to our own fullness. So experiencing the gracious God means falling in love with the earth and sticking around, imaging God in the way we can as the kind of creatures we are. Therefore, the only viable faith is a biospiritual one.

BEING WITH THE GRACIOUS GOD
MEANS LOVING JESUS
(CRUX SOLA NOSTRA THEOLOGIA EST)

> But ask the animals, and they will teach you;
>   and the birds of the air, and they shall teach you;
> ask the plants of the earth, and they will teach you;
>   and the fish of the sea will declare to you.
> Who among all these does not know
>   that the hand of the Lord has done this?
> In [God's] hand is the life of every living thing
>   and the breath of every human being.
>   Job 12:7-10 (NRSV)

Is not such wisdom enough? If we learned this and no more, would we not have everything necessary for an adequate eco-justice ethic? Luther thinks not. Is he right?

Finitum capax infiniti expresses itself as a rich pan*en*theism. Yet Luther does not make nature or the creaturely as such the focal reality of God's revelation. Rather, the compelling glimpse of God is in the humanity of a particular poor Jew from Nazareth in the region of Galilee during the season when Augustus happened to be the Roman caesar. What we can most reliably know of God's own way we know in the way of this man Jesus. God is like this Jesus. God is not more divine than God is in Jesus' humanity, Luther insists. God is not more powerful than God is in the power seen in Jesus. God is not more majestic than God is in the *kenosis* of Jesus. God is not greater than God is in this servant.[15] As this particular Jesus is, so also is God.[16]

Jesus is not a fleeting docetic visitor, nor a ghostly bearer of gnostic truth, but real, mortal flesh and blood from the countryside. Joseph tickles his bare bellybutton and covers his bare bottom; Mary puts his hungry mouth to her bare breast. He is, to be sure, not the *exclusive* revelation of the ubiquitous immanence of God. All creation manifests God. But he is the most compelling and definitive revelation, says Luther. Thus while "God is [always] in the facts themselves," including the facts of nature, the facts are best "read" via God-in-Jesus.

Yet Jesus, and above all Jesus on the cross, is a very strange revelation. In one sense, a dying Jesus is akin to all revelation of God in that it is only indirect—itself a rather strange attribute for revelation! But that's how it is with God. Just as Jesus is a human male, so all evidence of God and God's presence is masked. It is hidden in something else. We have no direct evidence of God at all; we see only what Luther calls the "rearward parts" of God (*posteriori Dei*). (The reference is to Moses and the Jewish notion that none would survive a direct encounter with the majesty of God.)

Yet the cross is not only indirect exposure of God, it is God's presence *sub contrario*—under the opposite. This is not only the rearward parts, but it is the indecent exposure and scandal of a God who is crucified as well as hidden (*Deus crucifixus et absconditus*). God is concealed in a vilified and broken human being. Jesus is God made poor and abused.

Reason and all theologies of glory expect and insist upon something else, namely, God in power, majesty, and light, in triumph, happiness, and wild success. God is found, however, in weakness and wretchedness, in darkness, failure, sorrow, and despair. God is not found only there, but God *is* found there in a special, crystallized, and saving way. God is present in a kind of suffering love and as a kind of power on the home turf of deadliness itself.

What does a crucified and hidden God mean for ethics? And what might the preferential option of God for the suffering mean? Gazing from the foot of the cross to the man of sorrows, how does the heart of the universe manifest itself here for the well-being of all creation? Isn't falling in love with the earth sufficient to discern the way of God? Why is it necessary to fall in love with Jesus as well? The question is for books, not a few paltry paragraphs. But the brief version must suffice for now.

Jesus as the way of God among us and as "a model of the godly life" (*Lutheran Book of Worship,* p. 94) shifts our attention in ethics decisively, in a way that panentheism alone does not. The standard attention in modern ethics concentrates on our own limited resources to effect good, to see what we might do to leave the world less a mess than we found it. The attention is to me and my capacities as a morally autonomous and responsible agent armed with natural powers. The way of Jesus, however, means entering into the predicaments of others who are suffering. There is a major moral and a major theological assumption here, but they merge so as to be indistinguishable in practice. The moral assumption is that the farther one is removed from the suffering present in creation, the farther one is from the central moral reality of the situation; and the closer one is to the suffering, the more difficult it is to refuse participation in that life, human or extrahuman. Compassion (suffering with) is the passion of life itself, even as joy is. Both are a corollary of the fact that the only way we can be human is to be human together. In fact, compassion is not, as we often think, something high and religious. Compassion, as the Dalai Lama says, is

> the common connective tissue of the body of human life. . . . Without it children would not be nurtured and protected, the slightest conflicts would never be resolved, people probably would never even have learned to talk to one another. Nothing pleasant that we enjoy throughout our lives would come to us without the kindness and compassion of others. So it does not seem unrealistic to me: compassion seems to be the greatest power.[17]

Apathy contrasts with compassion. It is the denial of the senses and of our inherent connectedness to all things. It is a rejection of our constitutional sociality and of the pathos of life. The corrective is a return to our senses and to "the imaginative ability to see strange people as fellow sufferers," in Richard Rorty's words. (Rorty's "strange people" should be extended to include other strange creatures.)[18]

The theological assumption of the way of Jesus is that discipleship or, for that matter, simply being human, means to participate in God's sufferings in and for the life of creation itself. That is where and how God is a saving God, and that is the way of the cross as a human and divine way.

This renders compassion (suffering with) the key virtue for a Christian ethic and solidarity (standing with) the key means. The quest of cross theology is precisely for a power that overcomes suffering by entering into it and leading through it to abundant life for all (the sabbath condition of redeemed creation). God's goal is newness of life; God's means is overcoming by undergoing. And God's way is best seen in

Jesus, who is the full compassion of God in full human form. What is discovered via Jesus, and is experienced in imaging him, is this: only that which has undergone all can overcome all. In this sense, cross ethics is an utterly practical necessity. Massive public suffering, or any one of its many expressions, will not be redemptively addressed apart from some manner and degree of angry,[19] compassionate entry into its reality, some empowerment from the inside out, some experience of it as both a burden and a burden to be thrown off, and some deep awareness of it as unhealed but not unhealable suffering. Of course it's frivolous to simply call this no pain, no gain ethics! But it's not frivolous to recognize, with Kuzoh Kitamori, that until our pain is intensified at the sight of creation's pain, as God's is, there is no redemption; that until we enter the places of suffering and experience them with those entangled there, as God does, our actions will not be co-redemptive.[20]

The simple logic here is that any power that does not go to the places where community and creation are most obviously ruptured and ruined is no power for healing at all. This is the impotence of what we wrongly call "power"—wealth, fame, legions of soldiers and ships, triumphalist ideologies, and arrogant, wasteful ways of life. Such "power" does not truly know the disasters of the spirit, the catastrophes of the psyche, the acidity of rain, soil, mind, or household, and thus cannot help heal wounds from within battered flesh itself. Or, if such "power" *does* recognize the normal pathologies of everyday life—they are, after all, as unavoidable as death itself—it treats them as rabid leprosies and as sectors of life to be quarantined out of sight, beyond notice and beyond feeling.

The only power that can truly heal and keep the creation[21] is power instinctively drawn to the flawed places of existence, there to call forth from the desperate and needy themselves extraordinary yet common powers that they did not even know they had. This is the power seen in Jesus. It is strength in weakness, life in the midst of death, joy within suffering, and grace where only wrath and pain and the rearward parts of God are most obvious. The ironic thing, one worthy of reversing standard accounts of wisdom and foolishness, is that this weak kind of power, learned in suffering and expressed as compassion, is what moves history. If Friedrich Nietzsche is right that "thoughts that come on doves' feet guide the world," how much more is it the case that simple actions coming on doves' feet do. Perhaps this is why in the emotive region of the cross and in the awful silence before a dying Christ one hears the seismic whisper of none other than the power of God. It feels like that. Even temple curtains are torn in that moment.

The cross does not oppose all suffering, since not all suffering is negative.[22] Some suffering is part of muddling through human development to greater maturity. The suffering the cross opposes is the suffering that negates life and destroys the realization of creation. Such suffering is the particular kind of death that is "the wages of sin." The forms of this suffering are multiple—psychic, physical, political, economic, cultural, familial, sexual, racial, environmental. What they share in common is disintegration of that which is created to be whole within its limits. What they need in common is restorative healing.[23] *This* suffering is the kind the cross, in *its* suffering, opposes. The way of the cross as the ethic of the human Jesus fastens, then, on that which negates and threatens the life of creation. What is held foremost is the integrity of creation. The suffering entailed in pursuing justice and peace is to serve this. Suffering here fastens on God's intention, through incarnational solidarity with the world's suffering, to turn history toward life rather than death.[24]

Dorothee Soelle, Bonhoeffer, Kitamori, Koyama, and Jon Sobrino have all explicated in profound terms the way of the cross and its relationship to suffering, pain, justice, and peace.[25] Therefore it is not enough to say simply, "Being with the gracious God means loving the earth." We must also say, "Being with the gracious God means loving this Jesus." That means Jesus on the cross, and it means the way *of* the cross as God's ethic and ours. Love the earth, yes, but to redeem the planet, go to the places of suffering and find God and God's power there. As we see in Jesus, God strangely, offensively, makes the margin the center and hefts the rejected stone to set the corner itself. The cross is erected "outside the gate" in the place of the damned. For redemption's sake, the periphery has become the center, and solidarity has become the way of stewardship.

> The "lordship" of the Crucified, if seriously grasped radically, transforms our preconception of dominion, exchanging for the concept of superior form one of exceptional and deliberate solidarity (being-with), and for the notion of mastery a vocation to self-negating and responsible stewardship.[26]

BEING WITH THE GRACIOUS GOD
MEANS GOING HOME

Cross theology is definitely focused on Jesus, but it is always contextual theology/ethics. God is everywhere, but God is only found *somewhere*. God is eternal, but God is, for us, only known *some*time. God's presence, like the facts themselves, is always concrete. The infinite is found in the finite, and the finite by definition is tied to time and place.

This means that an adequate theological ethic works relentlessly to discern the signs of the times. It includes and promotes analysis and interpretation, study and judgments. It asks, What time is it? Where is our some-where? What stance and action pertains now, in view of the eco-crisis and in order to inch toward ecological justice/social justice as a single justice?

Douglas John Hall's contribution here is massive, and mine far more modest.[27] Both are abbreviated in what follows. Both mean to say what we might find if we were to "go home" and look around. Both insist that our own closest reality is the subject, despite the strong middle-American tendency to avoid reflecting on its own social experience. (Some prefer to learn from a largely mythical past that "made this nation great." Others prefer to learn from a mythical "Third World" and from minority traditions not their own.)

The master image in the West since the Enlightenment has been the image of mastery itself. Humanity, as master in history, fashioning a world in accord with human design, has seen this kind of creating as the unspoken human vocation. That it was not "humanity," but imperial European, white, male, and North American humanity, did not deter us from totalizing claims and aspirations. The reigning psychology has been one of impulses to conquer and control, whether the object has been nature, space, the psyche, or sectors of humanity (nations, races, classes, women, and indigenous peoples). The means have been heavily those of science married to technology, including military technology, with a confidence that knowledge is power and power is the key to control. Knowledge/power, particularly as exercised through the mass organizations of industrial-technological society, is still regarded as key; the goal of fashioning a plastic world in accord with our own image, in order to make history turn out right, remains the operative goal. There is no sense of limits here, nor any genuine humility.

Ironically, the quest for human autonomy and dignity that the Enlightenment fostered and in some degree accomplished is also the remorseless quest to outstrip finitude itself and deny both our humanity and nature's essential character. In Luther's terms, it is a *theologia gloriae* of gourmet quality.

The economic engine that has driven this quest must be part of our analysis. The Industrial Revolution, in both capitalist and socialist incarnations, assured a certain kind of progress with a certain facilitating view toward nature. Nature, in this view, is taken to be "free goods"

(Karl Marx, Adam Smith), and history is regarded as the arena of human agency alone (socialists and capitalists share this atheistic tenet). The dominant stance set human beings over against (the rest of) nature and, with the right tools and structures, helped launch an economy of growth that raised large segments of the human population from their misery for the first time in recorded history. This happened and continues to happen, albeit with massively uneven results and at enormous expense to the planet, including many of its people. But it has happened with sufficient success to secure unlimited economic growth as the essential meaning of progress itself and the economic goal of the post-Enlightenment West. Furthermore it has, after World War II, found its way around the globe to become the hope of the poor and security of the rich in North and South, East and West alike. Growth is no longer simply a strategy for desirable ends in this scheme. It is the core metaphor itself. Thus "the limits to growth" was and is an oxymoron that could not and cannot penetrate the modern (largely male) mind.[28] This is not an anthropocentric ethic only, but an androcentric one with a vengeance.

Nevertheless, and despite the unthinkability of any other mass model, we have increasingly come to realize that the same fingers "which hefted the axe and won for us against tiger, bear, and ice" (Loren Eiseley) now bring us death by increments. We who most benefited from modernity and were most socialized to its theology now see, albeit yet darkly, that the mindset of modernity produces along one morally polluted stream weapons of mass destruction and, along another, the exhaustion and degradation of Mother Earth. It is also destructive of organic human community. All this is ironic, since both the bourgeois project and its Marxist critique trumpeted a well-intended humanism of earthly happiness and heightened human dignity. Both also trumpeted the control of natural forces by scientific technology as the means of increasing the general welfare and securing the common good.

The irony only intensifies as we slowly realize that by pursuing mastery over nature, we, as part of nature, may end up the most pathetic victims of this particular quest for power. Affluence has produced a poverty of spirit in which, seeking a pain-free existence, we no longer feel pain when creation suffers and we as part of it. By some grand illusion we have persuaded ourselves that a fully lived life can happen without pain and grief. In fact, no fully lived life can happen that does not enter into creation's suffering. If we deny or turn from earth's pain, our compassion itself dies and with it our humanity.

A thesis from Luther's Heidelberg Disputation of 1518 is striking in its applicability here. *Theologia gloriae* calls evil good and good evil, while *theologia crucis* names the object for what it is. The particular theology of glory that has typified modernity, the mindset of confident control, has called all this "good"—imperial expansion; unlimited economic growth; the spreading Industrial-Technological Revolution; suppression of "inferior" cultures and the civilizing of "inferior" peoples; and nature as the passive "anvil" (Francis Bacon)[29] on which a world of human design is beaten into shape. Such a world *has* achieved unparalleled good in many sectors. Yet what is evil here has also been called good, or defended as inextricable to the realization of good, which is the same thing. And what we now look to as potentially saving "good" has hitherto been called "evil" and "irrational"—the "primitive" views and ways of indigenous peoples; women's sensibilities and ways of relating; the visions of mystics and the ancient ways of contemplation; the "insurrection of subjugated knowledges" (Michel Foucault)[30] the world over; and life-styles of renunciation and simplicity.

Dominant theology in the modern and often highly secularized era has consciously addressed the "cultured despisers of religion" in order to convince them that Christianity is relevant to modernity itself, both as strong support and as purging critique. But as part of the same movement, this Christianity has looked with often-unspoken disdain upon despised cultures themselves. It has called good evil while calling evil good. What cross theology has regarded as the supreme human *temptation,* namely, mastery, modern theology, assimilating the ethos of modernity itself, has regarded as the supreme human *vocation!*

The theological drama continues to the present. One example will suffice—biotechnology. How shall we appraise it? It offers potentially enormous good. It has already achieved benefits we gladly embrace. An unqualified, broadside rejection seems foolish, not to say out of reach, from a practical point of view. Such a rejection would be as foolish as an unqualified rejection of all theology since the Enlightenment or of the Enlightenment itself. But read in the light of the epoch that has delivered the eco-crisis, we must pause for a sober and searching analysis carried out on grounds other than what the current cultural mainstream itself supplies.

Biotechnology is a decidedly new twist, yet it is a twist with the same kind of logic as the reigning *theologia gloriae.* To wit: the driving force to master the planet to date has proceeded to work from the outside in. That is, we humans shape nature as it comes to us in long-evolved forms, in order to modify our environment. We take these forms, and we burn, melt, mix, fertilize, prune, harvest, process, package, dissect, explore, construct, deconstruct, reconstruct, put down, pluck up, wreck, rebuild, and start anew. But biotechnology proceeds otherwise. It works from the inside out. The fundamental building units of life itself and their informational codes are altered so as to modify life itself, from the inside. In some instances, we even create new forms of life and, in all cases, we deliberately direct evolution. Bill McKibben, on whom I draw here, cites Brian Stableford's *Future Man*. Stableford unabashedly says that genetic engineering "will eventually enable us to turn the working of all living things on earth—the entire biosphere—to the particular advantage of our own species."[31] A crisper declaration of the logic of mastery as the logic of modernity could hardly be found. It fails to recognize humus and humility altogether, or to honor the insight of the Bible and cross theology that tragedy awaits those who think they control what they create.

In short, an analysis of "this present age" reveals at least that we have not yet learned modernity's lessons, despite the signals from our antennae that something is deeply wrong. Yet this analysis, of itself, isn't the salient point. The point is that cross theology, as contextual, insists upon analysis. "God is 'always' God 'today.' "[32] Discerning God's way means judging the times themselves. To experience the gracious God, go home and look around. And when you find putrid death there, together with real remnants of life, take heart! God, the cross signals, enters the death to negate it, that life might emerge for those who, in humility, repent and believe.

GOD'S WORK MUST TRULY BE OUR OWN

Luther's cross theology as applied to society lands somewhere near the intersection of liberation theologies and creation theologies, though with a chastened sense of creational limits and human propensities to deny them idolatrously. Cross theology, like both liberation and creation theologies, is curiously optimistic. It has seen the worst and discovered a mighty power for life there, smack in the midst of death. This power is not an alien one. On the contrary, it is the power of God that inheres in all creation. It belongs to us at the very core of our being, even as it belongs to the rest of the earth. It is in our bones and it places sustainability, even redemption, within reach. This power is the power of the Holy Spirit, *Spiritus creator* itself. The peculiar twist of cross theology is that, like Jesus himself, it moves in the power of the Spirit to the places of negative suffering in order to discover and uncover power for life there. As an ethic of compassion and solidarity it seeks out the places of oppressive suffering in order to overcome suffering's demonic, or disintegrative, manifestations. It goes to the victims in order to stand with them in their reality. Its quest is not for victims (!) but for the sources of suffering and the empowerment needed to negate the negations that yield victims. Its goal is the end of victims, human and otherwise. It insists that eco-justice is also social justice and that all efforts to save the planet begin with hearing the cry of the people and the cry of the earth together.

Whence the power for this? As a panentheistic ethic, cross theology, like much feminist theology and creation theology, says, "In creation itself, where God is." A power is present in the cosmos and in nature as we know it. It is God's own power and it is sufficient for the redemption of all things (*ta panta*). We are not cocreators—an insufferably arrogant notion—but we are coparticipants, together with all else "in heaven and earth."

Power as cosmic energy identified as God's own and as an expression of the Spirit is no new Christian theme. It is an ancient catholic one, perhaps most nurtured over the centuries by millions of Christians in the Orthodox communions. The Lutheran variation only insists on a steady focus on the crucified, human Jesus as the place and as the way this power concentrates for the redemption of creation. The focus on Jesus, and never *finitum capax infiniti* apart from the revelation of God in Jesus, is essential. Otherwise most rich-world Christians will work to save nature but not creation. They will sever ecological justice from social justice and treat the environment in a way so as to sustain their own interests alone. The issue for an adequate environmental ethic is not an upgraded view of nature, even a religiously sensitive one. That might be no more than a romanticist's notion of *finitum capax infiniti*. (Remember that romanticism's theme is its love of directly experienced nature.) The issue is the discovery of a power throughout creation that serves justice throughout creation. Nonhuman nature does not have intrinsic value, nor do human beings, as separate entities. Value is in the relatedness of all things to one another, in God, and justice is the rightful relation of creatures to one another. The question is always whose justice and what power, rather than the moral status of a (supposedly) independent "nature."

Jesus' crucifixion should have been the last one, and he should have been the last victim. But it was not and he was not, and God's sovereignty and Christ's lordship remain contested to this very day and hour. Thus, as Paul says, the sufferings of disciples are now added to Jesus' own in the same cause of redemption. He suffered ahead of us, rather than instead of us, and the way of the cross as God's own way remains ethically paradigmatic. He is both "a sacrifice for sin and a model of the godly life" (*Lutheran Book of Worship,* p. 94). For the present age, and with a view to survival requirements, cross theology's concern is with the power *in* creation (*finitum capax infiniti*) as a power to exorcise the demons that inhabit affluence and the deprivation that inhabits poverty. (Both affluence and poverty are massive causes of the eco-crisis.)

Exercising this power is a profoundly human and divine task. As Luther insisted, human actions are God's masks. Bonhoeffer called us to mature moral responsibility and its exercise for the sake of future generations, a moral responsibility we would learn only by living *etsi deus non daretur*—"as though [the] God [of religion] did not exist." Luther himself proposed the same. In general, he wrote, civil authorities "should proceed as if there were no God and they had to rescue themselves and manage their own affairs. . . ."[33] He similarly addressed another group of responsible citizens, "Nor will God perform miracles as long as [people] can solve their problems by means of the other gifts [God] has already granted them."[34] In short, and like both liberation theologies and creation theologies, cross theology asks us to find God deep in the gifts we naturally possess or those we might develop as the exuberant creatures we are. It means returning to our senses. This echoes a famous line from President John F. Kennedy's inaugural address, a line probably uttered as a mild expression of a *theologia gloriae!* "God's work must truly be our own." More importantly, in an era of heightened human impact on the entire planet, our own work must truly be God's.

3

HEALING THE PROTESTANT MIND
Beyond the Theology of Human Dominion

H. Paul Santmire

As the earth groans in travail, it appears that those who stand in the traditions of Luther and Calvin are ill-equipped to respond to the global environmental crisis theologically.[1] It appears, indeed, that in this critical instance the Protestant mind is suffering from a severe case of hardening of the categories. The Protestant mind has become fixed, not to say fixated, on what Karl Barth called "the-anthropology," the doctrine of God and humanity. This has meant, in turn, that Protestants generally have approached the earth almost exclusively via the theology of a divinely mandated human dominion over nature.

What is required, therefore, is a certain kind of theological healing, inspired by one of the great principles of the Reformation: *sola scriptura.* The Bible begins with the creation narratives of Genesis and ends with the Book of Revelation's vision of a new Jerusalem established in the midst of a new heavens and a new earth. The Protestant mind needs to be made whole, so that the voice of the Reformation tradition in our day can claim the entire creation for God once again, rather than focusing almost exclusively on God's history with humanity, while the natural world is interpreted as a kind of staging area for that divine-human drama.[2]

That such a theological healing is required will become evident as we review the course of the Protestant theological response to the environmental crisis during the last two decades. The typical Protestant response to this crisis has been repeatedly to prescribe the theology of human dominion, in various forms. There is a better solution—a wholistic solution adumbrated both in the Scriptures and in the classical Western theological tradition.

THE PROBLEMATIC OF THE PROTESTANT MIND:
FROM EARTH DAY 1970 TO EARTH DAY 1990

As we marked Earth Day 1990 in the United States, we also witnessed a pronounced increase around the globe in environmental awareness. The churches have been a part of this international discussion. Consider the World Council of Churches' new emphasis on "Justice, Peace, and the Integrity of Creation."[3] That accent on creation is new. Justice and peace have been longstanding emphases of the WCC.[4]

Given the immense scope and profound urgency of our global environmental crisis, this apparent greening of the public mind in general and of the Christian mind in particular can only be welcomed. But it all sounds disquietingly familiar. We have been here before, at least in the United States, particularly within the circles of North American Protestantism. Indeed, calls for increased environmental awareness and for the development of a theology of nature or a theology of ecology or a new land ethic have been issued in this country with an almost monotonous regularity for two decades or more, at least since the first national Earth Day in 1970. But whether we have finally begun to witness the greening of the Protestant mind in America can be debated.

For those who were around for the first Earth Day and its theological aftermath, there is surely a feeling of *deja vu*. A work like my *Brother Earth: Nature, God, and Ecology in a Time of Crisis* (1970), for example, was intended to be among the first of a wave of serious theological responses to the global environmental crisis, as that crisis was perceived by many with clarity already at that time.[5] But works like this were soon forgotten, and that wave of serious studies in ecological theology never emerged, as the nation and its Protestant churches quickly became preoccupied with other issues.

Notwithstanding that turn of events, during the ensuing twenty years a few theologians, notably John Cobb, Joseph Sittler, and, most recently, Jürgen Moltmann, valiantly continued to explore theological issues related to the concerns of ecology and the environment.[6] Each, as it were, staked out the territory of one of the Trinitarian persons: the vision of a Creator who persuades all things and thus bestows value on all things (Cobb); the vision of a Redeemer who is the universal fountain of divine grace, the *Pantokrator* or Cosmic Christ (Sittler); the vision of a Sanctifier who feels with and indwells all things, nurturing them, and shepherds all things to their final sabbath rest (Moltmann). But these thinkers have found few influential audiences of any size either within the churches or beyond. During the last two decades, Cobb, Sittler, Molt-mann, and others like them tended to remain solitary explorers with small followings, as far as their ecological interests were concerned.

Other voices were also raised in the wake of that first wave of environmental awareness circa 1970, many of them speaking from the margins of the American church: feminist thinkers and exponents of Native American, Asian, or African religions.[7] But these voices scarcely received any hearing within the American Protestant mainstream apart from romanticized environmental interludes, usually played out at church camps or on wilderness treks.

In light of twenty years of often fitful and largely unfruitful theological starts, are we now to begin the process all over again in the wake of Earth Day 1990? Do we need still more calls for increased environmental awareness in our churches and for new theologies of nature or a new land ethic? Will such utterances do anything more than assuage the mounting environmental guilt among our members, providing temporary and symptomatic relief for those who issue them and for those who hear them? Do we not have to wrestle here with a deeper malaise of mind that requires a more thoroughgoing kind of therapy?

It is sobering to consider that the very Protestant mind that has sanctioned such calls for increased environmental awareness and for new theologies of nature during the last two decades has been largely preoccupied with other, sometimes antithetical interests. Thus many of the most vocal Third World spokespersons in our churches understandably have championed theologies of liberation. These theologies have been projected as historicized, humanistic theologies par excellence.[8] Characteristically they have betrayed little direct concern for the earth, except insofar as they have, rightly, identified how the resources of the earth have been grossly maldistributed. Protagonists of liberation theology have also been suspicious, rightly, of those who espouse environmental concerns, since appeals to the order of nature in the past have often served to lend support to the unjust structures of the established socioeconomic order. A concern to save the whales, for example, might just be a subterfuge, consciously intended or not, to distract the public from focusing attention on the shocking numbers of children dying in our cities.

Meanwhile, back in the First World, establishment practitioners of the theological arts have addressed themselves to global issues mainly in cultural and political contexts, such as pluralism, science and technology, world peace, and democratic capitalism. Or they have found

themselves, willy-nilly, swept up by more parochial ecclesiastical concerns, such as hermeneutics, the doctrine of the ministry, and church
growth.

This situation almost inevitably has driven those Protestant church
leaders who have cared about environmental issues to fall back on long-
established and little-examined theological assumptions, most of them
having to do with the theological concept of human dominion over the
earth. In the process, they have also tended to ransack the Scriptures
to gather what have appeared to them to be environmentally relevant
texts, usually without the assistance of seasoned biblical scholars.[9]

Thus espoused as a kind of emergency solution by Protestant church
leaders who have not been able to find any other readily available options
in the Reformation tradition, the theology of human dominion over
nature has generally taken two forms during the last twenty years.[10]
Those who have identified chiefly with Third World concerns sometimes
have spoken of "new visions of eco-justice."[11] Those who have been
more at home in a First World milieu have tended to speak of "a new
theology of responsible stewardship."[12]

Whether promulgated under the banners of eco-justice or responsible
stewardship, all these theological options amounted to the traditional
Protestant theology of human dominion all over again. Their long
introductions describing the environmental crisis and impassioned affirmations of the need for a theological response, with a liberal sprinkling
of environmental proof-texts thrown in along the way, did not challenge
the underlying theological paradigm.

True, the theme "care for the earth" has emerged again and again
within Protestantism during the last twenty years, and this would suggest
a certain respect for what the World Council of Churches is now calling
"the integrity of the creation." But that theme has almost always been
emphatically attached, like an appendix, to the issues of *distributing* the
fruits of the earth justly (an eco-justice perspective) or *managing* the
productivity of the earth wisely (a responsible-stewardship perspective).[13] The theme "the integrity of the creation," in contrast, implies
contemplating nature as a world with its own life and its own value, in
short, caring for nature enough to allow it to have its own history with
God. But that theme, in the mind of many contemporary Protestants,
has been accorded little or no standing of its own. The advocates of
eco-justice or responsible stewardship may mention it, but they seem
to be nervous or unsure about the whole idea.

Could it be that the venerable Protestant theme of human dominion
over the earth is itself problematic? Could it be that the many environmental critics of Christian thought, beginning with Lynn White, Jr.,

have had a point all along?[14] Could it be that the reason that Protestant responses to the environmental crisis have not converted the church—or influenced substantial numbers outside the church—is because these responses have been part of the problem rather than part of the solution?

THEOLOGICAL ROOTS OF THE PROTESTANT PROBLEMATIC: THE-ANTHROPOLOGY AND HUMAN DOMINION OVER NATURE

The Protestant theology of dominion has its problems. It all began with a the-anthropological concentration in the thought of Luther and Calvin and came to its most notable modern fruition in the christological concentration espoused by Karl Barth.

The thought of Luther and Calvin is predicated on a vision of God and humanity in dynamic interpersonal communion, through the gracious Word of God.[15] God relating Godself graciously to humanity, and humanity responding to God in faith and love—that is the shape of the Reformation tradition's fundamental theological intuition.

Luther characteristically focuses his attention on justification by faith alone. That is obviously a theanthropological focus. It pertains to God graciously declaring the sinful human creature forgiven and the forgiven human creature appropriating that declaration in faith. Accordingly, Luther can observe at one point: "The knowledge of God and of man is the divine and properly theological wisdom" (*Luthers Werke* [Weimar], 40.2.7). For Calvin, the most important doctrine is the doctrine of the knowledge of God. And here, as in the doctrine of justification, God and humanity become the chief objects of attention. Calvin accordingly introduces his *Institutes* with words much like Luther's: "Our wisdom, in so far as it ought to be deemed true and solid wisdom, consists almost entirely of two parts: the knowledge of God and of ourselves" (*Institutes*, 1.1.1).

While the Reformers in a variety of ways also show a profound concern with the whole creation (which is highly suggestive and worth careful attention today), it nevertheless remains that *in accent*, if not always in substance, they repeatedly direct our attention to the dynamics of God's relationship with the human creature. Thus they tend to be preoccupied exegetically with the second creation narrative in Genesis, which highlights the human creation and fall (or so it had been read in the received tradition) and with New Testament texts such as Galatians and the first chapters of Romans, concerning justification by grace through faith alone, apart from works of the law. This focus on human sin and human salvation characterizes their biblical interpretation. They do not highlight the cosmic immensities portrayed by Genesis 1 and the apocalyptic universalities depicted in Revelation.

By the time of Karl Barth, the Reformers' the-anthropocentric focus had been systematized, especially by theologians who wrote in the tradition of Immanuel Kant and Albrecht Ritschl.[16] Such thinkers taught that God cannot be known in nature, and they often implied that God cannot even be encountered in nature. Both Kant and Ritschl maintained, systematically, that the divinely posited purpose of nature was to provide a place in which God could create, educate, or redeem "a kingdom of spirits." Kant and Ritschl also accented the theme that the proper relationship of the human creature to nature is dominion—a concept that often was taken by their followers to mean domination.

Theirs was a pristine logic. If the raison d'être of nature is essentially instrumental, why not use nature like the instrument it is for the greater glory of the underlying divine purpose, which is the creation and exaltation of the human creature? That nineteenth- and twentieth-century theologians like Ritschl, who stood in the Kantian tradition, also were serving scientific, technological, and economic interests is also noteworthy in this context.[17]

Karl Barth's theology exploded in the midst of this scenario with a resounding no.[18] In the name of his famous christological concentration, he took issue with what he considered to be the all-too-easy nineteenth-century identification of bourgeois progress with the coming of the kingdom of God. But he did so, as one of his most important essays states, in the name of *The Humanity of God*. He was chiefly concerned with God and humanity, in Christ Jesus. Howevermuch he might have distanced himself from his nineteenth-century predecessors in other respects, he essentially held firmly to their systematic subordination of nature to God and humanity. Remarkably, in the context of his extensive exegesis of the Genesis creation texts, Barth also argued that the Bible does not permit us to espouse a theology of nature at all, only a theology of God and humanity.

Nature only comes into view in Barth's thought in two respects: first, as the stage for God's covenant history with humanity; second, as the field in which the human creature exercises a limited but undeniable lordship, akin to the divine lordship over the creation. Strikingly, the same Barth who could celebrate the great beauties of Mozart's music found little or no opportunity to celebrate the beauty of the Swiss Alps, in the midst of which he lived. Wonder in Barth's thought almost always had to do with the glories of the divine-human drama, not with the glories of the divine creativity in the cosmos, as depicted, for example, in Psalm 104. Thus, what has rightly been called the "triumph of grace" in Barth's thought had this unintended result: the abnegation of nature. Did it ever cross Barth's mind that God might want the world God created to be blessed with the Alps and great whales, with hummingbirds and lilies of the field? It is doubtful that Barth ever entertained such thoughts.[19]

The problems of this kind of Protestant the-anthropology of nature are many. To begin with, it is intrinsically unstable. The theology of dominion too easily can become the ideology of domination. On the one hand, Barth does set limits for human dominion over nature so that it does not become domination of nature. Barth does not want to encourage what he thinks of as mindless exploitation of nature. But notice that these are the limits of prudence, not of essence. The human creature, in this sense, must not mindlessly exploit nature lest nature be destroyed and human life thus be undercut, or likewise lest some humans be enabled to exalt themselves unjustly over others through the accumulation of natural resources as their private domain. Barth was a socialist. He believed firmly in the just distribution of the goods of creation and the preservation of the earth for future generations. But, on the other hand, nature in itself essentially amounts to very little, according to the same Barthian logic. It has only an instrumental value, at best. Then what are we to believe when we read Barth, that human manipulation of nature must be restrained *or* that such manipulation is an essential datum of human life, to be taken for granted and even encouraged to the point of domination for the sake of social justice?[20]

In this connection, it is important to note that Barth knows of only two kinds of *ad extra* relationships on the part of persons: I–Thou relationships and I–It relationships. Authentic human relationships, in his view, are all I–Thou relationships. They are characterized by allowing the other his or her *Lebensraum*, because the Thou intrinsically, as one elected in Jesus Christ, requires that kind of respect. In this sense the Thou is a *Selbstzweck*, an end in himself or herself, *qua* elected. In contrast, according to Barth's schema, relationships with nature can only be I–It relationships. The creatures of nature have no raison d'être of their own. They are essentially mere objects, waiting to be used by persons. In this respect, Barth's thought seems to encourage the domination of nature, notwithstanding his explicit calls for prudent restraint.

Barth never finished his *Church Dogmatics,* in particular the section that would have dealt with eschatology, so we will never know how he would have envisioned the world to come. Would the world to come in his view be a world, as depicted in the Bible, where the lamb will lie down with the lion, where the whole earth will be renewed in abundant fecundity and majestic beauty as the desert blossoms, where the whole creation will end its travail and experience the glorious liberty of the children of God, where all the nations will gather at the holy mountain of Zion? Or would Barth's vision of the world to come be a divine-human world only, as Thomas and other classical theologians had maintained, with no plants and animals and mountains, since they are not essential constituents of the human essence?[21] Since in Barth's schema only humans, not plants and animals, not stars and galaxies, are elected in Jesus Christ, Barth's depiction of the world to come would have to have been humanistic to the extreme. Do not look for the greening of eternity in the thought of Karl Barth.

Barth's legacy, as far as the theology of nature and the ethics of the environment are concerned, leaves the minds of those who would be Barth's followers constantly vulnerable to the inroads of a spirit of domination. The line between eco-justice and responsible stewardship, on the one hand, and environmental exploitation, even destruction, on the other hand, can sometimes be ethereal. We know that Barth's thought stands as a Rock of Gibraltar against all forms of interhuman exploitation. But he offers us no strong guarantees for the Rock of Gibraltar itself. From Barth's perspective that rock could legitimately be here today and gone tomorrow, if its disappearance did not inhibit the well-being of the human creature in any essential respect.

The problem with an instrumental theology of eco-justice or the theology of responsible stewardship is not that these theological approaches to nature are necessarily wrong, but that they may be much too reticent; it is not that they are obviously incorrect, but that they may be too susceptible to distortion. And while it is true that the abuse of the principle should not discredit its validity, it is also true that probable abuse of the principle in a time of crisis certainly should discredit the principle's obvious utility, especially if other principles are available that may be less vulnerable to abuse.

Some of the most thoughtful of the post-Barthian exponents of eco-justice and responsible stewardship have recognized the vulnerability of their positions in this respect.[22] Thus one finds references in their writings regarding the need to respect nature in itself (nature as *Selbstzweck*), not only for its usefulness. Sometimes these thinkers even draw on extrabiblical sources, Native American religions, or romantic poets, and they opine that these heterodox perspectives have something to teach us! That may well be the case. But it is striking that these Protestant thinkers feel driven to exercise this rather odd theological maneuver. These exponents of eco-justice and responsible stewardship typically derive everything else that they hold to be theologically essential from the Bible and the classical theological tradition. Yet here they feel compelled to reach out, so uncharacteristically, to nontraditional theological sources in order to support their argumentation.[23]

For example, Douglas John Hall, a champion of the theology of responsible stewardship, finds it necessary to develop a relational anthropology, according to which the human creature is essentially, not just instrumentally, a part of nature. He even discusses the need to recognize "the spiritual element in matter." He explains that "the corollary of the statement that human being is being-with-nature is the recognition that nature, from its side, has a capacity for relatedness." We cannot conceive of the material world, he stresses, as though it were totally devoid of spirit—as though it were simply "it"! Accordingly, he talks about a sacramental approach to nature that resists the "thingification" of nature.[24]

The point here is not that writers such as theologian Hall do not have theological warrant, according to their own assumptions, to think in terms of the intrinsic value of nature or a sacramental vision of nature, although that is a question that must be raised in another context.[25] The point here is that when these writers seek to reaffirm the modern Protestant theology of dominion—that Barth exemplifies—either in terms of eco-justice or responsible stewardship, they find themselves compelled to affirm the value of nature in itself, the ultimate value of nature in the eyes of God, and the concrete indwelling of God in all things, not just the history of God with the human creature. Their attempt to qualify the modern Protestant theology of human dominion over nature, even as they seek to reinterpret that theology, shows the liabilities of that theology from the perspective of the insider.

If, following the inherited tradition of Luther and Calvin—which was brought to a radical conclusion by the christological concentration of Karl Barth—we discover that the modern Protestant theology of dominion has so many liabilities, must we not ask whether there might be a better alternative? Can this Protestant hardening of the categories be healed? In the tradition of Luther and Calvin, can one only espouse some kind of theanthropological interpretation of nature?

A NEW PARADIGM: CONSTRUCTING A WHOLISTIC PROTESTANT THEOLOGY

There is a better theological alternative. To identify it, it is necessary to invoke a concept that has become tediously familiar, the concept of the paradigm shift. What is needed is a new paradigm for Reformation theology, not a completely new theology. The parallel with the paradigm shift in the natural sciences in this instance appears to be exact. Einsteinian physics did not abrogate Newtonian physics. In the context of the former, the latter still remains true, as a general rule, insofar as the latter refers to the forces studied by Newton, such as those operative on a billiard table.

It is possible to reclaim the thought of Karl Barth in a new context, just as Einstein's science reclaimed Newton's. The laws of the billiard table remain true in the matrix of this new way of thinking, but in this case one pauses to look out the window as well, at the garden and the mountains on the horizon. This seems to be a highly promising project because, upon completion, it will allow us to open the door to paths that lead to a variety of theological options in this context, at least a few of which seem worthy of our attention. The theologies of John Cobb, Joseph Sittler, and Jürgen Moltmann have not gained the widespread, serious hearing in the churches precisely because the views of these thinkers have been informed by the new paradigm.[26] As Thomas Kuhn instructed us some years ago in *The Structure of Scientific Revolutions* (2nd ed., Chicago: Univ. of Chicago Press, 1962), the adherents of the old paradigm are simply ill-equipped to understand the insights of those who write from the context of the new paradigm. The defenders of the old, by temperament, can only reject constructions that emerge from the context of the new.

It is a question of identity that is before us here. Whatever negative responses some of Karl Barth's ideas might have elicited (Lutherans troubled by his understanding of Law and Gospel; feminists scandalized by his theology of man and woman), he remains the twentieth-century interpreter of the traditions of Luther and Calvin par excellence, in the eyes of most historically informed interpreters of the same traditions. Karl Barth is, or comes close to being, the Protestant Thomas Aquinas— for better or for worse.

Barth's thought embodies a self-conscious allegiance to the two most important principles of the Reformation: *sola gratia* and *sola scriptura*. Barth's thought does represent "the triumph of Grace," on the one hand, and a devotion to the Scriptures, on the other. This is nowhere more apparent than in his treatment of the doctrine of creation, which is an uncommonly lengthy exegesis of the two Genesis accounts of creation, predicated on a theological vision of the gracious eternal election of Jesus Christ and the people of Christ.

It is appropriate and necessary to turn to Barth's thought in this instance, where the concern is with the theological paradigm more than the theological particulars. For it is a question of identity we face here, not doctrine. And Barth certainly represents the theological identity of the traditions of Luther and Calvin.

If it is possible to hold firm to the essentials of Barth's thought while broadening its scope, and to show explicitly how this twentieth-century Protestant the-anthropology can be incorporated into the matrix of a more inclusive twentieth-century Protestant wholistic theology, then the requisite paradigm shift will have been clarified in a way that may enable protagonists of the old to step forward to claim the new without sensing a loss of identity. Then it might be possible for those visionary representatives of the new paradigm, such as Cobb, Sittler, and Molt-mann, to gain a fresh hearing in this respect.

A New Ecological Paradigm for Protestant Theology

To identify a new ecological paradigm, in the matrix of which this wholistic Protestant theology might be developed, we first take one historical step backward. We will discover that the new ecological paradigm we are seeking to identify is not so new at all, howevermuch it has been forgotten. This paradigm has been one of the two dominant modes of thought, or motifs, that have informed even the earliest Christian theologians.[27] Both motifs are related to a primordial human experience—the encounter with the overwhelming mountain. From the rites of primal religions to the intuitions of moderns such as Paul Cezanne, who passionately contemplated Mount Saint-Victoire again and again, mountain heights have universally captivated the human imagination and its religious sensibilities. This primordial experience characteristically has taken historical form in two related but distinct modes, one projected from the perspective of the mountain heights, contemplating the ethereal regions above, the other projected from the same heights, but, instead, contemplating the global vision of the manifoldness of being on every side. From these two originating experiences of the overwhelming mountain two metaphors have come to expression in many forms and various cultures. One grows out of the contemplation of the ethereal above and can be called the metaphor of ascent. The other grows out of the contemplation of the fullness of reality around and can be called the metaphor of fecundity. The itinerary of the mind, in the first instance, is upward. It moves away from the manifoldness of being below toward some exalted experience of pure and all-transcending spiritual unity above, the One. The itinerary of the mind

in the second instance is outward and circuitous. It moves out toward
the surrounding manifoldness of being and embraces its fullness, a vision
of the Many.

The ancient Hebrew people were captivated by yet another metaphor
drawn from the force of the Exodus experience: the metaphor of migration to the good land. In this instance the itinerary of the mind is
forward, moving toward a wholistic, earthly future—from materially
deprived wilderness experience toward an experience of earthly abundance—toward a land flowing with milk and honey.

On the basis of these three metaphors, operative in many cultural
contexts in the West, two motifs developed in classical theology. One,
predicated on the metaphor of ascent, is the spiritual motif. The other,
predicated on both the metaphor of fecundity and the metaphor of
migration to the good land, is the ecological motif. This motif depicts
the world at the beginning, the Alpha, in terms of a primordial fecundity;
and it envisions the ending, the Omega, in terms of arrival at the earthly
abundance of the Promised Land. Both the spiritual and the ecological
motifs are attested in the Scriptures, and both are in evidence in the
classical theological tradition in the West. The "new" ecological paradigm, then, is an itinerary of the mind that begins with the experience
of fecundity and moves toward a fulfilling experience of overflowing
earthly blessings.

In Barth's thought the spiritual motif dominates. For Barth, theology
begins when we lift up our eyes to the heights of eternal election, where
we see a world constituted by mainly spiritual creatures: God and humanity, united in Jesus Christ. Only in service of that primal vision does
the manifoldness of the created world come into being. The spiritual
motif shapes Barth's thought from beginning to end. The ecological
motif comes into view only when a place is required in the midst of
which the primal spiritual story of God and humanity can unfold. Barth
is not really interested in the fecundity of nature, except insofar as it
offers a congenial stage for the playing out of the divine-human drama.
Nor does Barth characteristically think of salvation in terms of a "land
experience," akin to the one in the Hebrew Scriptures. Characteristically,
when Barth is interpreting Romans 8 concerning the whole creation
groaning in travail, awaiting the liberation now enjoyed by the children
of God, he suggests that this expression, "the whole creation," in fact
refers to human creatures alone, not to the cosmos!

Now let us begin to think theologically in terms of this paradigm
shift. What happens if we appropriate the Barthian schema no longer
on the basis of the spiritual motif (the metaphor of ascent), but rather

on the basis of the ecological motif (the metaphors of fecundity and migration to the good land)? This paradigm shift is permissible for inheritors of the Reformation tradition, since both *sola gratia* and *sola scriptura* can be variously affirmed within the matrix of either paradigm. The difference is this. With our vision enlightened by the ecological paradigm, the grace we can see is the life of God overflowing, predicated on self-giving love, to the whole creation, not primarily to the human creature. The promise proclaimed in the Scriptures can be heard not just as the gift of human salvation, but also as the gift of a new heavens and a new earth in which righteousness dwells for the sake of all creatures.

In the context of the ecological paradigm, then, *sola gratia* can remain the fundamental norm of all theological reflection. But this grace will now be displayed in terms of cosmic universality, not just in terms of anthropocentric particularity. Also, this expansion of the theological horizon can be accomplished in terms of *sola scriptura*. Texts such as the following, along with the formative texts so often cited by Luther and Calvin from Romans and Galatians, can take on a formative significance.

The first text depicts the cosmic scope of God's gracious activity *ad extra*, as God's reign moves toward its fulfillment: "For from him and through him and to him are all things. To him be glory forever. Amen" (Rom. 11:36). The second describes the reign of Christ in, with, and under God's universal history with all things, as that history is ultimately to be consummated: "For he must reign until he has put all enemies under his feet. The last enemy to be destroyed is death. . . . When all things are subjected to him, then the Son himself will also be subjected to him who put all things under him, that God may be all in all" (1 Cor. 15:28). A third hints at the cosmic work of the Spirit of God, nurturing all things, and suggests, as Ireneaus and Luther maintained, the image of the brooding of the mother hen over the nest of the whole creation: "When God began to create the heavens and the earth, the earth was without form and void, and darkness was upon the face of the deep; and the Spirit of God was moving over the face of the waters" (Gen. 1:1-2). A fourth text depicts the landscape of the consummated future of God: "Then I saw a new heavens and a new earth; for the first heavens and earth had passed away, and the sea was no more. And I saw the holy city, new Jerusalem, coming down out of heaven from God . . ." (Rev. 21:1-2). Such texts point to a normative biblical warrant for the ecological paradigm and show the significance of *sola scriptura* for this exposition.

It remains, then, to depict how this universal divine ecology unfolds, in contrast to the more narrow divine-human economy in Barth's thought. One difference becomes immediately apparent. In keeping with the promissory character of the metaphor of migration to a good land, and in response to the eschatology that shaped the teachings of Jesus and the theology of Paul, the *final fulfillment* becomes the integrating construct in this ecological theology, rather than the *eternal beginning*, as is the case in Barth's thought. Still, the prologue in heaven, the covenant, must be allotted its own definitive significance.[28]

The Covenant

The "whence" of the divine ecology is the covenant, or the originating commitment that the infinite living God makes to initiate, sustain, and complete a history with a finite world, in the midst of which this God wills to call forth the human creature. This, in the most compact language available, is the originating divine covenant:

> God resolves in eternity graciously to communicate God's infinite life to interrelated and interdependent communities of finite beings in fitting ways, and to enter into communion appropriately with every community of finite being, mediated by the eternal Logos of God and energized by the eternal Spirit of God, in order to manifest the divine glory through a universal history, which God wills to bring to its completion when the time is right, so that all things, in appropriate ways, might enter into the eternal sabbath rest of God.

Perhaps the most radical departure from Barth's thinking suggested by this summary statement of the covenant is the description of the prologue in heaven in general terms, as a prologue. Hence the classical theological distinction between the eternal Logos of God and the incarnate Logos of God (the *logos asarkos* and the *logos ensarkos*) is preserved here, whereas Barth collapses the two. The name Jesus Christ is not yet mentioned in the context of the covenant, precisely to preserve the historical particularity and the eschatological concreteness of the incarnation and the promised parousia.

God has a real history with all things, not a predetermined history. What is sure and certain in God's primordial eternity is God's resolve to carry out God's purpose. What is not sure is the way in which that resolve is to be enacted in cosmic history. God must struggle to bring that history to the fulfillment God intends for it from the very beginning, by the mediation of the Logos and the energizing of the Spirit. In Barth's thought, in contrast, "first things" are so completely defined that little is left to be added when we describe the unfolding of the divine covenant in time and space and its subsequent eternal fulfillment.[29] The promissory character of the metaphor of migration to a good land requires us to envision the original, initiating intention or commitment of God in open-ended terms, as the beginning of a genuine history with all things.

The originating divine plan is not to establish a world in order to educate or redeem a "kingdom of spirits," as Kant and Ritschl taught and as Barth believed, but it is something more expansive and more encompassing. The divine purpose is to establish and shepherd a universal history of nearly infinite variations and to bring that history to its fulfillment in the eternal sabbath rest of God.

The God of the Covenant

As we continue to reflect within the context of the ecological paradigm, it becomes apparent that three major emendations should be made to Barth's doctrine of God, two of them developed by Jürgen Moltmann and the other espoused by the medieval theologian Bonaventure. The first has to do with the inner-trinitarian principle, attested throughout the course of the classical tradition, that the Father is the source of the whole Trinity (*pater fons totius trinitatis*). Barth takes this principle as a given. But it now appears that this principle is an afterglow of ancient Greek metaphysics and the metaphor of ascent. The principle was predicated on the conception of a hierarchy of being, with the undifferentiated, purely spiritual One at the apex. Moltmann argues convincingly that a more communitarian and egalitarian image of each of the divine persons in relation to the others does more justice to the biblical notion of the living God who has a history with all creatures.[30]

We have seen in the covenant vision how God graciously wills to bring into being and to enter into communion with interrelated and interdependent communities of beings. Since the world God creates is itself communitarian and since our doctrine of God will shape our image of the world, it is important also to be able to envision a deity who is fundamentally communitarian. It will then be all the more fitting that such a God should create and redeem a communitarian world.

The second emendation has to do with the richness of the inner-trinitarian life. If space permitted, it would be highly instructive to draw on the trinitarian insights of Bonaventure extensively at this point.[31] Bonaventure understands the life of trinitarian persons to be characterized by an infinite fecundity in themselves, which for him is the inner-trinitarian ground for the extra-trinitarian divine creativity in terms of fecundity. Since Barth is not really concerned with the theme of fecundity, this thought does not emerge in his trinitarian thought. But it certainly commends itself for our attention as we seek to outline a doctrine of God that is shaped by the ecological paradigm.

The third emendation of Barth's doctrine of God, this one also suggested by Moltmann, has to do with a new accent on God's self-limitation, on the one hand, and God's mothering of the creation, on the other hand, especially by the nurturing energy of the Spirit. This God creates a space within the divine being, withdrawing to allow the cosmos to have its own place.[32] In this schema the cosmos is not dominated by a distant and therefore overpowering divine otherness, as some Protestant images of God, including Barth's, have sometimes suggested. This God is one who calls into being by eliciting and who rules by nurturing, as John Cobb has suggested. This God is not a king, akin to the Persian emperors of old, as Alfred North Whitehead once reminded us. This God is one who is most characteristically revealed in the humility of the cross, whose power is weakness. This is a God who can enter intimately and immediately into an interactive history with all creatures, not one who controls them like puppets.

The Integrity of Nature

The expression the "integrity of creation" is one that the World Council of Churches has lately given some currency.[33] That is a promising development, but this new terminology will remain a *flatus vocis* if it is not firmly rooted in some appropriate theological conceptuality. The inherited Protestant theological tradition, as that tradition is exemplified by Karl Barth's theanthropological thought, seems ill-equipped to do that. What is required is a triangular mode of thought that corresponds to the trinitarian structure of the divine life. The line between God and nature must be drawn just as visibly as the lines between God and humanity, and between humanity and nature. Barth maintains that we cannot know anything about the line between God and nature. In his thought, therefore, nature is inevitably interpreted in terms of its instrumental value; it has no divinely bestowed standing of its own.

Nor will it be sufficient only to redraw the line between humanity and nature, with heavier strokes toward the pole of nature, as Douglas John Hall has sought to do with his concept of a relational ontology.[34] He argues that the relationship with nature belongs to the human essence and that nature therefore is not merely an object posited by God for the sake of human manipulation. This is an improvement on Barth's the-anthropological narrowness. But it is doubtful whether Hall and others who move in the same direction actually demonstrate theologically that nature is a genuine other, with its own integrity, not merely an object at human disposal. Even in this relational anthropological schema, the integrity of nature will finally have to be understood chiefly in terms of *human* being. Thus Hall discusses "the three dimensions of human relatedness," being-with-God, being-with-the-human-counterpart, and being-with-nature.[35] While he acknowledges that the first, being-with-God, means being with "the source and ground of all being,"[36] Hall actually does not depict that third line in the triangular set of relationships, the one between God and nature, with any sustained attention. He is chiefly concerned with the lines between God and humanity, and humanity and nature.

In practice, that kind of relational ontology will also soon become vulnerable to the spirit of domination, since the relationship of the human being with nature is understood in this context chiefly in terms of the human actor who takes responsibility for nature.[37] The human creature, in this schema, plays a kind of *Paterfamilias* role vis-à-vis nature, not owning nature outright but being "truly responsible for what happens in the household."[38] The human creature, according to this way of thinking, is never responsible *to* nature as a genuine other, but is typically responsible *for* nature as a dependent other.

In the past, many theologians thought of woman in a similar way—that she is Adam's rib and gains her meaning from *his* responsible and caring relationship with her. Now that the voice of women has been heard with resounding clarity, it has become apparent that it is dehumanizing to interpret female being in terms of male being, howevermuch the interpreter takes pains to indicate that the woman has her own integrity. Ultimately that leads to "the rape culture." Likewise for nature. If nature is interpreted mainly in terms of human being, then the spirit of domination, the rape of nature, cannot easily be kept at bay.

So it is important to say that God has a history with nature that is independent of God's history with humanity, although the two, nature and humanity, are also intimately interrelated and interdependent. This is suggested by the covenant stated above: God resolves in eternity graciously to communicate God's infinite life to interrelated and interdependent communities of beings, and to enter into communion with them in appropriate ways, through a universal history.

God has a history with the galaxies, communicating God's infinite life to them gloriously. The white heat of the stars reflects the divine majesty in a way that humans, who are like grasshoppers, never could.

Likewise, God has a history with the dinosaurs and the ichthyosaurs and all the sea monsters and every great beast of the forests and the fields, however threatening they might be to us when we cross their paths. The Siberian tiger thus reflects the divine majesty in a way that humans, who were not there when God laid the foundations of the world, never could:

> Tiger! Tiger! burning bright,
> In the forests of the night,
> What immortal hand or eye
> Could frame thy fearful symmetry?
>   William Blake,
>   "The Tiger"

There is a time, especially in the night, when it is best for the tiny human creature to withdraw like a grasshopper into some protective niche, to allow the great ones of the cosmos to thunder and to frolic with God. When you are huddled by the hearth in the middle of the night and you hear the lightning crack or the lions roar, then you may first begin to understand the integrity of nature. Then with the coming of the day, with the sun blazing down on the fields, you might see still more, with the eyes of a Vincent Van Gogh: the richness of the soil and the beauty of the lilies, to which even Solomon in all his glory could not compare. Then you will all the more understand the integrity of nature.

The Vocation of the Human Creature

Although every community of being within the universal history of God with the creation mirrors the glory of God, only members of the human community are created according to the image of God. The human creature, created in community like all other creaturely beings, is unique in this respect: the human creature is called to enter into self-conscious communion with God, along with other humans, through confessions of praise and acts of obedience. We have much to learn from Barth at this point, in particular as he accents the uniqueness and the responsibility of the human creature.

But Barth's theology of the human creature also needs to be expanded. Barth's vision is too qualified by the theme of human uniqueness, and he overemphasizes human dominion. Thus his image of the human creature in relation to nature accents human manipulation and even exploitation of nature. However, given the ecological paradigm, the image of God as the one who elicits all things, and the vision of nature as communities of beings with their own integrity, it is fitting to think of the human creature no longer as *homo faber* (humans as those who "make"), but as *homo cooperans* (humans as those who cooperate).[39]

Given the familiar Protestant proclivity to allow the idea of dominion to be interpreted and enacted as domination, it may be best to call a moratorium on the use of that conceptuality altogether. It appears that the Protestant concept of dominion has, at least for the foreseeable future, lost its viability, notwithstanding some heroic attempts to salvage the idea.[40] Likewise for the closely related and for the church financially rewarding idea of stewardship. It may not be worth the effort to keep trying to interpret it "the right way," since it is so tainted with the nuances of manipulation and exploitation.[41] The vision of humanity as *homo cooperans* is much more in tune with the biblical vision of shalom than is the popular image of human dominion.[42]

In order to think wholistically in terms of *homo cooperans*, and not just anthropocentrically, it will be necessary to revise the Protestant understanding, taken for granted by Barth, of human *ad extra* relationships. If the only human *ad extra* relationships are I–Thou and I–It relationships, then human relationships to nature must be depicted in terms of dominion or domination, since (notwithstanding speculations by Martin Buber to the contrary) human beings do not enter into I–Thou relationships with the other creatures of nature. That is suggested by the image of Adam alone in the Garden of Eden. He was not fully himself when he was alone with the animals. He could not communicate with the animals. He could not give himself fully to the animals. He needed another human being. Human beings speak and respond, with meanings too deep for words at times, but with meanings nevertheless. Hence it is important for us to have available a conceptuality of I–Thou, I–It, *and* I–Ens, the latter pointing to a relationship of contemplation and cooperation with nature.[43]

The I–Ens relationship is a bonding of two beings from different communities of being, one capable of personal communion and the other not. Unlike the I–Thou relationship, which is always verbal at some level and always reciprocal in some way, the I–Ens relation is always nonverbal and only sometimes reciprocal, as in the case of some relationships between humans and animals. This is part of the significance of the account of Adam naming the animals.

The I stands before the Ens, contemplating another creature or aspect of creation with its own integrity before God, called forth by God with its own value. With wonder and awe the I contemplate the mysterious givenness and beauty of the Ens. Luther's remark is significant: "If you really examined a kernel of grain thoroughly, you would die of wonder" (*Luthers Werke* [Weimar], 29.496). Sometimes such wonder is transmuted as repulsion when the I contemplates the dark side of nature, as symbolized by Melville's white whale, Moby Dick. At other times, the wonder of the I before the Ens is transfigured as delight, as when with Jesus one contemplates the lilies of the field. The I of the I–Ens relationship never seeks to manipulate or exploit, but always wills to receive this other as a divine creation with its own integrity and inviolability, as a sign of grace, even when the Ens might be found to be repulsive.

Furthermore, the I always stands before the Ens with gratitude, never with greed. The Ens can never be property. The Ens always belongs to the Creator alone. The Ens is never mine. The Ens is always Thine. Once it is mine, greed begins to take over. Greed breeds mindless manipulation and finally ruthless exploitation. But when the other creature is Thine, the I stands before the Ens in gratitude, which brings with it contemplation and celebration, sometimes with joyful abandon.

Homo cooperans lives with the creatures of nature as Entia, creatures called forth by God for the sake of God's own history with them and for the purposes of blessing human life. *Homo cooperans* is attentive to the Ens and its needs, as a creature to be honored and served. As God once stepped back and created a space so that the whole world could have its *Lebensraum,* so, imaging the divine restraint and the divine ministry, *homo cooperans* stands back and contemplates the Ens and sees that it is good. *Homo cooperans* waits with humble and caring attention for opportunities to know and to serve the Ens.

To speak in terms of humanity as *homo cooperans* is not to reject what René Dubos has called "creative intervention in the earth."[44] The argument here should not suggest passivity on the part of humans as the only divinely mandated relationship with nature. On the contrary, *homo cooperans* should, on occasion, intervene creatively in the systems of nature. How else are humans to build up their own communities of shalom, given the ravages of the elements and God-given human needs such as food, shelter, security, sex, culture, and festivity? The point, then, is that intervention in natural systems should be predicated on the attending and the caring of the I–Ens relationship.

I do not intend here to foreclose discussion about vegetarianism, animal research, or, more generally, human development of the world of nature. Nor do I intend to foreclose discussions about issues of distributive justice in human history, vis-à-vis nature. The Scriptures propose homocentric values ("are you not of more value than they?"

[Matt. 6:26b]), as well as cosmocentric values ("to serve it and to protect it" [Gen. 2:15]).[45] All such discussions must be carried on under the rubric of *homo cooperans*. The only divinely mandated way for the human creature to develop the resources of nature, when that is the moral choice of the moment, is within the context of a relationship of co-operation.

The Cosmic Vocation of Jesus Christ and the Cosmic Ministry of the Holy Spirit

Ireneaus thought of the Word and the Spirit as the hands of God.[46] We have seen that the covenant of God with all things is mediated by the Logos and energized by the Spirit. We now name the Logos and the Spirit Jesus Christ and the Holy Spirit, while, in the context of the ecological paradigm, we still confess the cosmic scope of their works. The cosmic vocation of Jesus Christ is depicted in Col. 1:15-16, and the cosmic ministry of the Holy Spirit is adumbrated in the first verses of Genesis. These themes belong at the heart of this wholistic theological reconstruction. Karl Barth would have nothing to do with such themes, nor will many Protestants today.

But in the triangular shape of this ecological theology the line between God and nature completes the picture, along with the lines between God and humanity, and between humanity and nature. Jesus Christ as the Lord of life is the firstborn of creation, in whom all things cohere and to whom all things tend. Jesus Christ is the cosmic Christ, the *Pantokrator,* as Joseph Sittler suggested.[47] The Holy Spirit is the *Spiritus Creator,* the lifegiver, according to the Nicene Creed, who dwells in all things and sanctifies all things, as Jürgen Moltmann wrote.[48]

The vocation of Jesus Christ does not only relate to human sin, as shown with pathos and power on the cross.[49] But as the resurrected one who comes from the future of God, Jesus Christ is also the perfecter of the whole creation.[50] His coming signals therefore the beginning of the ending (in the sense of *telos*) of all things, when they shall cease from their groaning in travail and also enjoy the liberty that the children of God now enjoy, on the day when the Son hands the Spirit-filled cosmos over to the Father, when God shall be all in all.

Furthermore, the advent of Jesus Christ, as the one who has come to blot out human sin, also means that he has come to restore the sinful human creature to a right relationship with God and therefore to a right relationship with nature, as well as with other human beings. Insofar as believers live in communion with Jesus Christ, therefore, believers know what was never theirs as sinners alone: the primal realities of life in the creation as the garden of God, living as *homo cooperans*. Insofar as they live in communion with Jesus Christ, likewise, believers also can have a foretaste of the feast to come. They can savor tastes of that great cosmic banquet, when as citizens of the new Jerusalem they will contemplate the glories of the Lord shining not only within that city, but from every creature of nature that will dwell in a new heaven and a new earth.[51]

4

ECO-JUSTICE AND LIBERATION THEOLOGY
The Priority of Human Well-Being

Heidi Hadsell

*W*hat possibilities emerge when we explore Latin American liberation theology and ethics in thinking about eco-justice? While liberation thought has not taken eco-justice as a central category of reflection, its distinctive approach to ethical questions in the human world can be very useful in shedding light on questions about the environment. This chapter focuses on several of the elements that compose this approach: anthropocentrism, a central interest in justice, a critique of capitalism, and a critique of scientific neutrality.

LIBERATION THOUGHT IS ANTHROPOCENTRIC

Liberation thought is centered on the human world. It emphasizes and gives priority to human relationships and to human history. The normative questions it asks have to do with human beings. In other words, liberation thought is thoroughly anthropocentric.[1] It works within the dualistic separation of humanity from nature that has been characteristic of much of modern philosophy and modern theology. The anthropocentric emphasis in liberation thought is evident both in its theological affirmations and in the themes and events in contemporary life that are its central ethical concerns.

Theologically, liberation thought affirms the human-centered focus of Christianity by emphasizing God's primary interest in, and action in, the human world. The symbol of God's concern with humanity is the central Christian theological affirmation that God became human in

Jesus. In the opening pages of *A Theology of Liberation*, Gustavo Gutierrez underlines this fundamental Christian anthropocentrism with a quote from Karl Barth: "The God of Christian revelation is a God made man, hence the famous comment of Karl Barth regarding Christian anthropocentrism—'Man is the measure of all things, since God became man.' "[2]

Liberation thought adds emphasis to this anthropocentric understanding, with a Christology in which the humanity of Jesus is accented.

> Being a Christian does not mean, first and foremost, believing in a message. It means believing in a person. Having faith means believing that a certain human being of our own history, a Jew named Jesus, who was born of Mary, who proclaimed the Father's love, the gospel, to the poor, and liberated those in captivity, who boldly confronted the great one of his people and the representatives of the occupying power, who was executed as a subversive, is the Christ, the Messiah, the Anointed One, the Son.[3]

This human-centered theological understanding undergirds the ethical concerns of liberation thought. It allows, and even demands, liberation theologians to put concrete human life at the center of their reflection.[4]

Born in the context of extreme economic and social inequalities and massive human suffering, liberation ethics has concentrated on the following: an insistence on the full humanity and dignity of the poor; a social analysis of the systemic roots of their misery; and the search for a Christian understanding of the praxis of human liberation. It has devoted itself to human social relationships,[5] and has had neither the motivation nor the luxury of scrutinizing human relationships with nature, or nature itself.[6] To the extent that nature has become an object of reflection, it is due to its effect on and interaction with human individuals and communities and not as an object in itself. What therefore is the value of nature in an ethic so centered on the human?

The value of nature in liberation thought is derived from the value of human life. This is not to say that nature has no value. Rather, its value is in relation to human life. Nature in and by itself, unrelated to human life, is not valued; it acquires its value by reference to human life and human communities, and its value remains secondary to that of human life. In this as in other respects, liberation ethics takes the form of ethical utilitarianism. The end is human well-being. To the extent that nature contributes to human well-being it is to be valued, but it is viewed primarily as having instrumental rather than intrinsic value. The concern for human well-being involves concern for the well-being of nature. The reverse is also true: the concern for the natural

human habitat can be one way of taking human welfare seriously. Enrique Dussel clearly expresses a concern for nature that remains human
centered: "Its destruction is the annihilation of the locus of human
history, of humanity, of the incarnation, and hence the gravest of ethical
misdeeds."[7]

LIBERATION THOUGHT IS JUSTICE-CENTERED

As stated above, the theology of liberation takes human relationships
as its point of departure. But it does not stop there. Rather, it establishes
as a central element of its thought the idea of justice. To talk about
human relationships is not enough; it is also necessary to evaluate those
relationships in the light of justice.[8]

While different authors stress varying nuances in the concept of
justice, they agree that the central normative claim of Christian social
thought for all human social practices is love, manifested in the social
world as justice.[9] The ethical dialogue about eco-justice therefore must
be first and foremost a dialogue about the requirements of justice,
particularly justice toward the poor. It is the *fil conducteur* through the
maze of conflicting claims and languages about the environment, and
it orders all other commitments and values.

Justice in liberation thought is primarily a social category. It refers
to human institutions and routinized human social practices, both of
which are independent of individual motivations or feelings. To ask the
question of justice in relation to environmental questions is to embed
environmental questions in a network of other characteristics in the
social world, some of which, at first glance, may seem to have little to
do with the environment. Such characteristics include human forms of
production and distribution, human patterns of consumption, human
habits of leisure and work, human ideologies and beliefs. These patterns
of social interaction mediate our social relationships and our relationships with nature and must be carefully scrutinized.[10]

In its radical commitment to justice in the human social world,
liberation thought meets and challenges certain tendencies in what may
be characterized as a "naturalistic" approach to the environment. Justice
insists on the fundamental priority of human responsibility to humans,
particularly to the poor. So, for instance, to focus on the intrinsic rights
of nature, in a world where the intrinsic rights of many humans are
honored only in the breach, is to distort priorities and to romanticize
nature.

To put this question in another way, the location of human well-
being at the center of ethical concern prevents the placing of the natural

world over against the social world, so that the natural world becomes a new human fetish. This fetishizing of nature contributes to human self-alienation. Nature becomes the subject and humans become its object; human life is valued in relation to nature, rather than the natural valued in relation to the human. Humans become a problem of nature, rather than the protection of nature being a human problem; meanwhile, justice slips from view altogether.[11]

Examples of this fetishizing of nature are not difficult to find. In the United States today, there is considerable concern over the destruction of the Amazon rain forest. With some exceptions, the concern is just that: concern about the rain forest and not about the people who live in it. A human-centered ethic committed to justice, by contrast, starts with the human inhabitants of the rain forest and takes their welfare seriously. In order to save the Indians, one must save the forest. The welfare of the human inhabitants will be the welfare of the forest. The two are not separate nor antithetical, but humans remain the central ethical concern.[12]

A current example of a political movement using this logic is that of the rubber tappers in the Amazon, whose leader, Chico Mendes, became an international environmental *cause célèbre* when he was killed by ranchers in December 1989. In the last decade the rubber tappers have organized in order to protect the rain forest from growing numbers of cattle ranchers and farmers who burn the forest in order to pasture cattle and grow crops. The tappers seek to protect the forest, but they seek its protection, not as an object in itself, unrelated to human communities, but as a part of nature that they depend on for their own livelihood. Their economic survival is directly linked to the preservation of the forest.

Liberation thought's commitment to human liberation in human history is related to the Christian concept of the kingdom. Liberation thought affirms that there is a *telos* in the human project, there is direction in human history, and Christian normative obligations and claims are related to it. Christians are to live in the light of what could be, but is not yet, and to participate in the creation of the future.[13] The future here envisioned is not empty of normative content. Rather, it implies a time in which the human hopes for justice and the full flowering of human potentiality are possible.

The vision of the kingdom is another point at which liberation thought questions naturalistic assumptions. It underlines the affirmation that human life is indeed distinct from nature, although conditioned by it, by affirming a distinctively "human project."[14] It also establishes a normative perspective from which to evaluate this human project. It rejects the pattern of the actual Western human project, describing it as one of domination of both humans and nature, without abandoning the notion of the human project altogether. It thereby avoids collapsing what is distinctively human into the natural.[15]

LIBERATION THOUGHT CHALLENGES PREVAILING ECONOMIC ASSUMPTIONS

The utopian elements in liberation thought have led to a healthy mistrust of the various discourses that claim to be limited to the "real." One such discourse, and a dominant one, is that of economics. Much of the perceived conflict between the claims of justice, on the one hand, and the demands of environmental responsibility, on the other, center on assumptions made about economic growth.[16] Growth in the market economy is assumed to be the economic engine that will, eventually, produce enough so that everyone can live decently and thus will eventually enable societies to meet the minimum requirements of distributive justice. It is on the basis of such claims that growth models of development have been exported around the world, as well as "sold" to us here in the United States.

But growth is also identified as one of the, if not the, major causes of environmental destruction.[17] Growth involves production, which requires consumption, and both production and consumption damage the natural human habitat. The problem as posed leads to the conclusion that one must choose somehow between justice in the form of economic development, and the protection of the environment in the form of limiting growth.

These assumptions are widely shared in both the Third World and the First World and are a major focus of the polemic between them. Indeed, the expression eco-justice is precisely an attempt to hold in tension what are thought to be contradictory claims based on such assumptions about growth. Based on such assumptions, Third World nations are convinced that environmentalists are saying that these nations must stop growing and therefore abandon their hopes for development. First World nations are convinced that the protection of undeveloped parts of the Third World are increasingly the major source of hope for human survival.[18]

Liberation thought joins this debate in two major ways. One is an external critique, which emerges from the position of the Third World in the global economy. The other is an internal critique that questions the nature of capitalism itself.

The external critique is based primarily on an understanding of theories of dependency that come from Marxist political economy.[19] Dependency theory is an analysis of capitalism seen from its periphery. The major theme in dependency theory is, of course, that the poverty of the South is directly related to and even a function of the capitalist accumulation in the North, in a process that dates back to the first contacts between North and South. According to this theory, the economic exigencies of the North (center) are largely determinative of the nature of the economic life of the South (periphery). Accordingly, as the theory's name suggests, Southern economies are "dependent" on those of the North. The result is what one author calls the "disarticulation" of the Southern economies.[20] They are economies that once integrated in the world market in an inferior position, have never had the opportunity to control the economic process for their own ends.

While the stress on dependency may be somewhat overdone in an increasingly interdependent economic world, the insight into the varying and often contradictory dynamics and effects of international capitalism is valuable for thinking through environmental questions. First, dependency theory disagrees with the capitalist claims of being able to provide prosperity for all. In so doing, it brings the dynamics of capitalism themselves directly into the debate. The critique of capitalism, centered on the connection between the private accumulation of wealth (primarily in the North) and the exploitation of labor (primarily in the South) is one that attributes to the capitalist search for profits the increasing marginalization of millions of people in both center and periphery.[21] In other words, given the international hierarchy of capitalism and the internal structures it creates, growth tends actually to increase rather than to decrease the inequalities of distribution both among nations and among classes within nations. Growth itself therefore is questioned, and with it, the supposed necessary choice between growth and the environment.

Second, since dependency theory emphasizes the varying effects of capitalism (depending in large part on where an economy is placed in the international hierarchy), it is able to make distinctions that are important for thinking about the environment internationally. For example, center and peripheral nations are able to exert varying degrees of control over their economies and the corporations active in them. Peripheral nations, burdened by international debts and insufficient national capital have little choice other than to submit to the rules of the international market administered by such agencies as the International Monetary Fund and the World Bank. Such agencies require policies intended to promote rapid growth and profits, which are destructive of both the environment and the human labor force.[22] The destruction of the Amazon is precisely the result of such policies, which have "opened up" the region to capitalist activity.

Joining dependency theorists, the liberationist critique of capitalism simultaneously shifts the burden of responsibility for environmental destruction caused by economic activity to the North and calls for a radical reassessment and restructuring of the international market system.[23]

The internal critique of capitalism is one that focuses on the dynamics of capitalism itself and not simply on their effects on the capitalist world's periphery. The ethical critique is based on a normative commitment to justice, sharpened by the empirical evidence of the marginalization of millions that capitalism causes. One of the elements in the internal critique most relevant to issues of eco-justice is the comparison between the role of humans in the production process and the role of nature. Both human labor and the natural world are sources of economic value. Both nature and people are exploited in the search for profit, and nature, like human labor power, is appropriated and transformed, in the productive process, into private wealth. In both cases, the capitalist treats exhausted human labor and ruined nature as simply "negative externalities" or by-products of the process of production. Accordingly, capitalist logic refuses to take responsibility for the by-products of poverty, massive marginalization, and environmental destruction. Far from being in competition with each other, the garbage dumps and the people condemned to live on them are the products of the same economic logic. Or, to use again the example of Amazon, the marginalization of the Indians and Amazonian peasants and the destruction of the rain forest are the results of the same process of accumulation.

This analysis suggests that instead of remaining within the limits posed by the logic of the market system, one must examine the system itself. The debate then must move beyond false choices to discovering the mechanisms available or necessary for addressing the logic of capitalism itself, so that first, people and second, nature are no longer treated as mere externalities of the process of private accumulation. We need to discover how to bring the process of production and accumulation under wider human control.[24]

The thoroughgoing questioning of capitalism distinguishes the liberationist evaluation of capitalism from other evaluations that, while sharing much of the liberationist's normative critique, advocate reform without questioning capitalism itself. Daly and Cobb for example in their recent work *For the Common Good* advocate a limitation both of the scale of the market system and of its growth.[25] Their attempt to contain and reform rather than to replace the capitalist system is representative of much of the literature on the environment that views capitalism as problematical by virtue of its excesses and not by virtue of dynamics intrinsic to it.

LIBERATION THOUGHT IS PARTICIPATORY

In theory, if not always fact, liberation thought emerges from and encourages decentralized and nonhierarchical forms of organization in which everyone may participate. Born in the shadow of authoritarian military dictatorships and a hierarchical and authoritarian church, liberation thought has for the most part refused to reproduce the patterns of relationships of these institutions. Instead, it has sought to endorse democratic forms of decision making.[26] It has taken its cue from base communities that are, by and large, inclusive and horizontal rather than vertical and that consider the processes of decision making as important as the decisions themselves.

Liberation thought has also placed a high value on the organic connections between the local folk and their political and intellectual representatives. Indeed their roots within their communities legitimate liberation theologians far more than any claim they may have to special knowledge.[27] And liberation theologians are quick to critique themselves when they become too estranged from the base they represent.

This emphasis on the organic grounding of and the legitimation of liberation thought is important to eco-justice concerns. It encourages the demystification of scientific expertise through an identification of the ideology in scientific thought itself, and a questioning of scientific autonomy.

Science, far from being nonideological, has, as Jürgen Habermas has suggested, become the dominant ideology of this era.[28] It bases its claims and derives its legitimacy on its own science-based technology, rather than on any connection to human communities. As such, science is self-legitimating, requiring no referent beyond itself. It understands itself as neutral and above the human fray. Daniel Bell, convinced by such claims, has even proclaimed the "end of ideology" altogether, since scientific wisdom seems destined to become the great arbiter, rendering political and economic ideological conflict obsolete.[29]

Liberation thought, by contrast, with its grounding in "the people," implicitly suggests that knowledge of any kind that is self-legitimating is also self-serving and therefore to be viewed with a highly critical eye. It further suggests that rather than fostering democratic processes, an over-reliance on scientific expertise tends toward a new form of authoritarianism.

The role of scientific expertise therefore is to be questioned to the extent that it promotes its own self-aggrandizement and pushes the questions of the environment to a level that is less accessible to most people. In so doing, it is ultimately destructive of the kind of society in which both the environment and human justice are prominent concerns.

In its evaluation of the uses and misuses of technology, liberation thought comes close to many other voices in the dialogue about eco-justice. It shares, for instance, much of the analysis of those who question economic development as a goal in and of itself and who urge a rethinking not only of the goals of economic development, but also its process, as well as the use of qualitative indices to measure "development" rather than merely quantitative ones. Similarly, as is consistent with its own commitment to local, popular control and management of industry and agriculture, liberation thought may easily support such environmentally sound techniques as those that entail the use of appropriate technologies, as well as labor-intensive rather than capital-intensive economic production, and other such techniques that at the same time help protect the environment and empower the poor and the marginalized.

LATIN AMERICAN LIBERATION THOUGHT AND OTHER LIBERATING THEOLOGIES

Latin American liberation theology is not the only form of liberation thought. Today there are many liberating theologies from many contexts, some of which contribute more to the ongoing dialogue about eco-justice than others. Feminist thought, for example, which shares with liberation thought a concern for human social life and human social relationships, has begun to explore specifically female ways of knowing and of acting as moral subjects.[30] Indeed it is by virtue of their engagement with women's social reality that feminists have searched for the epistemological and theological roots of women's oppression. Thus feminists have developed a critique of many of the dualisms embedded in the foundations of Western thought such as that between body and spirit and that between nature and humanity that have contributed to the human misuse of nature as well as to male oppression of women.

Feminist thought of this kind contributes substantially to current thought on the environment. It also challenges other kinds of liberation thought such as that from Latin America to reconsider the epistemological assumptions embedded in their own thought.

In a manner similar to that of the feminist exploration of womens' reality, Latin American liberationists motivated by their political and social engagement with the poor have searched for analytical tools that can illuminate economic and political marginalization. One such tool has come from Marxist thought. From this base, the liberationists' challenge to feminists is to make explicit the class bias implicit in much of feminist thought. More recently, many liberationists have committed themselves to an exploration of "popular" religiosity and culture. This has been and promises to continue to be a source of innovation and growth in liberation thought, and there may be elements in this thought that contribute specifically to the question of eco-justice.

CONCLUSION

After exploring the possibilities of liberation thought in contributing to reflection on eco-justice, we conclude that liberation thought provides concepts and tools of analysis important to an adequate ethical understanding of eco-justice. Fundamentally, eco-justice ethics derived from the theology of liberation is a political ethics. Its contribution is contained in its assumptions regarding the ethical primacy of the human social world, and the claims of justice contained therein; in the critique of capitalism both as it is experienced in the Third World and in its intrinsic nature; and in its suspicion of the ideological elements and authoritarian tendencies of viewing science as the only expertise. Certainly liberation thought, as a creation of the southern hemisphere, has some limitations for thinking about ecology in both the context of the capitalism of the northern hemisphere and in the content of the social questions it addresses. Aside from such contextual issues, it appears clearly adequate for the analysis of both realities.

THE NEW STORY

Redemption as Fulfillment of Creation

George H. Kehm

*T*here is an urgent need today for a theology that includes the whole of creation in redemption. Only such a theology can correct the constriction of the Christian message that has been allowed to go on virtually unchallenged within the churches until recent times. The constriction is anthropocentrism. H. Paul Santmire has called it the-anthropocentrism.[1] It is found in both individualistic and social versions of the gospel, the one centering on the salvation of the individual soul, the other on the transformation of society and individuals in the direction of the justice of God's kingdom. Neither version of anthropocentrism promotes a vision of the world that would include all species, ecosystems, and the entire biotic community (including the earth itself) as included in the salvation promised by God according to the Christian story.

Even if an ethic of stewardship of the earth and its "resources" is included in the theologies underlying these anthropocentric outlooks, that ethic inevitably falls into some form of utilitarianism with respect to the extrahuman creation. Both the theology and ethics of anthropocentric versions of the Christian story are unwarranted constrictions of the biblical story, and they contribute more to the problem than to the solution of the present ecological crisis.

Thomas Berry has described the main features of the flawed version of the Christian story.[2] While his descriptions reflect his experience in the Roman Catholic church, American Protestants can easily recognize the features he singles out in their own hymns, sermons, and confessional standards.[3] The story focuses on the soul or the self; the struggle for deliverance from personal sin or inauthentic selfhood; the turn to faith in Jesus as one's Lord and Savior as the crucial breakthrough to personal salvation, authentic freedom, wholeness, and so on. In mainline Protestant churches the story includes participation in the believing community and one's ability to work with others for social justice and world peace. Nevertheless, it remains a story about what God has done and still does for the salvation of humankind (or only a segment, according to some Protestant doctrines). Berry is right that such a version of the Christian story "is no longer the Story of the Earth, nor is it the integral Story of [Hu]Mankind."[4] He considers it tragic that many Christians have accepted this version of their story as "normal." The truth is that the anthropocentric character of this version, its neglect of the inter-relatedness of human and extrahuman creatures, and its constricted view of redemption constitute fundamental distortions of the Christian story as normed by the fullness of the biblical story.

H. Paul Santmire has formulated a question that must be faced when Christian theologians try to displace the old, constricted version with one that is new and recovers neglected, essential elements of the Bible. Here is Santmire's question:

> Is the final aim of God, in [God's] governance of all things, to bring into being at the very end a glorified kingdom of *spirits alone* who, thus united with God, may contemplate [God] in perfect bliss, while as a precondition for their ecstasy all other creatures of nature must be left by God to fall away into eternal oblivion? Or is the aim of God . . . to communicate [God's] life to another in a way which calls forth at the very end new heavens and a new earth in which rightness dwells, *a transfigured cosmos* where peace is universally established between all creatures at last, in the midst of which is situated a glorious city of resurrected saints who dwell in justice, blessed with all the resplendent fullness of the earth, and who continually call upon all creatures to join with them in their joyful praise of the one who is all in all? (Emphasis mine.)[5]

I present in this chapter biblical and theological arguments in support of the second option, particularly that portion of the second option I hold to be essential to the Christian story, namely, the inclusion of the whole creation in the "final aim of God."

Santmire argued for this option on the basis of his "ecological reading of the Bible." He thought that "a large majority of biblical scholars" would have chosen the first option.[6] Yet many fine biblical scholars today are not only open to the second option but have written in support of it. Today there is greater awareness among scholars of philosophical challenges to dualistic distinctions (human/nonhuman, nature/history) and also a new openness to explore the appropriateness of other categories in biblical interpretation.[7] Dualistic distinctions virtually forced interpretations of the Bible in the direction of anthropocentrism, that is, the first option. The time seems ripe to promote the second option.

I will not here examine all the relevant biblical evidence, nor shall I retrace matters widely agreed upon by biblical scholars and systematic theologians. I also assume certain doctrines and beliefs shared by Christian theologians, which are firmly rooted in the Old Testament and are presupposed by the New Testament literature.[8]

What follows is my tracing of the themes of God's commitment to the earth or to the whole created world in the Bible (outside of Genesis creation narratives). The materials or themes most pertinent to this study are (1) the Noachic covenant; (2) Israel and the land; (3) the inclusion of creation in prophetic eschatology; (4) the inclusion of creation in the teachings of Jesus; (5) the redemption of creation in Pauline and Deutero-Pauline eschatology; and (6) the vision of ultimate salvation in Revelation. I shall rely on the work of competent exegetes for detailed textual support. My concern as a systematic theologian is with the question of the essentiality of the claim that the earth or even the whole created world is included in the redemptive work of God and ultimate salvation. The question of essentiality (essential to the Christian story, that is) is a properly systematic theological question, not a historical one. It is not settled simply by reconstructing "the biblical story" and demonstrating the presence in it of the theological claim in question.[9] Nor is it settled by an authority argument that says because the Bible contains this claim it is obligatory for Christians to believe and affirm it since the Bible is the norm of the church's proclamation of the Christian story.[10] Rather, the argument for essentiality has to demonstrate the *indispensability* to the Christian story of an idea or theological claim: that this idea or claim must be in the story or else the story would not be *that* story.[11]

What I show below is that the biblical material examined brings to light a divine commitment to the redemption of the whole creation. Moreover, the purpose of cosmic redemption is the glorification of God by a final triumph over all evil that promotes all creatures to their proper fulfillment and issues in a kind of praise of God that is indispensable to the full manifestation of God's glory. This value of creatures for God, which cannot be reduced to value for humans, is the ultimate and necessary basis in Christian theology for a Christian environmental ethic premised on the intrinsic value of created beings.

THE NOACHIC COVENANT

Bernard Anderson has called this an "ecological covenant."[12] Anderson warns against interpretations of the opening chapters of Genesis, the "primeval history," that separate them from the history that extends to the Exodus-Sinai events and beyond. It is especially important not to separate the creation narratives from Genesis 9, as we shall see.

The history from creation to Exodus-Sinai is "periodized into a sequence of covenants, each of which is called a *berith olam*, a covenant in perpetuity."[13] This type of covenant stresses "the unilateral initiative and sovereign grace of the covenant maker who 'gives' or 'establishes' the covenant, in comparison to the more bilateral covenant type in which the covenant initiator imposes conditions and sanctions on the other contracting party (e.g., Exod. 24:3-8)."[14] According to the Priestly scheme, the first period extended from creation to the end of the Flood. This period was concluded with a *berith olam* between *Elohim* (God) and Noah, his family, and his descendants. "This was a universal covenant in that it embraced all peoples (the offspring of Noah's sons) and an ecological covenant in that it included the animals and a solemn divine pledge regarding the constancy of 'nature' (Gen. 8:21-22)."[15] Anderson goes on to describe the second period of the P history that extended from Noah to Abraham, with whom *El Shaddai* (God Almighty) made a *berith olam* promising to "be God" to him and his descendants, and granting the land as a "possession in perpetuity" (Genesis 17). The third period extended from Abraham to the sojourn at Sinai where God fulfilled the pledge to "be God" by giving God's personal name and presence in the tabernacle in the midst of the people. At this point the sabbath is regarded as the sign of the *berith olam* between God and the people (Exod. 31:13-17). "Thus the sabbath, which was 'hidden in creation,' (Gen. 2:2f.) and which became a cultic reality at Sinai, provides both the literary and theological *inclusio* that binds together the whole history with its system of covenants."[16]

The later covenants do not displace or abrogate the earlier ones, nor do they ignore their commitments. While Anderson, following Frank Cross, regards the later covenants as more ultimate with respect to the degree of revelation and divine commitment to "dwell" with human beings, he does not seem to suggest that the earlier are abrogated or ignored by the later. Anderson's remarks suggest the opposite, namely, that the later covenants include the commitments made in the earlier ones, and that God is still committed to bringing about aspects of the earlier covenants not yet fulfilled in history. Not only shall Abraham's descendants be blessed, but all nations shall share in the blessing. Not only shall the descendants of Noah, the nations, be blessed, but the earth and all living things upon it shall be blessed.

It is the Noachic covenant and not the creation narratives that provides the source of hope for a new creation. This covenant came in the wake of the corruption of the original creation by human "violence," which provoked God's decision to destroy all living creatures on the face of the earth except Noah, his family, and the remnants of each species he took into the ark. After the destruction, God permits a new beginning and resolves never again to curse the soil or destroy every living creature because of human sinfulness. God promises this despite the persistence of the evil imagination in the human heart, which had caused such havoc in the first place (Gen. 8:21ff.). God makes an "everlasting covenant" with "every living being of all flesh that is upon the earth" (9:16), and even with the earth itself (9:12, 13). Anderson concludes: "In the first and last analysis, the hope for the human and nonhuman creation is grounded in the *sola gratia* of God's universal, ecological covenant."[17] I would add to this the suggestion that the Noachic covenant makes explicit and unambiguous the divine commitment to the preservation of creation that was only implicit and ambiguous in God's recognition of the original creation as "very good" (Gen. 1:31). God's commitment to the earth in the Noachic covenant may be taken as a sign of God's commitment to creation as a whole. Despite the fact that the creation is no longer in a condition of pristine harmony, God is committed to its continuation and flourishing (the latter being implied in the prospect of many seedtimes and harvests to come, and that not just for Israel but for all the peoples of the earth).

The Noachic covenant is the only one of the covenants referred to in the Bible that is not made with people but with the earth and all its inhabitants, human and nonhuman.[18] Interpretations of the Bible that jump from the creation narratives to the Abrahamic and Sinai covenants, and on to the covenant with David and the new covenant of Jeremiah, winding up with the new covenant in the New Testament writings— all the while ignoring the Noachic covenant—easily slide into an anthropocentric understanding of the Bible. Karl Barth's theology is a case in point. H. Paul Santmire has amply demonstrated the "theanthropocentric" character of Barth's theology.[19] Barth also gives skimpy treatment to the Noachic covenant and in his fullest discussion bypasses God's commitment to the earth.[20] If Barth had followed a hermeneutic like Anderson's and developed a doctrine of creation ordered to an eternal covenant that included a divine commitment to the earth "in

perpetuity," we might have seen greater emphasis on the intrinsic value
of created being as such and a more cosmic view of reconciliation and
redemption than can be found in Barth's *Church Dogmatics*.

ISRAEL AND THE LAND

The theme of God's commitment to the earth appears again in the
biblical traditions relating to Israel and its land. A number of scholars
have seen that the very idea of "Israel," the special people with whom
God covenanted at Sinai and bound to the Torah, is inconceivable
without the land promised to them. Israel was called to be a landed
people, to live by the Torah on the land God gave to it.[21]

The Torah contains interesting legislation concerning the land itself.
Of particular interest is the legislation pertaining to the "sabbath of the
land" (Lev. 25:1-7) and to the Jubilee year (Lev. 25:8-55), which are
integrally related. They have to do with the obligations God, to whom
the land properly belongs,[22] imposed on the "tenants" to whom God
gave it in order that by "keeping" them the land, too, would be kept
fruitful and its inhabitants would be able to "dwell in the land securely"
(Lev. 25:18). Note that the inhabitants the land was intended to support
include not only its human inhabitants (the Hebrew landlords and
everyone in their households, including slaves and resident aliens), but
also the animals who lived on it, wild as well as domestic (Lev. 25:6;
cf. Exod. 23:10-13). It is as if the land and its human and nonhuman
inhabitants were a community whose diverse members suffered or flour-
ished together depending upon whether the "ecological" stipulations
of Israel's God, the Creator of heaven and earth, were kept.

At first glance, the Jubilee legislation seems to be concerned only
with people, specifically the Israelites who had been forced to give up
their property in the interval between Jubilee years.[23] They and their
children were to be freed to return to their ancestral lands in that year.
In this way, the allotments of land made by God when Israel occupied
the land were to be kept intact, thus honoring God's sole ownership of
the land. Furthermore, Israelites who had been forced into slavery were
restored to freedom—the only proper status for those chosen to be
God's servants (Lev. 25:42, 55). Implied in these provisions, however,
is the assumption that the loyal service to God required of Israel was,
in part, the keeping of the sabbath legislation both for people and for
the land (including its animal inhabitants). The right kind of people
with the right way of life were required to keep the land rightly, it
seems. What is implied here is an "ethical ecology" that sees people,

animals, crops, and land as interrelated in a living whole whose well-being depends on honoring the Creator's will for each to exist and to have its rightful place in the whole. It was an ecology in which flourishing life was contingent upon doing justice, and ecological decline was a consequence of injustice—contempt for the Creator shown by violating what was right for God's creatures. This "ethical ecology" is even more evident in the prophetic traditions, as we shall see.

The reference to the sabbath connects this legislation with the creation narratives. It is as if the obligations of "keeping" the earth left unspecified in those narratives are made more specific, at least as they applied to Israel and its land, in the sabbatical legislation. Paul van Buren has contended that Israel's way of living on its land is in fact its "witness to creation."

> Every creature has a place in God's creation. Israel's sense of place . . . should be heard by all creatures as its witness to God's purpose for [God's] creatures. From the testimony of this nation, every nation may take courage to believe that it, too, is in the hands of the God who gives it a place—strictly of its own—in which important words can be spoken which "establish identity, define vocation, and envision destiny." Israel's discovery of the meaning of place is an invitation to all peoples to make a similar discovery.[24]

In the previous section we noted the international scope of the Noachic and Abrahamic covenants. Van Buren and others see this theme continuing in God's covenant with Israel and thus giving to Israel's "specialness" a representative function. Israel is to be "a light to the nations" (Isa. 42:6). With respect to the way Israel is called to live on its land, its witness to the nations would be to disclose to them the relationship between earth and people that was intended by God's work of creation. Thus, Israel's "land ethic"[25] may be construed as a pointer to a universal ethic of care of the earth. The theological principle that justifies such an interpretation has been well stated by George S. Hendry. "[T]he God of biblical faith," he writes, "elects," that is, "introduces [God]self and relates [God's] action to particular people." But, "the election of the particular is from the first instrumental to the attainment of the universal; it is the method, or strategy, of God to begin with the particular and advance to the universal."[26]

THE INCLUSION OF "NATURE" IN PROPHETIC ESCHATOLOGY

We can see further evidence to support Hendry's claim in the expansion of Israel's eschatological hopes to include universal peace among all

nations and all creatures and not simply hope for a restoration of Israel
to security and prosperity on its land. Donald Gowan has catalogued
and described the various pictures of eschatological salvation found in
the Old Testament.[27] He finds in most of them references to transformed
persons, transformed relations between Israel and the nations, and a
transformed nature. The global expression for this total transformation
is, of course, shalom. What shalom means is perhaps best illustrated in
peace pictures such as Isa. 11:1-9 or Ezekiel 34 (the latter even speaks
of a "covenant of peace," v. 25).

Taking just the Isaianic picture, the recovery envisaged for Judah
includes the renewal of faithfulness ("knowledge of God"), social justice,
and peace throughout the land. Justice for the poor is restored through
the reign of a righteous king. "Peace" between humans and animals
accompanies this social transformation. It is depicted in mind-boggling
ways: carnivores ceasing to hunt prey, poisonous snakes ceasing to be
threats to humans. The obvious point of the imagery is that all forms
of "violence," hurting or killing, have ceased on God's holy mountain,
indeed, not only on Mount Zion but throughout the earth (v. 9).[28]
Isaiah's imagery portrays an inclusive vision of salvation that is the
obverse of the inclusive visions of doom, both of which presuppose
what we have called the "ethical ecology" grounded in creation.

The most succinct expression of the ruin brought about by the violation of this ecology is in Hosea, although this same pattern can be
found throughout the prophetic writings.

> Hear the word of the Lord, O people of Israel;
>   for the Lord has an indictment against
>   the inhabitants of the land.
> There is no faithfulness or loyalty,
>   no knowledge of God in the land.
> Swearing, lying, and murder, and stealing and
>   adultery break out; bloodshed
>   follows bloodshed.
> Therefore the land mourns, and all who
>   live in it languish;
>   together with the wild animals and
>   the birds of the air,
>   even the fish of the sea are perishing.
>   (Hos. 4:1-3)

The message of Isaiah to the people of Judah and Jerusalem exhibits
these same features: (1) rebellion against God issuing in estrangement

from God (1:2-4, 21-23); (2) rampant injustice flowing from this de-
fection from God, the rich and powerful oppressing the poor (3:13ff.;
5:8); (3) ecological damage resulting from the economic oppression
(5:10).[29] The devastation of the land by invading armies and the removal
of the people are the reasons for the reversion of the land to wilderness,
however (6:10-12; 7:20-25; 35:12ff.). This devastation, though not
evidently a consequence of the injustices done within Israel, is thought
of as integrally related to them as though it was an inevitable outcome
of Israel's wickedness. According to the well-known act-consequence
pattern of thought in the prophetic traditions, acts invariably release
influences for good or evil into the community. The consequences may
emerge proximally or distantly, rebound upon the doer or upon others.
The consequences are also under God's power, however, so that their
occurrence is referred either to God's blessing or to the withholding of
such.[30] Thus, idolatry-driven injustice will have evil consequences sooner
or later, whether upon the perpetrators, the community, the land, or
all three. In Isaiah, both the ecological depletion of the land (evidently
related to overworking it, perhaps also monoculture farming) and the
devastation of the land by invading armies are God's "punishments" for
Israel's infidelity and injustice. But because of the ecological interrelatedness of people and land, and the continuity between acts and consequences, both consequences stem from the same root. By the same
token, any vision of salvation would have to include the reversal of the
evils affecting all aspects of the ecological system. And that is what we
find in the prophets.[31] What this means is that prophetic eschatology
inherently reaches for an eschatology that exhibits what Santmire calls
"symmetry" between the ultimate salvation promised by God and God's
commitment to the "ethical ecology" grounded in creation and eluci-
dated by the Noachic covenant and the sabbath legislation.

One other basic element in prophetic theology drives its eschatology
in this direction. That is the affirmation that the savior or redeemer of
Israel is none other than the Creator of heaven and earth. Deutero-
Isaiah makes this point repeatedly.[32] Israel could hardly think of God
in any other way. Its paradigmatic experience of redemption, the Exodus-Sinai events, showed God not only as its savior but as the "sole
Power" (Martin Buber) over all things. Think of the plagues, the crossing
of the sea, the thunderings and quaking earth at Sinai—"nature" at the
disposal of Israel's God. The thought is inevitable: Israel's savior is the
Creator. This means not only that Israel's God is the one true God and
all other pretenders to such status are deceivers. It also means the purposes of the savior must coincide with those of the Creator. God's saving

acts for Israel can only be a kind of "first fruits" of a salvation that would
extend to the ends of the earth, indeed, to the whole creation. It is not
surprising that someone from the Isaianic school produced a vision of
ultimate salvation as a transfigured cosmos, "new heavens and a new
earth" (Isa. 65:17ff.; note the repetition of Isa. 11:9ff.). "New" here
means a renewed, fulfilled version of the old, not a replacement of it
by a totally new production, as if the old were simply abandoned. What
we have here is another peace picture that centers on a restored and
exalted Jerusalem but alludes to a cosmic transformation as if the salvation imagined for Jerusalem required a universal peace. The logic of
the identity of the savior with the Creator requires that God's saving
action contribute to the promotion of the creation to its fulfillment. It
is not simply a counteractive measure aimed at restoration of a prior
order. Moreover, even if that saving action is focused on a particular
people, it must contribute to healing and fulfillment for all peoples and
for the earth itself, and even for the good of the whole creation, as
unimaginable as that may be. In sum, the thrust of prophetic eschatology
is toward the promotion of the created world to the richer patterns of
right relations (justice) among all creatures, to attain that harmony and
satisfaction among all creatures that is called shalom.

THE INCLUSION OF CREATION
IN JESUS' ESCHATOLOGY

The central theme of Jesus' preaching is "the reign of God." This expression was an evocative symbol, not a clearly defined concept.[33] Its
content is difficult to pin down from the references to it in the Gospels.
At the heart of it was the old, prophetic concern for "righteousness,"
right relations in all aspects of life. This was what God demanded of
people and what God's actions as "king" aimed to bring about. The
programmatic statement in Luke 4:16-21 indicates the scope of the
new initiative of God that Jesus proclaimed.

> The Spirit of the Lord is upon me,
> because he has anointed me to bring
>   good news to the poor.
> He has sent me to proclaim release
>   to the captives
> and recovery of sight to the blind,
> to let the oppressed go free,
> to proclaim the year of the Lord's favor.
>   (Luke 4:18-19)[34]

Comparatively new in Jesus' message was his claim that the new and ultimate manifestation of God's reign was already breaking forth in history in conjunction with his own words and deeds. Also new, and shocking to the religious authorities, was his teaching of the radical, unconditional mercy of God that extended salvation to the "wicked" (blatant sinners, and Jews who had "made themselves Gentiles," i.e., put themselves beyond the pale of salvation). One "entered" God's reign (and so was "saved") by subjecting oneself to God's limitless mercy and care and by enacting one's faithfulness to God by showing a like mercy and care for all others (including enemies). Such a life fulfilled the righteousness required by the commandments, which Jesus summed up in a great commandment and a second one like it (Matt. 2:36-40), these being the bedrock of "all the law and the prophets." Such was the heart of the message Jesus preached and which provided the platform for the renewal of Israel he and his followers sought to bring about.

One might have expected Jesus to have declared himself openly on the issue of whether God was about to restore Israel to sovereignty over its land. Apparently that was a much-debated subject among the Jews at that time, and the nationalistic parties affirmed such a restoration. In his exhaustive study of the teachings of Jesus bearing upon the theme of Israel's land, W. D. Davies concluded that "Jesus . . . paid little attention to the relationship between Yahweh, Israel and the land."[35] As we have seen, the theme of the land connects with the "land ethic" found in Leviticus 25 and parallel sources in Exodus and Deuteronomy. We would like to have Jesus' interpretation of this material, especially something about the obligations to care for the earth and its nonhuman inhabitants. Unfortunately, the Gospels provide no decisive evidence on this matter.

There are a couple of explicit references to "the earth" in Jesus' teaching that offer some clues as to what he thought about the destiny of the created world. First, there is the saying in the Beatitudes, "Blessed are the meek for they shall inherit the earth" (Matt. 5:5). This saying probably refers back to Ps. 37:11, "the meek shall inherit the land." The Hebrew text uses the word *eretz*, which means, in this instance, the land promised to Israel. The Matthean text translates this word by the expression *tēn gēn*, which means "the earth."[36] Was Jesus moving from specific restorationist language to the language of a more universal hope? It seems so. Then it would follow that his vision of the ultimate form of the reign of God moved in the direction of a universal shalom like that found in the prophetic traditions, especially in the later chapters of Isaiah.

The second text referring to the earth is the petition in the Lord's Prayer, "Thy kingdom come, thy will be done, on earth as it is in heaven" (Matt. 6:10). The Lukan version is probably more original. It leaves unanswered the question whether the ultimate form of God's reign would be achieved on earth or in some transcendent realm. The Matthean version answers this question in favor of realization of God's reign on earth. Was this Jesus' view or only Matthew's? We think it was Jesus' view and that Matthew rightly interpreted the shorter petition. This interpretation fits the conclusion we reached above about the meaning of "the meek shall inherit the earth." It is also supported by the consensus that has emerged in the past decade among Gospel scholars in North America that Jesus did not expect a cataclysmic end of the world but held a this-worldly view of the expected reign of God.[37]

Sean Freyne has provided the most judicious and insightful interpretation to date of Jesus' attitude toward the land. He shows that Jesus continued the tradition of interpreting Israel's "specialness" as having a representative function. It was to be a means of conveying to the nations instructions about God, human beings, nations, and nature that contain something of universal validity. Freyne's words deserve to be quoted at length:

> The boundaries of the land were very definite reminders of Israel's separateness, and the experience at the time of the hellenistic reform led to increased sensitivity in that regard subsequently, among all strands of Second Temple Judaism. In that climate the primary purpose of the symbol [viz., the land—my comment], God's care and concern for Israel, was in grave danger of being distorted into an ideology which generated violence, xenophobia, and isolationism. These were not features of the earlier Mosaic dispensation, or of the prophetic reinterpretation at an earlier period of Israel's history, especially that of Isaiah. Just as [Jesus'] healing and exorcising ministry in Galilee did not directly attack the temple symbolism, but transformed its range and scope, so too his treatment of the land-symbol did not regard the confines of the land as important. In dealing with this theme of universal care, images taken from the land in its primordial significance of the created universe, rather than in its capacity to symbolize Israel's special election—the birds, the trees (olive and vine), flowers and seeds—are used to probe the depths of the vision and to instil in his hearers a confidence in the message, based on everyday experience of the land.[38]

In other words, we find in the sayings of Jesus bits of wisdom about how to live under God's reign with and from the earth and its creatures, especially now that the advent of the powers of ultimate salvation—

God's transforming word of unconditional forgiveness and the Spirit
of God—had come into history through his ministry. The more par-
ticularist symbols of Israel's tradition are used to promote the universal
intentions of the creation traditions. A conception of the ultimate fulfillment of God's reign in the form of a universal peace brought about
by the flourishing of right relations among all God's creatures would
be consistent with the tenor of Jesus' teachings. The apostle Paul was
the first among New Testament writers to draw out the theological lines
that lead to such a conception of ultimate salvation.

THE REDEMPTION OF THE WHOLE CREATION IN THE PAULINE AND DEUTERO-PAULINE EPISTLES

J. Christiaan Beker has pointed out the fundamental importance of the
"apocalyptic world view" for Paul's thought.[39] The resurrection of Jesus
Christ meant, for Paul, that the "new age" of the consummation of all
of God's ways and works with creation had dawned. It signaled God's
victory over "the last enemy," death, and the beginning of the release
of the powers of the new age into history.

The resurrection of Jesus was understood by Paul to be essentially
related to the resurrection of all who are (or who would be found to
be) "in Christ" (1 Cor. 15:22-23). It was the "firstfruits of the harvest
of the dead" (NEB). This harvest was understood, in turn, to be essentially related to the subjection of every kind of anti-God "rule" and
"authority" and "power" (1 Cor. 15:27). Tracing the expansion of
Christ's redemptive work to its ultimate outcome, Paul concluded with
a vision of the inclusion of all things in God, a situation in which God,
the Creator of all things, is "all in all" (*he ho Theos panta en pasin;*
1 Cor. 15:28).

Paul goes on in this chapter to speak of the resurrection of the body.
The body is included in ultimate salvation, as the expression, "the resurrection of the body," already indicates. The body is essentially related
to what Paul calls "flesh," however (1 Cor. 15:38-39). By moving from
the term *soma* (body, v. 38) to *sarx* (flesh, v. 39), Paul links the human
body with the same kind of physical reality that animals, birds, and
fishes share in, albeit in different ways. In fact, by likening the human
body to the husk of a seed (v. 36f.) Paul even suggests a fundamental
connection between the human body and the plant world. What is
common to all who participate in this reality is that they are "perishable,"
that is, subject to death. What the resurrection from the dead means
for humans is that they thereby acquire a "spiritual body," that is, a

body that is imperishable or "immortal" (v. 44). That which was made from the "dust of the earth" becomes an imperishable reality, no longer subject to decay and death. The implication that there is an essential bond between humans and the earth itself is not developed in this chapter, but it emerges powerfully in Romans 8.

The eighth chapter of Romans opens a window to a cosmic eschatology that includes the whole of creation in redemption. Building on the axioms that all things are "from," "through," and "to" God (Rom. 11:36) and that the Lord, Jesus Christ, is God's executor, so to speak, in this originating and directing work of God (1 Cor. 8:6), Paul is led to the thought that the whole creation is destined for redemption (Rom. 8:21). The redemption from the powers of sin and death that has already been experienced in those who have received "the firstfruits of the Spirit" (v. 23) is here understood to be the harbinger of a universal redemption. What the creation is to be redeemed from is what Paul calls "futility" (*mataioteti;* v. 20) and bondage to "decay" (*phthoras;* v. 21). The first word is the same as the one in Ecclesiastes that is usually translated "vanity." It means emptiness, fruitlessness. The second term is roughly equivalent to what 1 Corinthians 15 means by corruptibility. Both terms refer to the realities of sin and death as endemic in the whole creation, especially the latter. The "futility" of which Paul speaks is related to the "subjection" to which the creation became victim in the aftermath of human sin (v. 20, perhaps generalizing from Genesis 3 to a creation-wide condition like being under a curse). "Bondage to decay" suggests that the hopeless being-unto-death Paul saw as the universal human plight is here understood to be part of a cosmic bondage. It should be noted carefully that the kind of suffering Paul imagines as afflicting Christians, people who have already experienced redemption from bondage to sin and death, is a suffering induced by the unredeemed state of the creation (v. 22f.). So long as they still live in their "earthly" bodies, even the redeemed will share in creation's groaning in travail til the time when the whole creation is redeemed from every last hold "death" has upon it.[40] The logic of this view of redemption is that unless redemption is cosmic, it cannot be complete for any part of the creation, not even the human part or some segment of the human part.[41]

The kind of cosmic Christology required by such a view of redemption emerges most clearly in the New Testament in Col. 1:15-20. Here is a vision of Christ as the agent of creation, the coordinating power "holding together" all things, and the mediator of the reconciliation of all things to God. Such a vision was anticipated in texts like Phil. 2:5-9.

Ephesians 1:3-10 (especially v. 10) reflects essentially the same vision of Christ, although the emphasis in this book is more upon the new community in which Jews and Gentiles had been united, this being understood as a precursor of the redemption and reunification of all things (a theme that appears in Colossians, too, e.g., 1:18 and 21f.).

Space does not permit discussion of the complex historical and theological problems connected with such things as the influence of the figure of Wisdom in Jewish sources on the understanding of Christ in Colossians.[42] Suffice it to say that Colossians shares the Pauline view that the new age of the consummation of creation had already dawned in the death and resurrection of Jesus Christ, in whom the "fulness of God" dwelt bodily (Col. 1:19). Perhaps even more than Paul this text emphasizes that God has already, in Christ, "reconciled" (note the past tense) all things to God, that is, made peace among all creatures on earth and in the heavenly places (Col. 1:20). The anti-God powers that Pauline epistles speak of as still needing to be brought under subjection are spoken of in Colossians as having already been "disarmed" and defeated (2:15). Nevertheless, the beneficiaries of this universal triumph of God in Christ are as yet only a small part of the creation, the part of the human race that has received the Holy Spirit. The gift of God's Spirit to the Christian community is understood as the power enabling it to be a precursor and communicator of redemption to the rest of humankind.

Though the Pauline and Deutero-Pauline writings do not develop the idea of a possible redemptive influence upon the extra-human creation that might accrue to the world-wide evangelizing mission of the church, their outlook supports the *hope* that influences of that sort are possible, and if possible, then obligatory for Christians to undertake. The idea that God subjected the creation to "futility" is but the background for the positive idea that God has done this to give it hope (Rom. 8:20), namely, hope of eventual redemption and ultimate salvation. Even if the ultimate fulfillment for which creation longs will not come til that future in which Christ "appears" together with all the transfigured children of God (Rom. 8:19), proximate or provisional forms of that fulfillment had already appeared in the lives of individuals and in the sphere of social life, according to the New Testament. The Pauline epistles emphasize this in talking about the new communal life made possible by the Spirit: the reconciliation of Jews and Gentiles; the emergence of new mutuality transcending authoritarian and oppressive relations between masters and slaves, Greeks and barbarians, men and women. To be sure, the historical performance of Christians fell short of the ideal of Gal. 3:28, but a breakthrough based on the power of the Holy Spirit had begun, and has continued to the present to inspire new initiatives and promote new advances in the direction of that ideal in the ongoing communities of Christ's people. There is no reason for Christians to hold back from attempting similar initiatives to promote liberation and reconciliation, the renewal of right relations, between humans and all the other creatures God loves.

THE INCLUSION OF CREATION IN THE
FINAL VISION OF REVELATION

There is one more piece of evidence to round out this overview of the biblical material most pertinent to our topic. It consists of two passages, Rev. 5:9-14 and Revelation 22. In the first passage, every creature in heaven and on earth and under the earth and in the sea (obviously, none is to be left out) joins the saints and the elders and the "four living creatures" who surround the throne of God and praise the Lamb who was slain for the world's salvation.[43] Matthias Rissi interprets this passage as a *prolepsis,* an anticipatory expression, of the final "universalism of salvation" that appears in the last chapter of the book.[44] Rissi's interpretation of the final vision of chapter 22 is worth quoting at length. It fits in perfectly with the hope for the redemption of the whole creation found in Romans 8.

> What lifts the final vision above all those that have preceded it is its *universalism of salvation.* While in the vision of the new Jerusalem with its open gates *promise* and the availability of unconditional grace is made manifest, the concluding vision prophesies the *realization* of this grace. Life and healing are now in fact imparted to all the nations. Jerusalem broadens itself out to become paradise. There is now no longer a "within and without," for the end of every curse and condemnation is announced: *kai pan katathema ouk estai eti.* ("there shall be no more anything accursed," 22:3). . . . This decisive, positively universal word of prophecy, which opens up the deepest meaning of the final vision, points towards a future which exceeds and brings to perfection the events of 21:10-27. The lake of fire, or the second death, is now done away with, for Israel, the nations, and the kings of the earth have entered into the fulness of the light of divine glory. Revelation exhibits a hope which embraces the entire creation.[45]

What Rissi says of the universalism of salvation in Revelation confirms what has been argued throughout this chapter. A biblical or Christian understanding of redemption must include the whole of creation, human and nonhuman, in ultimate salvation. Ultimate salvation, the end of all God's ways and works, cannot mean less than the fulfillment of the whole creation originated by God, the "reconstitution of all things" (*apokatastaseus panton*, Acts 3:20, an expression whose point is obscured by the RSV translation, "times of refreshing").

IMPLICATIONS

The logic of the biblical story requires that God's work of redemption or salvation complete God's work of creation. The God who acts to save the world is the God who created it. The end or goal of God's saving action can only be the same as the end of God's action as Creator. Furthermore, since everything God created was essentially good, fit for the end for which God made it, and sin did *not* denature any creature—turning it into something essentially evil and irredeemable—then there is nothing that could finally obstruct God's saving action from successfully bringing the totality of creation to its proper end. The evidence in the Bible for an inclusion of the totality of the extra-human creatures in ultimate salvation is clear. The answer to the vexed question of whether every individual human being will eventually be included in ultimate salvation (universalism, in the narrow sense) is not so clearly indicated in the Bible, so no conclusions about it are appropriate here. What follows are some important implications of the argument presented above. A brief sketch of them is presented below in the hope of stimulating needed correctives and further research.

1. It is unbiblical and theologically incoherent to constrict the Christian story to a message of salvation for one species (or a select portion of that species) alone. Since some people inside and outside the churches still think this way about "the gospel of Jesus Christ," the point deserves to be repeated. In the biblical view, ultimate salvation means fulfillment for the whole creation, and it is impossible for humans to attain it without the coparticipation of the extrahuman creatures.

2. Anthropocentric definitions of "the covenant of grace" or of God's "eternal decree(s)" or "the eternal covenant" must be revised so as to include the redemption of the whole creation in the conception of the end for which God created the world.

3. Only in this way can the eternal value *for God* of the whole creation, which is affirmed throughout the Bible, be guaranteed theologically. If any part of the creation is dispensable for the manifestation of God's glory in the "new heavens and new earth," then it can have no ultimate value for God. This would make it difficult to argue that such a part

of creation has any intrinsic value. However, the intrinsic value of all of God's creatures can be affirmed since none are dispensable to ultimate salvation.

4. The intrinsic value of created being is not completely secure theologically unless one holds to an eschatology (and corresponding Christology) that includes the fulfillment of the whole creation in ultimate salvation. The kind of philosophico-theological argument that tries to guarantee this point simply in biblical "axioms" that God is the Creator of all things and has made all things good is insufficient.[46]

5. The time is ripe for Reformed theology in particular to revive and rethink the old doctrine of a final "reconstitution of all things." It seems better to speak of "reconstitution" than "restitution" (the more customary English translation of *apokatastasis*) because it implies continuity between the old and the new orders of reality while at the same time suggesting a radically new way of integrating things. The expression is more a symbol than a concept. Heretical and nonheretical interpretations of the "reconstitution of all things" were proposed by some influential Greek fathers. John Calvin cautiously supported the idea. In his commentary on Rom. 8:21 he wrote:

> . . . since all created things [are] in themselves blameless, both on earth and in the visible heaven . . . all creatures shall be renewed [along with the sons of God] in order to amplify it [i.e., the ultimate manifestation of God's glory—comment mine].[47]

He goes on to say that the creatures shall participate in different kinds of glory, but concludes "that they, according to their nature, shall be participators of a better condition; for God will restore to a perfect state the world, now fallen, together with [hu]mankind."[48] He warns against over-subtle speculation about the conditions under which plants and animals might no longer be subject to decay, but asks his readers to be content with "this simple doctrine," viz. "that such will be the constitution and complete order of things, that nothing will be deformed or fading."[49]

While I have no interest in encouraging fantastic speculations about the prospects of restoring the created world to some "pristine" condition, I do think that the Christian hope for the renewal of the whole creation has important implications for the way Christians respond to the ecological crisis of our time. Surely, now is the time to work out those implications.

Part Two
Issues for an Eco-Justice Ethic

GLOBAL WARMING AS A THEOLOGICAL ETHICAL CONCERN

William E. Gibson

*W*e do not know that any planet supports life other than our own. The countless living forms that flourish on the earth emerged in the later stages of a process that began over fifteen billion years ago. The conditions of the biosphere in all their dazzling intricacy and unity had to be right in order for life to evolve and thrive. The atmosphere surrounding the earth functions as a major determinant of temperature. The gaseous mantle keeps the proper portion of the sun's heat from escaping back to space. Mars, with a much thinner atmosphere, cannot support life as we know it (Mars shows no evidence of any life at all), because it is too cold. Venus, with thick clouds as well as a closer proximity to the sun, is much too hot. The ranges of temperature in a given region of our planet enter into the determination of the forms of life it can support. The flora and fauna, in turn, adapt themselves to the climatic and other conditions that prevail. If conditions change too rapidly, some of the plants and animals will not survive. The stability of the atmospheric mantle protects them from stress and from extinction.

PERIL: THE GREENHOUSE EFFECT INTENSIFIED

The "greenhouse effect" comes from a change in the composition of this protective mantle. It has, of course, functioned like a greenhouse all along—by keeping heat from escaping. But now gaseous emissions generated in massive quantities by modern production and consumption enter the atmosphere. It traps more heat than before.

The peril that threatens the world is the intensification of the natural greenhouse effect. This undermines the atmosphere's capacity to maintain the stability of the climate to which ecosystems and living creatures have become adjusted. Major climatic changes have occurred in the past over many thousands of years. The change that looms is an increase in global mean temperature of something like 5° F in less than one hundred years. This would constitute an extraordinary spurt when viewed in geological perspective. Human and other creatures would face unprecedented problems of adjustment. The Worldwatch Institute authors, not given to extreme language, offer this assessment: "Indeed, [rapid warming] can be compared with nuclear war for its potential to disrupt a wide range of human and material systems, complicating the task of managing economies and coping with other problems."[1]

The year 1990 was marked by a succession of major international gatherings to review the threat and consider action. In June three working groups reported to the Intergovernmental Panel on Climate Change (IPCC), a panel of scientific experts that operates under the auspices of the United Nations Environment Programme and the World Meteorological Organization. In August the IPCC met in plenary session, reviewed the three reports, and approved an overview report, which served as the basic document for the Second World Climate Conference, 29 October to 7 November in Geneva. Meanwhile, global warming had been high on the agenda at international meetings of parliamentarians and at the World Convocation on Justice, Peace and the Integrity of Creation, convened in Korea by the World Council of Churches.

The international community moved in 1990 toward a considerable consensus as to some basic facts about climate change, even as it took note of major areas of need for further investigation. A procedure was set in motion for negotiating a formal international convention that might be ready for signing at the UN Conference on Environment and Development in June 1992. We may draw upon the 1990 reports and meetings for a summation of the danger that the planet faces.

IPCC Working Group 1 on the Scientific Assessment of Climate Change affirmed with certainty the natural greenhouse effect and the anthropogenic enhancement of it from increasing concentrations of the greenhouse gases: carbon dioxide (CO_2) (which is responsible for over half of the effect), methane, chlorofluorocarbons (CFCs), and nitrous oxides. If concentrations of the long-lived gases (all but methane) were to be stabilized at today's levels, there would have to be immediate reductions of emissions by over 60 percent.[2]

Drawing on current modeling results, employing a "business-as-usual" scenario, and acknowledging a rather large "uncertainty range," the group predicted an increase in global mean temperature during the next century at a rate of about 0.3° C per decade—for a total increase of 1° C (1.8° F) by 2025 and 3° C (5.4° F) before the end of the century.[3]

The full IPCC, however, regards these figures as probably understated.[4] And Working Group 2, using independent studies, projects an increase in the range of 1.5° C to 4.5° C between now and 2025 to 2050.[5] It is generally agreed that the increase will not be uniform around the globe; there will be little increase at the equator but more than the average in upper latitudes.

Working Group 2's assignment was to describe the environmental and socioeconomic impacts of possible climate changes. Here are some of its findings.

Agriculture. Studies do not yet show whether, on average, the potential for agriculture will increase or decrease for the world as a whole. "Negative impacts could be felt at the regional level as a result of changes in weather, diseases, pests and weeds . . . necessitating innovations in technology and agricultural management practices. There may be severe effects . . . particularly in regions of high present-day vulnerability. . . ."[6]

Forests. ". . . current forests will mature and decline during a climate in which they are increasingly poorly adapted. Actual impacts depend on the physiological adaptability of trees and the host-parasite relationship. Large losses from both factors can occur. . . . The most sensitive areas will be where species are close to their biological limits in terms of temperature and moisture."[7]

Natural Terrestrial Ecosystems. Significant shifts in climatic zones are expected. The rate of change is "likely to be faster than the ability of some species to respond. . . ."[8] "The socioeconomic consequences of these impacts will be significant, especially . . . where societies and related economies are dependent on natural terrestrial ecosystems for their welfare. Changes in the availability of food, fuel, medicine, construction materials and income are possible. . . ."[9]

Hydrology and Water Resources. "It appears that many areas will have increased precipitation, soil moisture and water storage, thus altering patterns of agricultural, ecosystem and other water use. Water availability will decrease in other areas, a most important factor for already marginal situations, such as the Sahelian zone in Africa. This has significant implications for agriculture, for water storage and distribution, and for generation of hydroelectric power."[10]

Human Settlements. "The most vulnerable populations are in developing countries, in the lower income groups, residents of coastal lowlands and islands, populations in semi-arid grasslands, and the urban poor in squatter settlements, slums and shanty towns, especially in megacities."[11] More people will become "environmental refugees."

Oceans and Coastal Zones. "A 30–50 cm sea-level rise (projected by 2050) will threaten low islands and coastal zones. A 1 m rise by 2100 would render some island countries uninhabitable, displace tens of millions of people, seriously threaten low-lying urban areas, flood productive land, contaminate water supplies and change coastlines. All of these impacts would be exacerbated if droughts and storms become more severe. Coastal protection would involve very significant costs."[12]

At the Second World Climate Conference over seven hundred scientists from more than one hundred countries issued a statement declaring that scientific and economic uncertainties must not be used to postpone strong societal responses to the threat of climate change.[13] The ministerial delegates of 137 governments adopted a compromise statement agreeing on the need to stabilize emissions of greenhouse gases while ensuring sustainable development of the global economy. To the disappointment of representatives of European and island nations, no specific targets for reducing emissions were set. Opposition from the United States led to their omission.[14] At that time and throughout 1991, however, the United States professed its intention to hold down the production of greenhouse gases overall, though not necessarily the most important, carbon dioxide. The United States is responsible for about a quarter of the five billion tons of CO_2 that human activity puts into the air annually.

The sober language of scientific assessment of global warming avoids words carrying emotional freight. Nevertheless, the findings presented to the Climate Conference clearly indicate a peril-laden prospect:

• Scientists do not project slow, steady change but erratic weather patterns, shifting unexpectedly, disrupting agriculture, as heat waves, droughts, storms, and hurricanes become more devastating than those yet known.

• Forest losses and the rapid climate changes that ruin large areas of habitat for wildlife will occur on top of the massive tropical forest destruction and wholesale extinction of plant and insect species already taking place.

• The rising sea will upset coastal ecology and aquatic life in ways beyond calculation but sure to be both environmentally and economically disastrous, as cities strain to build seawalls and dikes and vast numbers of people become refugees from the encroaching waters.

A picture emerges of natural processes made less dependable and life-supporting by human agency. "While the earth remains," God promised Noah, "seedtime and harvest, cold and heat, summer and winter, day and night, shall not cease" (Gen. 8:22). Industrial civilization now upsets the regularity depicted in that promise. Nations dependent on oil for industries and style of life resort to extreme measures, even war, to keep oil flowing. The ironic lesson of global warming is that the world has too much oil for its own sustainable well-being.

FAITH RESPONSE: PROTECTING CREATION, SHARING SUSTENANCE

The details of projection and speculation about impending peril leave one sobered, confused, and dismayed. Scientists know that the human impact on the atmosphere has profound implications for ecosystems in every region and for the all-encompassing planetary system. But they cannot say precisely how those implications will unfold. There are far too many factors, acting upon each other, defying quantification, for scientists to feed them into a computer model and get a dependable, adequately fleshed out scenario of the environmental and socioeconomic impacts. The evidence is massive that the impacts will be horrendous eventually, but the dangers may not be immediate enough to keep mechanisms of delay and denial from operating. We get a broad, alarming picture of a problematic future and numerous details of what could happen. The details constitute a challenge to keep what could happen from happening. Perhaps our next steps depend on first feeling that we are like Job—one who "darkens counsel without knowledge" (Job 30:2). The question comes to us: "Who has put wisdom in the clouds or given understanding to the mists?" (Job 38:36).

A new *humility* is the appropriate first response of faith to global warming. What have we done, we who belong to Western culture, industrial civilization, a capitalist economy? What have we done to God's good creation? Global warming looms as nature's ultimate retaliation against a culture that values it only as a resource. We are part of a civilization so intent on production that it cannot heed the evidence of limits and of an economy that institutionalizes selfishness and fosters inordinate concentrations of power.

Ironically, carbon dioxide is a nontoxic gas. As the energy base for industry shifted to fossil fuels, there was no idea of a dangerous atmospheric buildup. The case is similar with CFCs, which not only contribute to global warming but play the major role in depleting the ozone layer protecting the earth from harmful radiation. The CFCs were hailed as nontoxic, inexpensive chemicals, useful as propellants, coolants, and solvents. The destruction of the atmosphere's protective functions may stand as the supreme example of good intentions gone awry.

Nevertheless, it also exemplifies the damaging, often unforeseen effects of modern civilization's essential thrust. I refer to an anthropocentric, nature-conquering, growth-oriented, consumption-emphasizing paradigm for relating to the world and understanding the meaning of life. It has succeeded spectacularly in overcoming want for a portion of the human family (while perpetuating it for the rest), but the paradigm's inherently destructive and unjust tendencies are rendering it obsolete. Global warming was not intended, but it is the consequence of a relentless, ever more forceful pursuit of material security and affluence. Global warming challenges us to a fundamental critique of Western philosophical assumptions and economic institutions.

Perhaps only a faith characterized by the kind of trust that makes our finite creaturehood acceptable can respond to global warming with appropriate humility and freedom from defensiveness. In that humility one acknowledges complicity in the affliction of creation without engaging in self-castigation for inability to prevent it. Humility then moves one on from repentance and acceptance of forgiveness to look at the world with new eyes and to undertake the radical critique that has to precede systemic change.

Humility is preparation for *ethical responsibility*. The faith-filled ethical response to global warming is to become involved, with the Creator who is also the Deliverer, in protecting the creation, nonhuman and human, from further impairment and abuse.

Nature's revolt as epitomized by global warming exposes the unsustainable character of the way modern human beings have related to the rest of creation. Because much of that relationship has to do with economic arrangements for drawing sustenance from nature, the rebellion of nature exposes the unsustainable character of those arrangements.

Sustainability has become an urgent ethical norm for our time precisely because the industrial way of life, geared tenaciously to increasing the production and consumption of manufactured products, has become self-destructive. Various factors enter into this conclusion: pollution of many kinds, the demands of a still-growing human population, the degradation of renewable resources, and the depletion of nonrenewables. But underlying these considerations is the basic fact that the economy is driven by energy from fossil fuels whose combustion emits carbon dioxide, the chief cause of global warming.

Sustainability means the capacity to continue, not just to survive but to thrive, to function well. It entails the recognition of the obligation of the present generation to coming generations. We must recognize that the ways whereby people today satisfy their needs for sustenance, security, and fulfillment must not undercut the ability of people in the future to satisfy the comparable needs that they will have. But the norm does not center exclusively on human needs. It respects the integrity and recognizes the value of nonhuman creatures, ecosystems, and natural processes. It respects and values these for their own sake as well as for their indispensable functions in making human well-being possible. The norm requires that natural systems and societal systems thrive together.

Global warming's threat to sustainability is without precedent or parallel. To continue policies and practices that lead to further buildup of greenhouse gases constitutes a reckless violation of the norm.

Apparently it is already too late to prevent some warming. Although the six warmest years of the past century were all in the 1980s, most scientists are hesitant to concur with James Hanson of NASA that global warming has begun. Nevertheless, the time lag between the emission of greenhouse gases and their actual effect on climate is such that we must still expect to experience the consequences of what has already been sent into the atmosphere. The relevant questions are, How much warming will take place, and how fast will it occur? The norm presses upon governments, industries, and individuals the imperative of drastically cutting emissions in order to slow and limit global warming.

In one way or another what we do or do not do in this regard pertains to the way we humans relate to nature to satisfy our needs. Sustainability requires that as we "till the garden" we also "keep" it (Gen. 2:15). The shared human responsibility is to till with care, protecting the creation from impairment.

At the same time, in a faith-filled ethical response to global warming we must share equitably the sustenance obtained by tilling. The Creator intends creation's gifts for the well-being of all members of the human family. Justice requires that economic arrangements be designed to ensure *participation* by all and *sufficiency* of sustenance for all participants.

Participation and sufficiency, as norms of justice, combine with sustainability as norms distinctively applicable to the global eco-justice crisis. It is a crisis compounded of the assaults by violent technology and industry and wasteful consumerism upon the ecology of the planet, and the oppressive exclusion of masses of people from their rightful enjoyment of the good things that the Creator provides. The application of the three norms to the crisis of our time means that the overriding goal of public policy and personal practice in the societal arena is to achieve a *sustainable sufficiency for all.*

Underlying the three and giving them power and dynamism is a fourth norm, *solidarity.* This norm may be understood as a forceful affirmation of community. It gives strong, contemporary expression to the commandment to love the neighbor, as extended and indeed universalized by Jesus (see Luke 6:27 and 10:25-37; cf. Gal. 5:14 and 1 Thess. 3:12). It extends the idea of neighbor love beyond the human realm to entail the keeping and cherishing of all components of God's very good creation (Gen. 1:31). Solidarity, associated as it is with the struggles of the oppressed, indicates that extending and underlining the law of love, if it be more than romantic platitude, entails commitment and fidelity that may well be costly responses to the eco-justice crisis.[15]

The IPCC group on impacts of climate change points repeatedly to the greater toll that these will likely take where people and nonhuman species are already vulnerable or stressed. Brazil, China, Africa, and the Asian portion of the USSR are among the regions mentioned as likely to suffer declines in food production because their existing vulnerability will make it harder for them to adjust.[16] Sea-level rises and storm surges would be particularly hard on island nations and the coastal lowlands of Bangladesh, China, and Egypt.[17] Developing countries are generally more vulnerable than developed countries. Coping with disruption will be very difficult because of their limited resources, their debts, and "their difficulties in developing their economies on a sustainable and equitable basis." Nevertheless, says the IPCC group, "Global warming and its impact must not widen the gap between developed and developing countries."[18]

But the gap usually does widen in troubled times. The maintenance of total food production for the world will hardly salvage the situation in a Bangladesh whose rice fields are inundated by the sea. Cities like Miami, New Orleans, and London may somehow afford dikes against the sea, but this may be impossible for Cairo and Shanghai. Third World countries, deeply in debt, will be still more hard pressed to maintain the export crops upon which debt repayment depends, and people whose very survival becomes more problematic will give still less priority to environmental protection.

People of faith must insist that the issues posed by global warming have to do not only with sustainability but with participation, sufficiency, and solidarity. It will be ethically inadmissible to permit the costs of limiting the greenhouse effect, or adjusting to it, to fall overwhelmingly on those most vulnerable. The norms require that earth's sustenance be shared and basic needs be satisfied even in times of stress, disruption, and rapid, bewildering change. The standard of sufficiency applies to those who have too much as well as those who have too little. The responsibility of the affluent to bear most of the costs of global warming is clear. The kind of economic development that has mainly benefitted them imperils the planet.

POLICY MAKING: CLARITY AND CONTRADICTION

We have, on the one hand, a high degree of clarity as to appropriate policy for responding to the threat of global warming. The potential for reducing the emissions of the greenhouse gases is large and technically feasible. Substantial progress has actually been made in the international arena to phase out the production of CFCs on the basis of the Montreal Protocol and subsequent declarations in Helsinki and London. Included in these accords are commitments to seek safe substitutes for the offending chemicals and to enable developing countries to participate in the phase-out by giving them assurances of technology transfers from industrialized countries. The agreements on CFCs constitute the most encouraging instance to date of international cooperation on an environmental problem.

We have, on the other hand, formidable obstacles to the steps that could be taken to cut back on the emissions of carbon dioxide. CFCs are not essential to the existing economic system; fossil fuels are. There is every likelihood that CFCs can be eliminated without seriously impeding economic growth or affecting anybody's standard of living. The same cannot be said, however, about fossil fuels.

Policymakers, therefore, are pondering and debating what they can do to reduce CO_2 emissions without putting any brake on economic growth. They can do quite a lot. Whether it will be commensurate with the gravity of the peril remains problematic.

Working Group 3 of the IPCC focused on the formulation of response strategies. It divided these into measures for limiting the greenhouse buildup and measures for adapting to it. The latter have to do with disaster preparedness programs, comprehensive management plans for coastal zones, research on control measures for desertification, and research on adapting crops to saline conditions.[19]

The working group identifies five kinds of measures, feasible for early implementation, to reduce the emissions of greenhouse gases: (1) improved energy efficiency, (2) use of "cleaner" energy sources and technologies, (3) "improved forest management and, where feasible, expansion of forest areas as possible reservoirs of carbon," (4) the phasing out of CFCs under the Montreal Protocol, and (5) various management measures for agriculture and other human activities, including "improved livestock waste management" (to reduce methane releases), "altered use and formulation of fertilizers," and "improved management in landfill and wastewater treatment."[20]

Some recommendations are made for research and monitoring as preparation for longer-term, more intensive action. And a recommendation is made for "development of *new technologies* in the fields of energy, industry and agriculture."[21] The IPCC working group notes that the measures it proposes require a high degree of international cooperation and urges prompt negotiation of a "framework convention . . . [which] should, at a minimum, contain general principles and obligations . . . [and] be framed in such a way as to gain the adherence of the largest possible number [of countries]. . . ."[22] Industrialized countries, it states, have a responsibility to cooperate with developing countries in ways that include financial contributions as well as transfers of technology.[23]

These proposals for response strategies are actually rather cautious. The policy recommendations approved by the Presbyterian General Assembly in 1990 go farther in several respects. The Assembly, for example, asks the U.S. government for "vigorously stepped up research and development of energy efficient technologies" and, similarly, for stepped up research and development on "the various sources and technologies for solar energy." It calls for "incentives and disincentives to accelerate the transition to an economy based on renewable, safe, non-polluting, affordable energy"; strengthened "fuel economy and emission standards for automobiles, buses and trucks"; and "encouragement of alternatives to private automobiles . . . [including] municipal mass transit, railroads, bicycles, and walking."[24]

Similar measures were commended in 1990 to the Government of Canada by the General Council of the United Church of Canada. The Council urged a specific target—a 20 percent reduction in Canadian CO_2 emissions from 1990 levels by the year 2000.

Both the Presbyterian (U.S.A.) policy statement and that of the United Church of Canada set their recommendations within the context of increasing ecumenical concern. Both referred to the World Convocation on Justice, Peace, and the Integrity of Creation, which gathered in Seoul, Korea, in March 1990, under the auspices of the World Council of Churches. The Convocation in its Act of Covenant pertaining to the integrity of creation made "preserving the gift of the earth's atmosphere" its central focus. Delegates called for a global reduction in CO_2 emissions of 2 percent per year (with industrialized countries reducing theirs by 3 percent), through governmental measures to increase the efficiency of energy generation and use, active promotion of renewable, nonnuclear energy resources, and the transfer of relevant technologies to developing countries. They called upon their churches "to lead in the indispensable reversal of the thinking which supports unlimited energy consumption and economic growth."[25] The United Church of Canada resolution included a commitment to work for that reversal.

Yet IPCC Working Group 3 observed candidly: "It must be emphasized that implementation of measures to reduce global emissions are very difficult as energy use, forestry, and land use patterns are primary factors in the global economy."[26] Assessment of the difficulty to which the working group refers has divided the industrialized nations. On one side Europe, Japan, New Zealand, and Australia are convinced that they can make significant though limited reductions in their CO_2 emissions without slowing their economies. Moreover, they are serious enough to set specific targets and timelines for themselves. Germany, for example, has set a goal of reducing CO_2 emissions 25 percent by 2005. Denmark's targets are a 20 percent reduction by 2005 and 50 percent by 2030. The package of proposals announced by Germany to meet its goal includes improved heating technologies and insulation in buildings, increased use of industrial cogeneration, higher conversion efficiency at electric plants, greater dependence on renewable energy sources, improvements in public transportation, and either a tax on CO_2 emissions or additional taxes on fossil fuels.[27]

On the other side, the United States has refused to set any specific targets on CO_2 emissions and blocked the inclusion of timetables for industrialized countries in the final declaration of the Second World Climate Conference. The U.S. position led to friction at the July 1990 economic summit of the seven leading industrialized nations. "Participants such as West German Chancellor Helmut Kohl . . . took issue with White House Chief of Staff John Sununu regarding his position that the United States should not reduce CO_2 emissions at the expense of economic growth. Administration officials claimed that a stabilization of CO_2 emissions would be incompatible with the growth needs of the United States and developing countries."[28]

PROSPECT: AN ECO-JUSTICE PARADIGM

The United States and the other industrialized countries do not question the importance of maintaining economic growth. They disagree only on whether limited measures to address the threat of climate change by making CO_2 reductions would have an adverse effect on growth. At the Climate Conference the representatives of the other nations said that studies over the past year had shown that they could stabilize and eventually cut back CO_2 output "at no extra cost to the overall economy."[29] One such study, from the World Wildlife Fund and the Conservation Foundation, claimed that most industrialized countries could cut CO_2 emissions by 20 percent without reducing productivity.[30] By going ahead, then, with their policies and their targets, the industrialized nations are demonstrating their commitment to "sustainable development."[31]

But suppose the studies are incorrect, or that climate models overestimate the threat. Would that mean that Germany, Denmark, and the others are making a terrible mistake? Would it mean that the United States is wise in refusing to give priority to a reduction in the use of fossil fuels? In the face of the likely costs of agricultural disruption, added stress on forests, habitat loss and species extinction, sea-level rise, tens of millions of displaced people (environmental refugees), and the exacerbation of poverty problems, particularly in the Third World, do measures to limit global warming have to be cost-free and painless? Is economic growth the supreme value, even in the face of evidence that it is destroying the ecological basis of its own continuation—that sometime in the lifetime of people already living nature's revolt will bring it to a stumbling if not a screeching halt?

If policymakers responding to global warming were equipped with the norms enunciated in the previous section, the answer would be a resounding no. Instead, they remain captive to the obsolete paradigm that makes growth without limit the definition of healthy economics, a captivity that keeps them on an unsustainable course, even when confronted by the peril of global warming, even while they espouse sustainability.

If the norms of sustainability, justice, and solidarity are held together and allowed to determine policy and practice, what then? Clearly, we cannot accept a system geared blindly to economic growth, which fails to distinguish development that addresses the hitherto unmet needs of the poor from production that indulges the excessive demands of the rich or entices the not-quite-rich to buy what they do not need. Nor can we accept a system that justifies wastefulness and pollution in order to preserve jobs, or one that cuts educational and health facilities in order to pay the debts that have benefitted only the elite.

The threat of global warming makes sustainable development, as usually espoused, a contradiction in terms. Development, as understood by those who make government policy or run corporations, is almost always viewed as synonomous with quantitative economic growth, which in a crunch will take precedence over sustainability every time. Most proponents of sustainable development still expect justice to be cheap. The rich will still get richer, but something will trickle down to the poor. And technical fixes will somehow keep nature's revolt from getting out of hand.

Of course Third World countries need development geared to the essential needs of those who do not have enough. But they will not have it while the world remains stuck with an economic model and a life-style standard that require still more consumption by those whose material possessions are already more than sufficient. On a finite, fragile planet, nature's sustenance must be taken carefully and shared equitably.

I do not believe that the world can respond appropriately to global warming until the obsolete paradigm breaks down. The measures to achieve energy efficiency, which many countries are taking, point significantly in the right direction. But in a world where so much damage has already been done, a world whose population will probably double again, technical efficiencies alone will not halt the tide of global warming or permit the appropriate development that is so needed by the world's impoverished majority. As the obsolete paradigm breaks down, perhaps human intelligence and ingenuity may increasingly be applied to economic restructuring, both local and global,[32] that is expressive of solidarity and actually geared to sustainability, participation, and sufficiency.

WILDLIFE AND WILDLANDS
A Christian Perspective

Holmes Rolston III

*B*iblical faith originated with a land ethic. Within the covenant, keeping the commandments, the Hebrew people entered a Promised Land. That land is to be inhabited justly and charitably, and the twin commandments of biblical faith are to love God and to love neighbor. Israel is to be a holy people, a righteous nation, and the principal focus of biblical faith is not nature in the land, but the culture established there. At the same time the Bible is full of constant reminders of the natural givens that undergird all cultural achievements. Justice is to run down like waters, and the land flows with milk and honey.

The Hebrew covenant of redemption is prefaced by the covenant of creation. The Creator commands, "Let the earth put forth vegetation" and "Let the earth bring forth living creatures according to their kinds" (Gen. 1:11, 24). The fauna is included within the covenant. "Behold I establish my covenant with you and your descendants after you, and with every living creature that is with you, the birds, the cattle, and every beast of the earth with you" (Gen. 9:9-10). To use modern terms, the covenant was both ecumenical and ecological.

In subsequent developments, both Judaism and Christianity, emerging from Judaism, became more universalist and less land-based. In the Diaspora, the Jews were a people without a country, and, though this was widely regarded as tragic, Judaism remains a faith that transcends residence in Palestine. Christianity has often been regarded as more spiritual and less material, more universal and less provincial than its parent Judaism. Both these movements out of a geographically particular Promised Land, which are sometimes thought to make the land irrelevant to faith, can as well make every people residents of a divinely given landscape. In that sense the vision of many nations blessed in Abraham, is inclusive, not exclusive.

Jesus says, "My kingdom is not of this world" (John 18:36). Teaching as he did in the Imperial Roman world, his reference "this" is to the fallen world of the culture he came to redeem and to false trust in politics and economics, in armies and kings. God loves "the world," and in the landscape surrounding him Jesus found ample evidence of the presence of God. He teaches that the power organically manifest in the wild-flowers of the field is continuous with the power spiritually manifest in the kingdom he announces. There is an ontological bond between nature and spirit.

PROMISED LANDS

The North American landscape with its purple mountains' majesties, its fruited plains, its fauna and flora from sea to shining sea is divinely created no less than Canaan from the Negev to Mount Hermon. Exodus into a Promised Land has been a repeated theme wherever Judaism and Christianity have gone. All lands are to be inhabited justly and charitably, in freedom and in love. The divine imperative continues, addressed now both to Earth and to the humans who reside there, "Let the earth bring forth vegetation and every living creature." If this command was first biological, addressed to creation, it is now also ethical, addressing human duty. A people without a country is a continuing tragedy. Earth is a promised planet, chosen for abundant life.

The divine Spirit is the giver of life. "In the beginning God created the heavens and the earth. The earth was without form and void, and darkness was upon the face of the deep; and the Spirit of God was moving over the face of the waters" (Gen. 1:1-2). This wind of God inspires the animated Earth, and "the earth produces of itself" (Mark 4:28; the Greek says "automatically"). The days of creation are a series of divine imperatives. The wild creatures (as well as humans) are blessed and commanded to be fruitful, to multiply, and to fill the earth.

Only humans are made in the image of God; and humans, placed within Earth, are placed over, not under, the nonhuman fauna and flora. Humans are to be free on Earth, to live under God, and to care for this creation. Animals are biologically equipped for the ecological niches they inhabit; each is an impressive and satisfactory fit in its place. Humans are adapted for culture and inhabit the world ethically and cognitively. The animal lives within its own sector, but it cannot take an interest in sectors of the world other than its own. Humans can and should care beyond themselves; they can espouse a view of the whole. Adapting biblical metaphors for an environmental ethic, humans on Earth are and ought to be prophets, priests, and kings—roles unavailable to nonhumans. Humans should speak for God in natural history, should reverence the sacred there, and should rule creation in freedom and in love.

In contrast with the views of surrounding faiths from which biblical faith emerged, the natural world is disenchanted; it is neither God, nor is it full of gods, but it remains sacred, a sacrament of God. Although nature is an incomplete revelation of God's presence, it remains a mysterious sign of divine power. The birds of the air neither sow nor reap yet are fed by the heavenly Father, who notices the sparrows that fall. Not even Solomon is arrayed with the glory of the lilies, though the grass of the field, today alive, perishes tomorrow (Matthew 6). There is in every seed and root a promise. Sowers sow, the seed grows secretly, and sowers return to reap their harvests. God sends rain on the just and unjust. "A generation goes, and a generation comes, but the earth remains for ever" (Eccles. 1:4).

In Israel biblical faith was a focus of national life, and often in classical Christendom nations claimed to be Christian. In modern eras, with increasing separation of church and state, the connections between Christian conviction and national policy are more indirect. The twentieth century has seen increasing privatization of religion, but the same century has brought increasing awareness that the natural environment is a commons that cannot be privatized. Religion may be personal, each with his or her own creed, but the environment is a public domain. In America a land ethic can and ought to offset the interiorizing of religion to the neglect of its communal aspects. Divinely given earthen nature is the original act of grace. The commons is the fundamental sphere of divine creativity.

Facing the next century, indeed turning the millennium, there is growing conviction that theology has been too anthropocentric; the nonhuman world is a vital part of Earth's story. Certainly in a century of two world wars, a great depression, a cold war, the threat of nuclear holocaust, civil rights struggles, and increasing secularization and alienation, there have been, and remain, urgent human problems with which Christianity must cope. It is now increasingly obvious, in addition, that environmental welfare is an inescapable part of our global agenda. Nor does this require simply the conservation of a desirable human environment; duty requires preservation of the natural world and the coexistence of wild creation with the human community. In that sense Christianity, together with other faiths that influence human conduct, needs again to become a land ethic, to restore every living creature to the divine covenant.

This divinely given natural world is also vanishing. Recent centuries, especially the twentieth, have dramatically increased the built environment at the expense of the creation. After our generation comes and goes, Earth may not remain, or may remain only in a degraded state. God made the country; people made the towns, plowed the fields, clearcut the timber, dammed the rivers, and paved the roads. About 20 percent of the global land surface—almost all of the readily inhabitable land—has been drastically modified. In temperate countries the percentage of occupied land is much higher. Vast areas of land surface in high latitudes or arid lands have survived relatively unmodified because they cannot be inhabited, but that is changing with new technologies for exploiting tundra and sea, and with pollutants that travel to the poles, with ozone depletion and global warming.

About 96 percent of the contiguous United States is developed, farmed, grazed, timbered, or designated for multiple use. Only about 2 percent has been designated as wilderness; another 2 percent might be suitable for wilderness or semi-wild status, such as cut-over forests that have reverted to the wild or areas as yet little developed. National forests include about 14 percent of the American continent; they are public lands, sometimes with impressive wildlife, but, being lands of multiple uses (or multiple abuses!), they often have degenerate faunas and floras. We have only scraps of undisturbed once-common ecosystems, such as hemlock forests or tall grass prairies, and we have no chestnut forests at all. Acid rain is impoverishing the Adirondacks and the Great Smokies. In the western United States, our few old growth forests are being clearcut at the rate of 1,000 acres each week.

In the last two centuries the native fish flora of the North American continent has been more tampered with than have the fish floras of other continents in two thousand years of civilization. Hardly a stretch of landscape in the nation is unimpoverished of its native species—otters and peregrine falcons, wolves and bison. The higher up the species on the ladder of creation (the ecosystemic trophic pyramid), the more likely this is so. Americans regarded it as their manifest destiny to conquer the wilderness, and with this came profligate wasting of resources and prodigal slaughter of wildlife. The big predators have been decimated; the bison no longer roam the plains. The passenger pigeon is gone; bluebirds and many warblers are vanishing; we face a silent spring.

The natural world inescapably surrounds us, wherever we reside and work, and yet the built environment, necessary for culture, also is increasingly difficult to escape. Culture is and ought to be superimposed on the landscape, but not so as to extinguish wildlands and wildlife. This duty arises because of what the fauna, flora, and landscapes are in themselves, but it also arises because of human welfare. Humans need, in differing degrees, elements of the natural to make and keep life human. Life in completely artificial environments, without options for experiencing natural environments, is undesirable. A society attuned to artifact forgets creation. Life without access to the divine creation is ungodly.

LANDSCAPES AND WILDLANDS

Land, a gift of God, can also be owned as property. As did Israel before it, and as do most societies, America recognizes private property, the personal and corporate ownership of real estate. When property is developed within culture, its value reflects both the natural resources and the labor expended on it in varying proportions. Not only economic systems but all cultural values, beyond those of hunter-gatherer cultures, require modified natural systems; on completely wild lands modern culture is impossible. But land owned as a gift of God is imperfectly owned, and the creative processes on land transcend ownership. Property, even when domesticated, may also retain much naturalness, and some owned properties can retain elements of wildness. Regardless of whether lands are privately owned or in the public commons, the spontaneous natural givens can still be present. In this larger view of natural environment, land is always vastly more than real estate. The promised land is never a sector of private property, but a landscape, an environment in which one resides. The abundant life requires a larger landscape than the tract of property that supplies one's residence.

Land in this larger sense is crucially a "commons," that is, a public good. Whatever values are protected by the institution of private property, there is no invisible hand that regulates markets to guarantee an optimal harmony between a people and their landscape. Nothing ensures that the right things are done in encounter with fauna, flora, ecosystems, or regarding future generations. A test of the abundant life in a promised land, as we inherit biblical faith today, integrating it with other faiths that fund an American land ethic, is whether a people can see the whole commonwealth of a human society set in its ecosystem, and through this develop an environmental ethics. It is not simply what a society does to its slaves, women, blacks, minorities, handicapped, children, or future generations, but what it does to its fauna, flora, species, ecosystems, and landscapes that reveals the character of that society.

Despite the twentieth-century trend toward privatizing religion, national policy toward landscapes must involve collective choice producing a public land ethic. Some ethical choices are made by individuals, but in other cases citizens must choose together. Governments, like businesses, have large influence in our lives; both have vast amounts of power to affect the landscape for good or ill. Private conservancies are significant, and a conservation ethic is vital for landowners and their private lands, but unless landscapes, whether public or private, are protected by national, state, and local policy, they will be inadequately protected. In setting policy, citizens, including Christians who join other conservationists, can by mutual coercion, mutually agreed upon, do in concert what private persons cannot do alone. Christians, along with other interest groups, can unite to help forge this consensus. Christianity is thus forced to become public and to join in shaping the public ethic and reforming public policy.

There must be a management ethic for the landscape commons—about soil, air, water, forest preserves, environmental quality, the ozone layer, wildlife, endangered species, and future generations. This ethic will be voluntary in the sense that it is an enlightened and democratically achieved consensus with the willing support of millions of citizens. Such policy will also be written into law and therefore mandatory. No laws can be enforced without the widespread voluntary compliance of citizens. This voluntary compliance depends on the expectation that even those who do not wish to obey will be required to do so. Unless such an ethic is enforced, as well as encouraged, it is largely useless. There can be no effective merely private, voluntary land ethic.

Such concerted action can be taken with full or only partial agreement about reasons for so acting; it can sometimes involve agreeing about conduct while disagreeing about rationale. This is especially true in terms of minimum standards (for example, that game and timber harvests be renewable, that critical habitats be preserved for endangered species, or that surface-mined lands be reclaimed). Decisions here must be political decisions; but they are also taking place in the midst of a philosophical and theological reassessment, coupled with ecological and moral concerns, about how humans should value nature. They are political decisions entwined with reforming world views.

There should be many kinds of built environments, but an environmental policy also insists that natural sectors be preserved and incorporated into the built environments—greenbelts in cities, rural areas, waterfalls and cascades, mountains on the skyline, seashores and lake-shores unspoiled by development, spits and headlands, islands, swamps, oxbow lakes, and forests interspersed with pastures.

Most of the national landscape will be integrated with cultural activities. The landscape cannot and should not be entirely wild; but neither should it be entirely cultural. Culture should everywhere be mingled with nature. An environmental policy also insists that there be wild domains "where the earth and its community of life are untrammeled by man, where man is only a visitor who does not remain."[1]

For many persons today, especially in an increasingly urban society, the principal opportunities to experience wildlands and wildlife take place on public lands, as these have been designated for conservation and preservation. Most remaining wildlands are public lands—national forests, parks, wilderness areas, seashores, grasslands, wildlife refuges, lands under the Bureau of Land Management, state or county parks and forests. Many of these areas are largely managed for multiple uses and are only semiwild; still they constitute a major component of the natural environment. They also contain most of the relict pristine wildlands, as nearly as these remain anywhere.

Judgments about the extent to which natural landscapes are and ought to be rebuilt for culture are difficult to make. In view of the extent to which the American landscape has already been dramatically transformed, there should be a *maxi-min* principle in wildland preservation policy, something like the ratio of continental domestication to wildness. The relict, minimum level of wildland values needs maximizing (remembering the 96 to 4 domestication ratio) opposing a *maxi-max* principle (maximum consumption increasing to 100 percent our available acreage) to raise our already high standard of living.

Values carried by wildlife and wildlands, like the values for which Christians stand, are in critical part noneconomic. Christians have often and admirably focused on economic values where humans have been unjustly deprived of these, such as jobs, food, shelter, and health care. But in wildland decisions, where wildlands are proposed to be sacrificed to meet human needs, Christians should insist that these values be met instead on the enormous sectors of nonwild, domesticated lands, which are more than adequate to meet these needs, given a just distribution of their produce. Disproportionate distribution among humans is not to be cured by further disproportion of the human-built environment to the pristine, natural environment. The values that Christians wish to defend for remaining wildlands are often the softer, more diffuse, and deeper values essential to an abundant life. Without these experiences, the land cannot fulfill all its promise.

One cannot look to the market to produce or protect the multiple values that citizens enjoy on public lands, much less in wilderness areas, since many of the values sought here are not, or not simply, economic ones. A pristine, natural system is a religious resource, as well as a scientific, recreational, aesthetic, and economic one. To see a wildland as merely resource profanes such experiences and nature alike. A forest, mountain, or prairie is more than a resource instrumental to civilization and more than even a religious resource. It is primeval, wild, creative source.

Religious people can bring a perspective of depth to wildland conservation. They see forests as a characteristic expression of the creative process. In a forest, as on a desert or the tundra, the realities of nature cannot be ignored. The forest is both presence and symbol of forces in natural systems that transcend human powers and human utility. Like the sea or the sky, the forest is a kind of archetype of the foundations of the world. The central "goods" of the biosphere—forests and sky, sunshine and rain, rivers and earth, the everlasting hills, the cycling seasons, wildflowers and wildlife, hydrologic cycles, photosynthesis, soil fertility, food chains, genetic codes, speciation and reproduction, succession and its resetting, life and death and life renewed—were in place long before humans arrived, though they have lately become human economic and social resources. The dynamics and structures organizing the forest do not come out of the human mind; a wild forest is something wholly other than civilization. It is presence and symbol of the timeless natural givens that support everything else.

A pristine forest is prime natural history, a relic of the way the world was for almost forever. The forest as a tangible preserve in the midst of a culture contributes to the human sense of duration, antiquity, continuity, and identity. A visit there regenerates the sense of human late-coming and sensitizes us to our novelty. In the primeval forest (or on the desert or tundra) humans know the most authentic of wilderness emotions, the sense of the sublime. We get transported by forces aweful and overpowering, by the signature of time and eternity.

"The groves were God's first temples."[2] "The trees of the Lord are watered abundantly; the cedars of Lebanon which he planted" (Ps. 104:16). With forests, America is even more of a promised land than is Palestine. John Muir exclaimed, "The forests of America, however slighted by man, must have been a great delight to God; for they were the best he ever planted."[3] Such forests are a church as surely as a commodity. The forest is where the "roots" are, where life rises from the ground. Trees pierce the sky like cathedral spires. Light filters down as through stained glass. The forest canopy is lofty; much of it is over our heads. In common with churches, forests invite transcending the human world and experiencing a comprehensive, embracing realm. Forests can serve as a more provocative, perennial sign of this than many of the traditional, often outworn, symbols devised by the churches. The churches should welcome and seek to preserve such experiences. Muir continued, "The clearest way into the Universe is through a forest wilderness."[4]

Being among the archetypes, a forest is about as near to ultimacy as we can come in the natural world—a vast scene of sprouting, budding, flowering, fruiting, passing away, and passing life on. Mountaintop experiences, the wind in the pines, solitude in a sequoia grove, autumn leaves, the forest vista that begins at one's feet and disappears over the horizon—these generate experiences of "a motion and spirit that impels . . . and rolls through all things."[5] We feel life's transient beauty sustained over chaos. A forest wilderness is a sacred space. There Christians recognize God's creation, and others may find the Ultimate Reality or a Nature sacred in itself. A forest wilderness elicits cosmic questions different from those a town may evoke. Christians have particular interest in preserving wildlands as sanctuaries for religious experiences, both for themselves and for others inspired there.

A wildland is a wonderland, a miracle, standing on its own. "Praise the Lord from the earth, you sea monsters and all deeps, fire and hail, snow and frost, stormy wind fulfilling his command! Mountains and all hills, fruit trees and all cedars! Beasts and all cattle, creeping things and flying birds!" (Ps. 148:7-10). "Thou crownest the year with thy bounty; the tracks of thy chariot drip with fatness. The pastures of the wilderness drip, the hills gird themselves with joy, the meadows clothe themselves with flocks, the valleys deck themselves with grain, they shout and sing together for joy" (Ps. 65:11-13). "Who has cleft a channel for the torrents of rain, and a way for the thunderbolt, to bring rain on a land where no man is, on the desert in which there is no man; to satisfy the waste and desolate land, and to make the ground put forth grass?" (Job 38:25-27). God not only sends rain on the just and the unjust; God sends rain to satisfy wildlands. God not only blesses humans; God blesses the desolate wastes. These fierce landscapes, sometimes supposed to be ungodly places, are godly after all. God does not want all these places subdued and cultivated; rather, God delights in places with no people!

That the fair land of Palestine, with its cities and fields, should again become desert and wilderness is a frequent prophetic threat. The collapse of cultural life in the Promised Land is indeed a tragedy, and in that sense a relapse to the wild is sometimes used in the Bible as a symbol for judgment on an aborted, promised culture. Jackals roam the land, destroyed in punishment for sin. Such wildness is a tragedy only in foil to failed culture.

Certain biblical passages suggest that the natural world is implicated in the fall, resulting from human sin. It is incontestably true that human sinfulness can affect the natural world adversely, and in that sense human redemption also brings restoration of nature. But these passages are not to be taken to suggest that existing wildlands are fallen, nor can they be interpreted in terms of redemptive wildland management. Additionally, a peaceable natural kingdom, where the lion lies down with the lamb, is sometimes used as the symbol of fulfillment in the Promised Land. This too is a cultural metaphor and cannot be interpreted in censure of natural history.

Taken for what it is in itself, prior to using it to symbolize human hopes and disappointments, wildness in the Bible is never a bad thing. To the contrary, all creation is good. From this perspective, Christians can join with Aldo Leopold and his land ethic. "A thing is right when it tends to preserve the integrity, stability, and beauty of the biotic community. It is wrong when it tends otherwise."[6] Those who wish to reside in a promised land must promise to preserve its integrity, stability, and beauty. "That land is a community is the basic concept of ecology, but that land is to be loved and respected is an extension of ethics."[7] If so, we cannot inherit our promised lands until we extend Christian ethics into ecology. "The land which you are going over to possess is a land of hills and valleys, which drinks water by the rain from heaven, a land which the Lord your God cares for; the eyes of the Lord your God are always upon it, from the beginning of the year to the end of the year" (Deut. 11:11-12).

ANIMALS AND WILDLIFE

In theocratic Israel, animals belonged to God, as indeed did all property. "For every beast of the forest is mine, the cattle on a thousand hills. I know all the birds of the air, and all that moves in the field is mine" (Ps. 50:10-11). Though animals belong to God, they can also be owned by humans, and such ownership is a divine blessing (for example, Abraham at Hebron with his herds of goats and sheep). Such domesticated animals require care, morally as well as prudentially. "A righteous man has regard for the life of his beast" (Prov. 12:10). Cattle are to be rested on the sabbath (Exod. 20:10); the ox in the pit requires rescue, even at breach of the sabbath (Luke 14:5). The ox that treads out the grain is not to be muzzled (Deut. 25:4). Indeed, the care of a shepherd for his sheep is used as a model of divine care. "The Lord is my shepherd; I shall not want" (Ps. 23:1). The good shepherd searches for the lost sheep (Matt. 18:12).

Such metaphors presume compassionate treatment of animals, but they do not prescribe this conduct in detail. Whether and how far animals count morally is outside the central circle of ethical interests in the Bible, which is largely focused on interhuman relationships. But it is not outside the covenant nor is it outside the larger circle of moral relationships. Animal husbandry is compatible with Christian faith. Where animals suffer owing to human domestication, they are removed from nature, and compassion is warranted.

Animals in Israel were eaten and even ritually slaughtered in sacrifice, a practice in which Jesus participated. Some herbivores and all carnivores were considered unclean as food or sacrificial animals, but this does not demean their status as good creatures of God. Christians and Jews have abandoned animal sacrifice; both have continued to eat meat. Judaism seeks, in kosher slaughter, both to kill humanely and to eliminate the blood, the latter a symbol of reverence for life. "Every moving thing that lives shall be food for you; and as I gave you the green plants, I give you everything. Only you shall not eat flesh with its life, that is, its blood" (Gen. 9:3-4). This command suggests that humans were originally vegetarian and later, by concession, ate meat.

That divine permission and imperative authorizes meat hunting, which is not incompatible with monotheistic faith. A few biblical persons are admired for their prowess in the hunt: Nimrod "was a mighty hunter before the Lord" (Gen. 10:9). Esau brought game to Isaac, and David slew lions and bears to protect his sheep. Hunters used bows, arrows, spears, nets, traps, and pits, and wild game existed in parts of Palestine throughout the biblical period. Sport hunting, it should be noted, is not hereby permitted; killing merely for sport is nowhere endorsed in biblical faith. Orthodox Judaism has largely ceased to hunt, since kosher slaughter is difficult under the circumstances of hunting. Several of Jesus' disciples were fishermen. Jesus ate of their catch and gave fish to others to eat. Again, however, this is not sport fishing.

Though the ownership of domestic animals and the hunting of wild ones is legitimate, wild animals in biblical Israel were not private property, nor are they in the United States. In democratic America, wildlife are a commons, no matter whether on public or private land. Wild animals, birds, and stream fish in the United States, wherever they are found, on public lands or private, are held in public trust by the state for the good of the people. Hence the state fish, game, and wildlife commissions have power to manage, license, and regulate fishing and hunting. Landowners control access to their property, but when and what wildlife may be taken is the prerogative of the state. On public lands open to hunting, the wildlife present there is owned by no person until the occasion of legal capture, at which point it becomes the possession of the taker.

In traditional law, this was sometimes thought of as state ownership of wildlife, but in more recent law this has been subsumed under the state's power to regulate all natural resources, known as the public trust doctrine. We do not think that farmers own the migratory geese that fly over their fields, stopping there temporarily to eat corn, though we sometimes think of farmers as owning the rabbits that reside in their fields. This concept results largely from the mobility of wildlife; migratory birds have figured significantly in developing wildlife law. Large animals are also mobile. The elk shot in October on a private ranch, coming to lower elevations to winter, may have spent the summer in the national forest. The big predators inhabit a landscape as much as an ecosystem niche. Such animals are wild in the sense that they know no human property boundaries and cannot therefore be thought of as real estate.

Sedentary wild animals (barnacles and clams, possibly even the rabbits with restricted habitats, or pond fishes) do not know human property boundaries either, but nevertheless remain contained within them, and thus can successfully be owned by the landholder. Unlike the fauna, the flora, being rooted to the real estate, is considered to belong to the landowner. Mobile animals are also wild in the sense that they result from no human labor and are largely outside the control of humans. They are not livestock. So far as they are the product of game and fish management by the landowner, often thereby losing much of their wildness, they sometimes are thought of as coming to belong to their landowner and producer. There is also a widespread conviction that wild animals, differing from domesticated animals, ought not to be imprisoned without just cause, and thus states typically forbid the capture and continuing possession of wildlife without special permit.

Superimposed on the godly natural created order, biblical faith permits and enjoins humans to rebuild such orders in the interests of a just and loving culture. No forms of human life—hunter-gatherer, agricultural, or industrial—are possible without damage to the welfare of wild animals. A dominant view in national and state wildlife policy is that wildlife are a resource for humans to harvest, exploit, and enjoy on a sustainable basis. Certainly that view has precedent in the biblical outlook on animals. God utilized the first animals, for human benefit! "And the Lord God made for Adam and for his wife garments of skins, and clothed them" (Gen. 3:21).

But the resource view, unconstrained by appropriate respect for the full spectrum of animal values, is inadequate for forming a mature Christian environmental ethics. Under God, wildlife have intrinsic as well as instrumental value. When coats made of pelts taken in leghold traps are worn to flatter female varieties, this betrays an ethical stance that hardly seems to love wildlife intrinsically and theistically. Neither does shooting stags and mounting antlers to flatter masculine varieties. Nor does the keeping of wild animals for entertainment, as in circuses and some aquaria, or keeping them as caged pets. Even zoos have to be justified in terms of conservation and education, not simply as recreation. The fewer captive wild animals, the better, since captivity always degrades wildness. Despite the permission to capture animals for culture, Christians must remember that in God, animals are born free.

"Who has let the wild ass go free? Who has loosed the bonds of the swift ass, to whom I have given the steppe for his home, and the salt land for his dwelling place? He scorns the tumult of the city; he hears not the shouts of the driver. He ranges the mountain as his pasture, and he searches after every green thing" (Job 39:5-8). Letting wild animals "go free" provides a general orientation for the ethical treatment of wild animals. Christianity has no particular expertise in wildlife management, and many of the questions faced in environmental ethics have not been addressed by Christian thought. Thus, for instance, when a bison fell through the ice in Yellowstone National Park, some persons took compassion and attempted its rescue, but park policy forbade this, letting nature take its course. Policy also forbade mercy killing the suffering animal. On the other hand, United States federal and state wildlife personnel, joined by a Russian icebreaker, rescued two whales from winter ice at considerable expense, amidst international concern.

The bighorn sheep of Yellowstone caught pinkeye in an epidemic that partially blinded many sheep and caused their lingering death from starvation. They were left by policy to the ravages of the disease. On the other hand, in Colorado veterinarians treated an epidemic of lungworm, lest weakened sheep die of pneumonia. A relevant difference in the two cases is that the Yellowstone pinkeye epidemic was believed to be natural, while the Colorado lungworm was contracted from domestic sheep, and, additionally, these sheep have lost much of their original winter range due to human settlements.

Although Christianity cannot adjudicate the details of such cases, it can endorse a general principle that, among wild animals, nature ought to be left to take its course, even though this involves animal suffering. That is part of what it means to let them "go free" under God. In environments that humans preserve wild, we are under more obligation to respect nature than to reconstruct it. The ecological and biological processes of natural history reflect the will of God. Though Christianity has no particular insight into wildlife management practices, Christianity insists that the processes and products of natural history, being what they are under divine imperative, are good. "O Lord, thou preservest man and beast" (Ps. 36:6; KJV).

Compassion, which is appropriate and morally required for persons, can therefore be misplaced when applied without discrimination to wild animals. The Golden Rule, for instance, is prescribed for persons. If it can be extended at all to wild animals, this must be with due regard for their radically different circumstances. More often than not, the most compassionate benevolence respects their wildness and lets nature take its course. "As you did it to one of the least of these . . ." (Matt. 25:40) requires the feeding of hungry persons, but it does not require the feeding of wildlife. Wild creatures are in some sense neighbors to be loved, but the kind of love appropriate for them is neither agape nor eros. It is a love of their wildness for what it is, intrinsically and under God. Pointless suffering in culture is a bad thing and ought to be removed, where possible; but pain in wild nature is not entirely analogous to pain in an industrial, agricultural, and medically skilled culture. Pain in nature remains in the context of natural selection; it is pain instrumental to survival and to the integrity of species.

The nonhuman creation is wild, outside human ordering, outside culture. But it is not outside both divine and biological order. The Creator's love for the creation is sublime precisely because it does not conform to human purposes. Wild animals and wildflowers are loved by God for their own sake. That God is personal as revealed in interhuman cultural relations does not mean that the natural relationship of God to ground squirrels is personal, nor that humans should treat ground squirrels as persons. They are to be treated with appropriate respect for their wildness. The meaning of the words "good" and "divine" is not the same in nature and in culture.

Just as Job was pointed out of his human troubles toward the wild Palestinian landscape, it is a useful, saving corrective to a simplistic Jesus-loves-me-this-I-know, God-is-on-my-side theology to discover vast ranges of creation that now have nothing to do with satisfying our personal desires, and earlier eons of evolutionary time that had nothing to do with satisfying human desires. What the wildlands do "for us," if we must phrase it that way, is teach that God is not "for us" humans alone. God is for these wild creatures too. God loves wildness as much as God loves culture, and in this love God both blesses and satisfies wildness and also leaves it to its own spontaneous autonomy. To be self-actualizing under God is a good thing for humans, and it is a good thing, mutatis mutandis, for coyotes and columbines. That is the blessing of divinity in them. That the world is nothing but human resource, with nature otherwise value free, is sometimes taken to be the ultimately modern conviction, following which we will become fully human and be saved. It is in fact the ultimate in fiction, where the sin of pride comes around again to destroy.

> Is it by your wisdom that the hawk soars, and spreads his wings toward the south? Is it at your command that the eagle mounts up and makes his nest on high? On the rock he dwells and makes his home in the fastness of the rocky crag. Thence he spies out the prey; his eyes behold it afar off. His young ones suck up blood; and where the slain are, there is he. . . . Shall a faultfinder contend with the Almighty? He who argues with God, let him answer it.
>
> (Job 39:26—40:2)

> The high mountains are for the wild goats; the rocks are a refuge for the badgers. . . . The young lions roar for their prey, seeking their food from God. . . . O Lord, how manifold are thy works! In wisdom hast thou made them all; the earth is full of thy creatures.
>
> (Ps. 104:18, 21, 24)

In Earth's wildness there is a complex mixture of authority and autonomy, a divine imperative that there be communities (ecosystems) of spontaneous and autonomous ("wild") creatures, each creature defending its form of life. A principal insight that biblical faith can contribute, beyond its constraints on the exploitation of wildlife, is a forceful support of the concept of wildlife refuges or "sanctuaries" in national policy. A wildlife sanctuary is a place where nonhuman life is sacrosanct, that is, valued in ways that surpass not only economic levels but even in ways that transcend resource use in the ordinary senses. In that sense Christian conviction wants sanctuaries not only for humans, but also for wildlife.

ENDANGERED SPECIES

About five hundred faunal species and subspecies have become extinct in the United States since 1600, and another five hundred species are (officially or unofficially) threatened and endangered. In the American West, 164 fishes are endangered or vulnerable. About 56 percent of fish species in the United States and Canada are in need of protection. About 70 percent of the endangered and threatened fishes of the world are in North America. About 14 percent of the native continental United States flora, approximately 3,000 taxa, are either endangered or approaching endangerment. About 100 native plant taxa may already be extinct. In Hawaii, of the 2,200 native taxa, about 40 percent is in jeopardy and 225 species are believed extinct. Even where not nationally in danger, once-frequent species are locally extinct or rare. Utah, California, Texas, Oregon, Arizona, Nevada, Florida, and Michigan stand to lose plant species numbered in the hundreds. (See chart, p. 138.)

On global scales, about 20 percent of plant and animal species are projected to be lost within a few decades. These losses will be distributed widely throughout the faunal and floral orders, from large animals to insects, from trees to mosses. Losses will be heavier in the tropical rain forests than anywhere else, partially because of the inequitable distribution of resources in the involved nations, partially because of the biological richness of these forests, partially because, though naturally stable, these ecosystems do not absorb large-scale human interventions well.

Although Christianity does not have any particular expertise in endangered species management, biblical faith does have the conviction that these species originate in God. God ordered earth to "bring forth swarms of living creatures" (Gen. 1:20). "Swarms" is the Hebrew word for biodiversity! Adam's first job was, we might say, a taxonomy project, naming the animals.

Genesis also relates the first recorded endangered species project—Noah and his ark! Whatever one makes of the Flood historically, the teaching is abundantly clear. God wills for each species on Earth to continue, despite what judgments fall on the wickedness of humans. The fall of humans ought not to bring the fall of creation. Although individual animals perish in the Flood, God is concerned for preservation at the level of species. After the Flood, the covenant is reestablished with both humans and with the surviving natural kinds. "God said, 'This is the sign of the covenant which I make between me and you and every living creature that is with you, for all future generations: I

SOME ENDANGERED SPECIES IN NORTH AMERICA

Common name	Range
Mammals	
Ozark big-eared bat	Oklahoma
Brown or grizzly bear	48 conterminous states
Eastern cougar	Eastern North America
Columbian white-tailed deer	Washington, Oregon
San Joaquin kit fox	California
Fresno kangaroo	California
Southeastern beach mouse	Florida
Ocelot	Texas, Arizona
Southern sea otter	Washington, Oregon, California
Florida panther	Louisiana, Arkansas east to South Carolina, Florida
Utah prairie dog	Utah
Morro Bay kangaroo rat	California
Carolina northern flying squirrel	North Carolina, Tennessee
Hualapai Mexican vole	Arizona
Red wolf	Southeast to central Texas
Birds	
Masked bobwhite (quail)	Arizona
California condor	Oregon, California
Whooping crane	Rocky Mountains east to Carolinas, Canada
Eskimo curlew	Alaska and N. Canada
Bald eagle	Most states and Canada
American peregrine falcon	Canada to Mexico
Hawaiian hawk	Hawaii
Attwater's greater prairie-chicken	Texas
Bachman's warbler (wood)	Southeast U.S., Cuba
Kirtland's warbler (wood)	U.S., Canada, Bahama Islands
Ivory-billed woodpecker	Southcentral and Southeast U.S., Cuba
Reptiles	
American crocodile	Florida
Atlantic salt marsh snake	Florida
Plymouth red-bellied turtle	Massachusetts
Fishes	
Yaqui catfish	Arizona
Bonytail chub	Arizona, California, Colorado, Nevada, Utah, Wyoming
Gila trout	Arizona, New Mexico

Source: U.S. Fish and Wildlife Service, U.S. Interior Department; as of July 1989

set my bow in the cloud, and it shall be a sign of the covenant between me and the earth' " (Gen. 9:12-13). After the Flood, the command to humans is also repeated: "Be fruitful and multiply, and fill the earth" (Gen. 9:1). But this human development cannot legitimately be a threat to the diverse species that have just been saved from the Deluge; rather, the bloodlines are protected at threat of divine reckoning (Gen. 9:4-7). The Hebrews did not know anything about genes and so could not speak, as we do, of genetic diversity, but they spoke rather of protecting the bloodlines, a concept close enough to our modern concept of species.

These myriad species are often useful to humans, and on the ark clean species were given more protection than other species. After the Flood, plants were again given for food, and God gave permission to eat animals as well. Today, preservation of species is routinely defended in terms of human benefits. From a utilitarian viewpoint, species have medical, agricultural, and industrial possibilities. They can be used for scientific study; they can be enjoyed recreationally. Even species that are not directly useful may be indirectly useful for the roles they occupy in ecosystems, adding resilience and stability. High-quality human life requires a high diversity of species. But today we live on a sinking ark.

Humanistic justifications for the preservation of species, although correct and required as part of endangered species policy, fall short of a mature environmental ethic. They are inadequate for either Christian or Hebrew faith, neither of which is simply humanistic about species. Noah was not simply conserving global stock. He was not taking on board only those species with economic, agricultural, medical, industrial, and recreational value. Humanity is not the measure of things. What is offensive in the impending extinctions is not merely the loss of resources but the maelstrom of killing and insensitivity to forms of life and the biological and theological forces producing them. What is required is not human prudence but principled responsibility to the biospheric Earth. Indeed, for Christians, this is principled responsibility to God.

The Noah story is quaint and archaic, despite its profound insights. It is parable more than history. Yet, a floodlike threat is imminent. One form of life has never endangered so many others. Never before has this level of question been faced. Humans have more understanding than ever of the speciating processes, more power to foresee the intended and unintended results of their actions, and more power to reverse the undesirable consequences.

The United States Congress has lamented the loss of species.

The Congress finds and declares that—(1) various species of fish, wildlife, and plants in the United States have been rendered extinct as a consequence of economic growth and development untempered by adequate concern and conservation; (2) other species of fish, wildlife, and plants have been so depleted in numbers that they are in danger of, or threatened with, extinction; (3) these species of fish, wildlife, and plants are of esthetic, ecological, educational, historical, recreational and scientific value to the Nation and its people.[8]

A Christian position, endorsing all that is here said, will wish to add that these species are also of religious value, of value not only to U.S. citizens, but to God.

The protection Congress has authorized for species is a strong one. Interpreting the Endangered Species Act of 1973, the U.S. Supreme Court insisted "that Congress intended endangered species to be afforded the highest of priorities." "The plain intent of Congress in enacting this statute was to halt and reverse the trend toward species extinction, whatever the cost."[9] Notably, "economic" is not among the listed criteria of value, almost as though Congress by omission intended to deemphasize that value. But, since economic costs must sometimes be considered (and Congress itself has consistently underfunded the Act), Congress in subsequent legislation authorized a high-level, interagency committee to evaluate difficult cases, and, should this committee deem fit, to permit human development at cost of extinction or threatened extinction of species that impede development. Interestingly this committee has been termed "the God committee," and the nickname is not without some theological insight. God wills for species to continue, subject to natural processes, consonant with human development, and any who will to destroy species in the name of development take, fearfully, the prerogative of God. "Keep them alive with you" (Gen. 6:19).

In that light, at the level of species, all concepts of ownership ought to lapse, whether private, state, or national. Wildlife—individual deer, eagles, bears—are not owned by landowners, perhaps not even owned by government, but are a commons regulated by government for the benefit of all, in such way that wildlife ought to be perennially on the land. Landowners do not own species, whether fauna or flora, though they may own a field with rare plants in it, individual tokens of that endangered type. In legal terms, land ownership is imperfect and does not carry the right irreplaceably to destroy. In theological terms, land ownership is stewardship.

A species is a dynamic natural kind, a historical lineage persisting through space and time, typically over many millions of years. In that perspective, it is arrogant for even a nation to think of owning species. The United States would be a quite late-coming owner of such species.

From a biological point of view, several billion years' worth of creative toil and several million species of teeming life have been handed over to the care of this late-coming species in which mind has flowered and morals have emerged. From a political point of view, the United States inherits part of a continent over which life has flowed for a thousand times as long as the nation itself has existed. From a theological point of view, humans threaten the divine creation. These species belong not to us, either as persons or as a nation, but to God. There is something unchristian and ungodly about living in a society where one species takes itself as absolute and values everything else relative to its national or personal utility. It is more than appropriate for Christians to call for humans to respect the plenitude of being that surrounds us in the wild world, once so vast and now so quickly vanishing.

THE MEEK INHERIT THE EARTH

Biblical meekness is the controlled use of power, disciplined by respect and love. In the Beatitudes, the meek inherit the promised earth. That blessing is conferred upon peacemakers, upon humans who control their desires in their relations with other humans, but it is also conferred upon humans who control their desires in their relations with the land. The human power on Earth is divine gift, but it is divine gift to be used, reflecting the Creator God, in humility and in love.

To travel into such a promised land, monotheistic faith will orient for general directions of travel, something like a compass. But specific paths will have to be figured out locally. In wildland and wildlife conservation, with this general orientation, such strategies as the following apply:

- Avoid irreversible change.
- Optimize natural diversity.
- Optimize natural stability.
- Respect life, the species more than the individual.
- Increase options for experiencing natural history.
- Avoid toxic threats.
- Do not discount the future environmentally.
- Keep remaining public wildlands off the market.
- Optimize recycling.

- Accept no-growth sectors of the economy.
- The more fragile an environment, the more carefully it ought to be treated.
- The more beautiful an environment, the more carefully it ought to be treated.
- The rarer an environment, the more carefully it ought to be treated.
- Respect life, the more so the more sentient.
- Think of nature as a community first, a commodity second.
- Remember, morality often exceeds legality in environmental affairs.
- Work for environmental benefits that can only be had in concert.
- Avoid cutting remaining pristine forests on public lands.
- Preserve wildlands in all the diverse kinds of ecosystems.
- Restore degraded wildlands, reintroducing all the original native fauna and flora, where possible.
- Discourage trophy hunting and killing merely for sport.
- Make animal welfare high priority for all zoo and other captive wild animals.
- Strive for no net loss of wetlands.
- Place special concern on critical environments that support internationally migratory wildlife.
- Prefer the most environmentally sensitive alternatives for development over alternatives that maximize economic returns.
- Avoid below-cost timber sales on public lands.
- Preserve and restore wildlands adjacent to and integrated with urban areas.
- Support opportunities for environmental education for everyone.
- Provide interpretation and support for those persons whose lives and jobs must be altered in the interest of long-range environmental quality.
- Support Native American efforts to retain and restore wildness on their lands.
- Condemn all illegal trade in wildlife and wild plants, and products made from these.
- Keep life wild and free.
- Love your neighborhood as you do yourself.

Within their own community and life, Christians should:
- Include an understanding and appreciation of wildlife and wildlands in all teaching efforts.
- Include opportunities for experience of nature in church camps and conferences where possible.

- Provide opportunities for wilderness experience combined with Christian fellowship.
- Manage church lands and properties according to the most environmentally sensitive alternative.
- Integrate for maximum effectiveness the resources of church camp and conference centers across the nation.
- Support Christian ministries in national and state parks and on other public wildlands.
- Include in seminary education a theological understanding of creation, appropriate respect for wildlands and wildlife, and biological conservation.
- Support the annual environmental sabbath (first Sunday in June).

What on Earth are we doing? Humans cannot know what they are doing on Earth unless they also know what they are undoing. They can and ought to create their cultures, under God; but this ought not to be by undoing creation. Can humans genuinely gain by exploiting the fractional wilds that remain? What does it profit to gain the world, only to lose it—to gain it economically, to fence it in, pave it over, and harvest it only to lose it scientifically, aesthetically, recreationally, and religiously, as a wonderland of natural history, and as a realm of integral wildness that transcends and supports us—and perhaps even to lose some of our soul in the trade-off?

8

CREATION AS KIN
An American
Indian View

George E. Tinker

*H*eavily dressed for the half meter of snow covering the hillside, a
small group of people stood quietly around what looked like a
perfect, if rather large, Christmas tree. Mostly American Indians from
a variety of tribes and all members of an Indian congregation, the people
were speaking prayers on behalf of the tree. It could have been most
any annual congregational outing to harvest a Christmas tree for their
church, except that these prayers were a thorough mixture of Christian
prayers and traditional Indian tribal prayers. The two pastors held tobacco in their hands, ready to offer it back to the Creator, to offer it
for the life of this tree, to offer it to the four directions, above and
below, to offer it in order to maintain the harmony and balance of
Creation even in the perpetration of an act of violence. Someone
wrapped a string of colorful tobacco tie offerings around the trunk. As
four men sang traditional prayer songs around a drum, the people came
one by one up to the tree to touch it and say their prayers, some actually
speaking to the tree, speaking consoling words of apology, gratitude,
purpose, and promise.

A real sense of cultural value is being exposed in this gathering. This
attitude toward Creation and all the createds sets American Indians
apart from other Americans and most Europeans. Yet it is characteristic
of many of the world's indigenous peoples and represents a set of cultural
values that perseveres even in those indigenous communities that have
been converted to Christianity. Perhaps an outsider would describe the
attitude of these Indians as one of awe or wonderment. We American
Indians think of it as neither, but would prefer to call it "respect," the
appropriate attitude necessary to fulfill our responsibility as part of the

created whole, necessary to help maintain the harmony and balance, the interdependence and interrelationship of all things in our world.

The key word then, for the American Indian cultural context, is *respect*, respect for a tree. Even more important is the underlying notion of reciprocity. The prayers and the offering of tobacco are reciprocal acts of giving something back to the earth and to all of Creation in order to maintain balance even as we disrupt the balance by cutting down this tree. The question Indian cultures pose for Christian people, especially those of Europe and North America, is this: How can respect for a tree or rock, animals or eventually other human beings find any place in the industrial-commercial world that has emerged out of modernity and now threatens all of creation with "postmodern" extinction? And what sort of reciprocity do we or will we engage in; what do we return to the earth when we clear-cut a forest or strip mine leaving miles of earth totally bare? Perhaps more painfully, the same question can be put in terms of human justice: Where is the reciprocity, the maintaining of cosmic balance, with respect to those who are suffering varieties of oppression in our modern world, such as blacks in southern Africa, non-Jews in Palestine, Tamils in Sri Lanka or tribal peoples in Latin America? The World Council of Churches program for "Justice, Peace, and the Integrity of Creation" represents a crucial discussion that moves us in the right direction.

The WCC process called "Justice, Peace, and the Integrity of Creation" has resulted in an exciting and innovative document that seems to push our churches more decisively toward what I have described as the American Indian foundation of respect.[1] In spite of the historical tendencies of most of our churches and the sequence of words in the title that puts Creation at the end, the Final Document of the JPIC world convocation bites the bullet and puts concern for creation ahead of justice in its priority. I say this with a certain satisfaction, even though I sense a danger here. Like many other Third and Fourth World peoples, I, too, have worried that the growing concern for the ecological crisis facing all of Creation might again distract people of genuine conscience from their commitment to issues of justice and liberation. The concern for the survival of fish in mountain lakes polluted by acid rain, for instance, is noble. However, when that concern distracts our attention from the daily suffering of blacks in southern Africa, it becomes an actual participant in the oppression imposed on those human sisters and brothers by the terror of apartheid. For my part, I must constantly remind good Christian people in North America of the continued oppression of American Indians; of our 60 percent unemployment rate; the destruction of our cultures; the theft of our lands; and the greater victimization by disease and dysfunctionality resulting in a horrible longevity statistic of only 46 years. The need for justice, for churches that will proclaim that "good news to the poor and oppressed," is real, even in the midst of North America's wealth.

Nevertheless, I argue that respect for creation must be our starting point for theological reflection in our endangered world. More explicitly I argue, from an American Indian perspective, that justice and peace will flow as a natural result from a genuine and appropriate concern for creation. Hence the "integrity of creation" must be understood as much more than a concern for ecological disintegration. At a theological level, the sequence of words in the title Justice, Peace, and the Integrity of Creation is problematic for Native Americans and I expect for other Fourth World indigenous peoples. For us as for the early ecumenical creeds of the Christian church, creation must come first.

The World Council of Churches and many of our member churches have made the shift over the past two decades from "peace and justice" language to language of "justice and peace." The word order here has become more than just a curiosity. It reflects a definite prioritization, not so much in terms of importance but in terms of an appropriate sequencing of the whole agenda. This sensitivity of our churches is a response to the voices of marginalized people all over this world. Third and Fourth World peoples have been almost univocal that their primary need, whether within their own country or in the international community, has been for a measure of real justice and that peace in our context has first to do with justice. We have been equally clear that any sudden emergence of international peace in the world today would fall far short of satisfying the pervasive need for justice. It might function, quite to the contrary, to institutionalize further the injustices suffered, just as many peace movements have often functioned to steal peoples' energies away from some of the more immediate struggles for justice.

Just as concerned Christian people have begun to learn that true peace can only be realized through the establishment of justice and that peace is a consequence of justice, now we must begin to learn that justice and peace flow naturally out of a deep respect for all of creation. Thus for Native Americans and other indigenous peoples a more theologically intact title would be "Creation, Justice, and Peace." As it now stands, the "Integrity of Creation" reads as merely a tacked-on First World concern for environmental issues.

As Christians in the World Council of Churches, we need to rediscover our spiritual rootedness in the First Article of the ecumenical creeds as a clear biblical image and to allow that spiritual foundation to generate our decisive action for justice and peace. And it may be that the inherent spirituality of American Indians, Pacific Islanders, tribal Africans, and other indigenous peoples may help point us in the right direction. While it may be too late to change the title of the program, it is more important than ever to debate the issues involved.

THE CIRCLE AND *MITAKUYE OYASIN*

American Indians and other indigenous peoples have a long-standing confidence that they have much to teach Europeans and North Americans about the world and human relationships in the world. They are confident in the spiritual foundations of their insights, confident that those foundations can become a source of healing and reconciliation for all creation. Let me use a couple of simple examples from an Indian perspective.

My Indian ancestors had a relationship with God as Creator that was healthy and responsible long before they knew of or confessed the gospel of Jesus Christ. They had a relationship with Creator that was solidified in the stories they told around the camp fires in each of our tribes, in their prayers, and especially in their ceremonies. This relationship began with the recognition of the Other as Creator, the creative force behind all things that exist, and long predated the coming of the missionaries. In that relationship, the people saw themselves as participants within creation as a whole, as a part of creation, and they celebrated the balance and harmony of the whole of the universe in all that they did together.

In all that they did, our Indian ancestors acknowledged the goodness of the Creator and of all creation including themselves. That was the point of the stories, the focus of their prayers, and the purpose of the ceremonies. They recognized the balance and harmony that characterized all of the created universe: winter and summer were held in balance with one another. So also were hunting and planting, sky and earth, hot and cold, sun and moon, female and male, women and men. Our ancestors recognized all this as good, just as God did at the end of the sixth day (Gen. 1:31).

If all American Indian spiritual insights and hence Indian theology must begin with creation, this is reflected already in the basic liturgical posture of Indians in many North American tribes. Our prayers are most often said with the community assembled in some form of circle. In fact the circle is a key symbol for self-understanding in these tribes, representing the whole of the universe and our part in it. We see ourselves as coequal participants in the circle, standing neither above nor below anything else in God's creation. There is no hierarchy in our cultural context, even of species, because the circle has no beginning nor ending. Hence all the createds participate together, each in their own way, to preserve the wholeness of the circle. So when a group of Indians form a circle to pray, all know that the prayers have already begun with the representation of a circle. No words have yet been spoken and in some ceremonies no words need be spoken, but the intentional physicality of our formation has already expressed our prayer and deep concern for the wholeness of all of God's creation. It should be noted in this context that Indians do not hold hands when they pray thus, unless they have been tainted by the piety of a white missionary. There is no need to hold hands because we know it is enough to stand in the circle already joined together, inextricably bound, through the earth that lies firm beneath our feet, the earth which is, after all, the true mother of each of us and of all creation.

The Lakota and Dakota peoples have a phrase used in all their prayers that aptly illustrates the Native American sense of the centrality of creation. The phrase, *mitakuye oyasin,* functions somewhat like the word *amen* in European and American Christianity. As such, it is used to end every prayer, and often it is in itself a whole prayer, being the only phrase spoken. The usual translation offered is, "For all my relations." Yet like most Native symbols, *mitakuye oyasin* is polyvalent in its meaning. Certainly, one is praying for one's close kin, aunts, cousins, children, grandparents, and so on. And "relations" can be understood as fellow tribal members or even all Indian people. At the same time, the phrase includes all human beings, all two-leggeds as relatives of one another, and the ever-expanding circle does not stop there. Every Lakota who prays this prayer knows that our relatives necessarily include the four-leggeds, the wingeds and all the living, moving things on mother Earth. One Lakota teacher has suggested that a translation of *mitakuye oyasin* would better read: "For all the above me and below me and around me things": That is for all my relations. Perhaps one can begin to understand the extensive image of interrelatedness and interdependence symbolized by the circle and the importance of reciprocity and respect for one another for maintaining the wholeness of the circle. The American Indian concern for starting theology with creation is a need to acknowledge the goodness and inherent worth of all of God's creatures. We experience evil or sin as disruptions in that delicate balance, disruptions that negate the intrinsic worth of any of our relatives.

CREATION AND KINGDOM

In the remainder of this essay I want to pursue this American Indian image of creation in terms of the important biblical image of *basileia tou Theou*, the kingdom of God. In particular I want to suggest the benefits to Western Christianity of a Native American reading of the kingdom. I would like to do this with special attention to Mark 1:15 and the conjunction of the nearness of the kingdom and the need for repentance. But first we must make some decisions about the nature of the kingdom.

If the Indian image of creation is at all compelling, then we need to come to a new (or perhaps old) understanding of creation in our denominational theologies, one that begins to image creation as an ongoing eschatological act and not just God's initial act. We must begin to see creation as the eschatological basis even for the Christ event. If this is difficult, it may be so because the cultures in which the gospel has come to find a home in the West are so fundamentally oriented toward temporality and so disoriented toward spatiality. As a result the very categories of existence and all the categories of knowledge in the Western intellectual tradition function out of a temporal base and pervade our understanding of all reality.[2] This then characterizes our theologies and especially our interpretation of key biblical themes and texts.

Since the emergence of eschatology as a central aspect of the interpretation of the Gospels in Western biblical criticism in the work of Johannes Weis and Albert Schweitzer,[3] until very recently the kingdom of God has been given over completely to temporal interpretations.[4] That is, the only appropriate question to ask about the kingdom has been When? It is not that scholars did not consider other possibilities. In fact, the question Where? has been consistently disallowed. Norman Perrin spoke for some seventy years of scholarly dialogue in Europe and North America when he wrote in 1967: "[The Kingdom] is not a place or community ruled by God."[5] From Weis and Schweitzer to Perrin and beyond, the question had been: When will the kingdom of God happen? When will it appear? In the course of the dialogue a wide variety of answers has been proposed, each of them generating a new *terminus technicus* (Latin for "jargon") to label the theory. So we have argued between realized eschatology, actualized eschatology, immanent eschatology, or future eschatology, ringing all the changes on those themes.

Curiously enough, it was Norman Perrin and his student Werner Kelber who in the mid-1970s announced a major shift in interpretation of *basileia tou Theou*. Kelber first put forth arguments for a consistent spatial understanding of the kingdom in the Gospel of Mark, linking its meaning to expanding territorial-geographical developments in that gospel.[6] Perrin decisively articulated the metaphoric nature of *basileia* language, distinguishing between "steno" and "tensive" symbols and identifying *basileia tou Theou* as the latter. So we now can begin to understand the kingdom of God as a "symbol," which Perrin defines with Philip Wheelwright as "a relatively stable and repeatable element of perceptual experience, standing from some larger meaning or set of meanings which cannot be given, or not fully given in perceptual experience itself."[7]

It seems obvious that spatial categories do not necessarily exclude the temporal, nor vice versa. Yet the orientation assumed by the interpreter becomes crucial. Like M. Eugene Boring, I do not see how temporality can be excised from Mark's proclamation of the kingdom; yet I certainly disagree with his assumption that the kingdom of God sayings in Mark must be read in terms of an "overwhelming temporal orientation."[8] To the contrary, I want to argue for the possibility of spatial priority in language of the kingdom of God, perhaps in Mark particularly. The possibility becomes pronounced in any Native American reading of the text, because the Indian world is as decidedly spatial in its orientation as the modern Western world is temporal.[9] In fact any Indian reader of Mark or the Synoptics is bound to think first of all in terms of the question Where? with regard to *basileia*. And it is in this context that I want to pursue the discussion.

It seems safe to suggest that the image represents a symbolic value and that the parameters of the symbol might be filled in as follows: (*a*) The Gospels seem to view the divine hegemony as something that is in process. It is drawing near, it is emerging (Mark 1:15). Yet it is also "among us," in our midst (Luke 17). It is something that can be experienced by the faithful here and now, even if only proleptically. Its full emergence is still in the future. (*b*) The symbolic value captured by the imagery in no small part includes a view of an ideal world. And (*c*) the structural definition of that ideal world is, above all else, relational.

I am convinced that the imagery of divine rule is essentially creation imagery, that the ideal world symbolically represented in the image builds on the divine origin of the cosmos as an ideal past and an ideal future. It is relational first of all because it implies a relationship between the created order of things and its Creator, and secondly because it implies a relationship between all of the things created by the Creator. As the Creator of all, God is perforce the rightful ruler of all. And the

ideal world to which Jesus points in the Gospels is precisely the realization of that proper relationship between the Creator and the created.
Human beings may have been created as the last of all the created
(Genesis 1), or perhaps a human being was created first (Genesis 2).
That is really inconsequential. What is crucial is that the harmony and
balance of the created order was good. While that order has been
somewhat shaken by the human createds, it is still the ideal state toward
which we all look forward in Christ Jesus. The process is going on now,
and all of creation is a part of the process. As Paul says, all of creation
groans in travail, that is, in childbirth (Rom. 8:22).

REPENTANCE

Now to return to Mark 1:15, we need not discuss at length the nature
of the word for time. It is enough to suggest the cyclical seasonal nature
of *kairos* here over against the more linear concept of *kronos*. In any case
the mention of a time element should not distract us from a spatial,
now creational, understanding. Nor at this point would it prove fruitful
to pursue the verb *engiken* (has drawn near).

More important for my case is an understanding of the imperative
metanoiete (repent!). And here I want to argue for the underlying Ar-
amaic sense of *shuv* as "return" rather than the Greek notion of "change
of mind." Repentance is key to the establishment of divine hegemony
because it involves a "return," namely, a return to God. Feeling sorry
for one's sins is not a part of repentance at all, though it may be the
initial act of confession. Even in the most "Greek" narrative of Luke's
Acts of the Apostles, repentance is not a penitential emotion but instead
carries the Hebrew sense of return. In Acts 2:37-38, people feel penitential emotion as a result of Peter's sermon and come to him to ask
what they must do. His response is to say, "Repent and be baptized."
They already feel sorry for their sins. That's not what he requires of
them. The Hebrew notion of repentance really is calling on God's people
to recognize the divine hegemony, to return to God, to return to the
ideal relationship between Creator and the created.

The establishment of any ecclesiastical structure should be an attempt
to actualize this ideal as much as possible (proleptically). A church is
an attempt on the part of a community of believers to respond to God's
call to relationship, first of all to relationship with God as Creator, and
secondly with one another as fellow createds. A church is a response to
Jesus' vision of an ideal world characterized by love of God and love
of one's neighbor as one's self. But this ideal world can only be actualized

through repentance, that is, by returning to God as the Creator and rightful leader of all of creation. Hence church is a vehicle of repentance or return. Moreover, this ideal world that exists only within the divine hegemony is "good"; it is marked by divine balance and harmony.

CONFESSION, RETURN, AND THE INTEGRITY OF CREATION

It is my hope that the theological imagination of Native Americans, rooted as it is in the dynamic, generating power of creation, can help show new direction for the trinitarian theology of our churches. It should be clearly noted here again that the theological priority of creation is not a priority simply for environmental concern, but rather, *creation* is a firm foundation for *justice* and a vision for *peace*. If we can begin with a First Article affirmation of God as Creator and ourselves as created, then perhaps there is hope for a spiritual transformation that can bring us all closer to recognizing the kingdom of God in our midst (Luke 17:21). Then perhaps we can acknowledge our humanness in new and more significant ways, understanding that confession precedes return, and that both become the base for living in harmony and balance with God and all creation. Besides confession of our individual humanness, this means confessing the humanness of our churches, the humanness of our theologies, and the humanness of the world economic order in which we participate. Then it is possible to make our repentance, to return, to go back from whence we came, that is, to go back to the Creator in whom we like all of creation "live and move and have our being" (Acts 17:28). We must go back to a proper relationship with the Creator in which we confess our human inclination to put ourselves in Creator's place and renew our understanding of ourselves and our institutions as mere creatures. We must go back to a recognition of ourselves as a part of and integrally related to all of creation.

The Indian understanding of Creation as sacred, of mother Earth as the source of all life, goes far beyond the notion of such Western counter-institutions as the Sierra Club or Greenpeace. It embraces far more than concern for harp seals or a couple of ice-bound whales. It embraces all of life from trees and rocks to international relations. And this knowledge informs all of the community's activity, from hunting to dancing and even to writing grant proposals or administering government agencies. It especially concerns itself with the way we all live together. Perforce, it has to do with issues of justice and fairness and ultimately with peace. If we believe we are all relatives in this world, then we must live together differently than we have. Justice and peace, in this context, emerge almost naturally out of a self-imaging that sees the self only as a part of the whole, as a part of an ever-expanding community that begins with family and tribe but is finally inclusive of all human beings and of all of creation. All in this world are relatives, and we will live together out of respect for each other, working toward the good of each other. Respect for creation, for instance, must result in an ongoing concern for economic balance and resistance to economic injustices that leave many poor and oppressed while their white American or European relatives or Japanese relatives live in relative wealth at the expense of others.

Indian people have experienced and continue to experience endless oppression as a result of what some would call the barbaric invasion of America. And we certainly suspect that the oppression we have experienced is intimately linked to the way the immigrants pray and how they understand creation and their relationship to creation and Creator. Moreover we suspect that the greed that motivated the displacement of all indigenous peoples from their lands of spiritual rootedness is the same greed that threatens the destruction of the earth and the continued oppression of so many people. Whether it is the stories the immigrants tell or the theologies they develop to interpret those stories, something appears wrong to Indian people. But not only do Indians continue to tell the stories, sing the songs, speak the prayers, and perform the ceremonies that root themselves deeply in mother Earth, they are actually audacious enough to think that their stories and their ways of reverencing creation will some day win over the immigrants and transform them. Optimism and enduring patience seem to run in the life blood of Native American peoples.

Mitakuye oyasin! For all my relatives!

9

ECONOMICS, ECO-JUSTICE, AND THE DOCTRINE OF GOD

Carol Johnston

And the leaves of the tree were for the healing of the nations.
—Revelation 22:2

The biblical story of humankind begins in a garden—a pristine natural world that the first humans are charged to care for in a harmony of trust between God, themselves, and the rest of creation. When they break that harmony by distrusting God, the garden is forever lost to them, and they become strangers to God, to themselves, and to the world. There will be redemption, but redemption will not mean returning to the garden or to its innocent unconscious harmony of relations. Neither will redemption mean the escape of saved souls from a spoiled earth to a perfect heaven. The Bible ends with a vision of a new Jerusalem coming down from heaven to be established in a new earth (Revelation 21–22). With the city comes God, who will dwell with the people in the earthly habitation. In this vision, it is not earth that will be abandoned, but heaven.

While there will be no return to the primeval garden, the city envisioned in Revelation is not cut off from nature like a modern city. The "river of the water of life" flows from the throne of God through the middle of the city. On the bank of the river grows the tree of life, with its twelve kinds of fruits and its healing leaves.

This is a metaphorical vision of shalom, imaging a world of restored trust. God, human beings, and earth are reunited and dwell together in peace. The tree of life with its twelve fruits stands for the flourishing diversity of creation. There, from the leaves of the tree of life, "the nations" will find healing.

This image of healing can help us explore the problem of finding "healing for the nations" in the context of the eco-justice crisis. There are three dimensions of the image that give us clues to the problem. First, the healing is a healing of communities, not of individuals disassociated from their communities. Second, it is a healing that takes place by means of a flourishing nature filled with diversity. Third, the nations do not need to go outside the city to find healing, for nature and God are no longer separated from the city. After discussing these images, I will draw out some of their implications for a doctrine of God that is truer to the biblical vision of shalom.

HEALING OF "THE NATIONS"

The biblical images of redemption assume that human beings are social creatures, so we find redemption taking place in a community context. In fact, liberation and redemption consistently mean the creation of a covenantal community. From the Hebrews, whose identity was forged in intimate relation to the Law and its land ethic, and to the Christians, who knew salvation as members of one another in the body of Christ, individuals are not saved alone.

Yet the Western Christian tradition, especially Protestantism, has come to focus almost exclusively on the salvation of individual souls. The Bible is read with individualistic glasses, and the importance of community relations is missed. This individualism has come to pervade Western culture in numerous ways, including some that are highly destructive of persons and their human and natural communities. In this section I want to discuss the way individualism distorts or denies inherent relations and to propose an understanding that can better promote healing—one that preserves individual integrity and yet recognizes its inherent community context.

Relations as External

Calvin claimed that neither human beings nor nature could be "read" correctly until they were read with the "glasses of scripture."[1] Yet he himself read Scripture uncritically through the glasses of the dominant philosophical views of his day. That dominant philosophy was nominalism/voluntarism, a philosophical movement that helped the Reformers to argue against the entrenched authority and rigidity of the Roman Catholic natural law tradition.

In the natural law tradition, every entity was conceived as related to every other through its location in the "great chain of being." This created order was not only hierarchical, it was as fixed and as immutable as God. The advantage of the natural law tradition was that it protected both people and other creatures to some extent, because all were conceived as having their rightful place in creation, independently of their use to human beings. But it was rigid and reinforced the patriarchal social hierarchy of feudalism. Relations were not dynamic, but externally imposed. Justice was a matter of the obligation of authorities to render what was due based on one's place on the created ladder.

In reaction to the rigidities of the natural law tradition, nominalism/voluntarism went to the opposite extreme. It was individualistic and emphasized self-determined voluntary action, so the image of a natural order where all creatures have their place (including humans) began to come apart. This made it possible to break the stranglehold on authority wielded by the Roman and feudal systems and opened up new possibilities for the development of democratic movements. But it has worked itself out to an extreme of atomistic and arbitrary individualism that has infected every area of modern culture, including our images of God, human beings, and nature.

Read with the glasses of atomistic individualism, Christianity gives us a God who is self-enclosed and unaffected by the world. The biblical stories of a God passionately engaged with the Hebrew people—wrestling with them, arguing with them, weeping over them, suffering like a mother in travail for them—disappear. God is essentially remote, and it is difficult to imagine how God could relate to the world.

Similarly, human beings, like God, are conceived as atomistic individuals whose relations are secondary and external to their being. Nature itself is also conceived as composed of atomistic entities whose relations are only external. This has led to the mechanistic world view in which all entities, including humans, are thought to be made of interchangeable parts that can be taken apart and moved around to suit human desires.

Since relations are treated as external, modern economies, both capitalist and Marxist, have gone about industrialization by moving both human beings and natural resources to suit the needs of economic growth. Both believe that the improvement of human welfare depends on the increase of material goods, and both have readily destroyed communities and natural ecosystems in order to achieve it.

Even though Marxism emphasizes social relations as fundamental, the underlying assumption that relations are external gives license to the idea that a new society, shorn of old habits of oppression, can be achieved simply by dismantling traditional communities and imposing social equity. Capitalism sees social relations as both external and voluntary, so social equity is a matter primarily for voluntary charity or tax systems for welfare if there is enough popular support (thus in a social sense also voluntary).

Ecosystems are also readily abused when relations are conceived as external. First, human beings are assumed to exist independently of the natural environment; thus what happens to the natural world does not matter. Second, the environment itself is not thought of as essentially interrelated. Few understand that the economy, by extracting resources from the land, can cause chain reactions that mean widespread devastation. Both capitalist and Marxist economics assume that the scale of the economy can grow forever, with no reference to earth's productive or waste-absorption capacities and with no accounting for the fact that the earth is not an open, growing system, but a closed one.

Relations as Inherent

An alternative to conceiving of God, human beings, and the world in terms of external relations is to conceive of them as also inherently or internally related. Contemporary physics and the other sciences are pointing the way to reconceiving all entities as internally related, so that entities are constituted by their relations. Consequently ecosystems are characterized by intrinsic interconnections that reverberate in every entity, including the human beings who are also creatures.

If everything is inherently related, then human beings are not only essentially related to each other and the environment, but their very individuality is achieved through how they synthesize in novel ways their relations with others, including the natural world and God, and by how they contribute those uniquenesses to the experience of others. Social relations are thus inherent to a person's life and individuality.

Freedom therefore is always exercised in the context of these relations. The choices available can be narrower or wider depending on both what has been received from others and on what one can contribute to others. A child whose development has been stunted by impoverished relations both with other people and with the natural world has had its range of freedom narrowed. So has the adult who has been denied meaningful employment.

That relations are inherent need not mean that individuality and the human capacity for transcendence are lost in the social organism or natural ecosystem. Individuality is lost when external relations impose a role on a person that is defined wholly by the person's place in the system, which happens especially to women. We need to recognize that persons (male and female) and their human communities need to actualize their identities, particular to the uniquenesses of their natural environments and their own creative possibilities. Certainly, for example, the Swiss would not be who they are without their relationship with their alpine environment. And the American encounter with the vastness of North America has made its distinctive mark in forging American identity.

But we also need to recognize that both persons and communities are stronger when they are open to the kind of growth that comes from relationships with what is different. Ecosystems are richly distinct. Yet they have no sharp boundaries, but transition zones where there is much interaction between systems, which enriches both without dissolving the identity of either.

When relations are conceived as inherent, then the person is both influenced by relations with others and influences them. In this context, justice is not a matter of rendering what is due, but it is a matter of the quality of relationships between persons, so that all participate in deciding what is just for their situations.

When read through the glasses of inherent relations, the biblical images of salvation are much less individualistic and other-worldly and much more grounded in the redemption of community and natural relations. Individuals, in fact, cannot be fulfilled apart from community and natural relations. The possibility of achieving the full scope of their very individuality depends on the quality of those relations.

It should be noted that the quality of relations differs for men and for women. Women's individuality is more often underdeveloped, because their identities are submerged into that of dominant men. But men's individuality is also often deficient, because, while the self is in a sense "overdeveloped," it is also empty. A self based on largely external relations cannot find fulfillment, because it can neither be enriched by relations with others nor contribute to the enrichment of others.

The healing of the nations, then, depends first on the recognition that human persons, their communities, and the natural world are all inherently related, such that freedom and justice are dynamic dimensions of relationships characterized by participation and solidarity. Projects for liberation that recognize inherent relations will be much less likely to leave out the importance of maintaining the integrity of communities and the land and more likely to include the people affected as subjects of their own liberation.

HEALING BY MEANS OF THE LEAVES
OF THE TREE OF LIFE

Healing does not come from the throne of God, though God will "wipe away every tear from their eyes" (Rev. 21:4). Nor does it come from the Lamb, though the Lamb is the lamp of the glory of God, and the nations walk by its light (21:23-24). Nor does it come from the water of life, though the thirsty drink freely from its fountain (21:6). In the new Jerusalem, healing will come by means of the leaves of the tree.

Transformation through Continuing Relations
with the Natural World

Notice that healing does not come by fiat. God does not say, "Let them be healed," and the people are healed. The image implies that healing will come by means of this continuing relation of the people with the natural world. This is a further affirmation of salvation as depending on restored relations not only with God and other humans but also with nature.

The importance and character of this relationship with nature has been even more distorted and denied than the character of the Bible and the world when read with the glasses of external relations and anthropocentric individualism. In this view, the Genesis affirmation that human beings are made in the "image of God" and given charge of the earth to "subdue it," is easily interpreted as a license to do what humans please with the natural world. Arguments for restraint are usually grounded in a concern for nature fulfilling human need alone and not for other creatures in their own right. Calvin took for granted that the whole purpose of creation was for the sake of human beings,[2] despite his frequent affirmation that God's ruling and caring presence (and God's glory) is in all creatures and not only in that arrogant "five-foot worm" called human.[3] As long as the natural world is conceived as existing solely for the sake of human need and desire, and not also for its own sake and for God's delight in it apart from humans, the environment and humankind will not find healing and restoration.

Transformation at the Margins:
Value and Choice

The modern world views all value as dependent on choice—first on God's choice, then on human choice. Voluntarism[4] affirmed the absolute freedom of God to do as God pleases and insisted that God does not do what is good in itself, but whatever God does is good, simply because

God chooses to do it. A logical corollary of this view was the doctrine of double predestination: God has chosen to save some and chosen to damn the rest, which must be good, because God has chosen to do it.

Value became wholly subjective and arbitrary and reached its apotheosis in neoclassical (capitalist) economic theory, which is founded on the assertion that all value depends on the subjective choice of individuals, and on nothing else whatever. Economists go to great lengths to show that this individual choice, or "utility," cannot be compared or ranked in any way.[5]

It is in theory impossible to assert that the desire of individual A for more fur coats is not as important as the desire of individual B to avoid starvation. Value is subjective, individual, and in principle arbitrary. Individual A might decide to value charity for individual B. But this is strictly a gracious (arbitrary) decision on the part of individual A.

This theory of value has been applied in U.S. public policy since the early 1980s, when social welfare systems were gutted and the resulting social problems were left to charity. This value system also makes environmental integrity a matter of personal taste, and thus a luxury for those who can afford to care about pristine landscapes.

This intense focus on value as based on individual preference has permeated Western culture, including Protestant Christianity. Economists call this focus "marginal analysis," because they are looking at the choices individuals make in the market at the "margin," where they are choosing whether to buy one more of one thing or something else. Marginal analysis, or this attention to individual choice in the market, has dominated capitalist economics since the late nineteenth century. It has also characterized American Protestantism. What is chosen can vary, but individual choice is the focus of both evangelical revivalism and existential liberalism.

The irony of marginal analysis is the fact that it draws attention away from the real margins of society. What matters is the choice made in the center of action—the market in economics—not the consequences of that choice for what lies outside the system. In economics, everything outside the market is called an "externality" and is left out of consideration. This means that the pollution of the water supply is invisible until clean water becomes scarce enough to have a cost that shows up in the market. It also means that as long as the economy as a whole is "booming," the people and the ecosystems that have been left out or damaged are not considered.

One response to this problem is to shift focus from the market to the real margins, to the "marginalized" and suffering. But this response does not go far enough, as long as it still relies on the method of marginal analysis, because it ends up only reacting to crises generated by the whole system, instead of working to transform the system so that these kinds of crises do not get generated in the first place.

One way to explain this is to look at the U.S. medical system. The method of marginal analysis means that medicine has focused on crisis response: the deterioration of the arteries (through abusive diet, lack of exercise, and stress) is invisible until the heart stops. Until very recently medical research has concentrated on responding to the crisis of heart disease with high-tech machines, rather than on preventing it with low-cost health maintenance.

Analogously, in U.S. social justice movements the method of marginal analysis has tended to a preoccupation with attempts to distribute the fruits of production through social welfare and tax transfer programs. The social/economic system keeps generating more homeless people, more unemployment, more school drop-outs, more toxic dumps, more industrial accidents—in other words, more disintegrating communities and ecosystems—and the social welfare and charity systems keep trying to pick up the pieces. These crises of human need have to be met, but we will never get beyond them until we figure out how to create and maintain a healthier system.

Intrinsic Value and Healthy Relations

Instead of more crisis management and more distribution, we need inclusive participation and power sharing based on the recognition of the inherent relatedness of every entity and on intrinsic value. Recognition of inherent relatedness establishes the need to take marginalized people and externalized ecosystems into account. Recognition of their intrinsic value establishes their right to be included as entities on their own account. For human beings, this means a right to participate as subjects of their own lives, not as objects of what someone else decides they are due.

When value is taken to be subjective, then human beings, like God, are free to decide what is of value and what is not. But the biblical witness, in contradiction to the voluntaristic assertion, does not depict value as subjective. In the first creation story, each time God created, God paused and considered what had been created, "and God saw that it was good." This phrase appears six times. The creation was not good because God assigned value to it, which in principle might be high today and low later if God became bored with what God created. The creation was good because it contained value within it: it *was* good, and God *recognized* its goodness.

Once brought into existence, the value realized in created entities is inherent *in* the entities and not a function of anyone else's valuation, even God's. To exist is to be a realization of some measure of concrete value, and it is the discovery and recognition of this value that provides the foundation for treating creation with respect, not the idea that God, and not we, has the right of "ownership" because God is the creator. Even if God has right of ownership, and even if God is an omnipotent patriarch, and even if God created out of "nothing," all entities, once created, have intrinsic value and the right to recognition of that.

Intrinsic value does not mean "equal" rights between entities. That is an individualistic notion. Because all entities are inherently related, all come to existence through the sacrifice of other entities and are themselves sacrificed in turn. This means that all entities, including human beings, are both ends in themselves (with intrinsic value) *and* means to the ends of other entities (with instrumental value). The degree of their fulfillment depends on the degree to which they actualize both of these forms of value.

All entities have a right to be respected appropriate to their degree of intrinsic value and to their importance to the possibility of value in others. When intrinsic value is recognized rather than subjective value, the question becomes one of what is appropriate to human relations with and use of other entities. Degrees of value must be taken into account.[6]

For example, large mammals with highly developed nervous systems and conscious awareness have more intrinsic value than bacteria. This surely means, at least, that the torture of animals for human profit and convenience, as in factory farming and cosmetics testing, is inappropriate, but the use of bacteria for medical research is not.

On the other hand, most insects play some sort of key role in their ecosystems, for example as recyclers of waste. Their loss in large numbers would be a calamity to many other creatures, while the loss of individual members of the species is not a calamity, either to others or as experienced by themselves. Consequently human beings do not have the right to destroy species or to decimate their members to the point of threatening their ecosystems.

Concern for species diversity is nothing new to the biblical tradition. The story of Noah shows how God is concerned to protect species from the consequences of human sin, and there is no distinction of species deemed "useful" to humans. The legal codes of the Hebrew Scriptures include injunctions to protect the well-being of nonhuman creatures and allow them scope for natural behavior (for example, the prohibition against muzzling the ox while it treads out the grain [Deut. 25:4]).

Recognition of and effective respect for the intrinsic value and inherent relatedness of all entities is often objected to on the grounds that human welfare demands the sacrifice of other creatures and of ecosystems such as tropical forests. And increasingly this is true, because of the way economic development generates these kinds of crises. In the short run, as economic growth is being bought at the cost of environmental integrity, human need comes in conflict with the natural world.

But this is marginal analysis again, with all the attention focused on the trade-off between jobs and environment and no consideration of how we came to be reduced to such a no-win choice. A closer look reveals in case after case that it was not the needs of the poor that sacrificed environmental integrity, but economic growth for the sake of profits that rarely benefit the poor. Poor Brazilians are pushed off fertile farmland by powerful landowners and move into the rain forest *after* corporations have logged the valuable hardwoods and left a desert for the poor to try to live from. The poor know better than we the cost of degraded ecosystems, for it is they who must try to live in them.

Details of how to apply the recognition of intrinsic value have to be worked out in the context of the specifics of human relationships with other creatures and the biosphere as a whole. The point is that human beings both *need* (inherent relations) to share the planet with other creatures in the context of healthy ecosystems, and other creatures have the *right* (intrinsic value) to exist on their own terms.

This brings us back to the image in Revelation of healing for the nations as coming from "the leaves of the tree" of life. The atomistic individual of Western culture is essentially incomplete, even crippled, by the denial of inherent relations and intrinsic value. Healing can only come when these are recognized and healthy relations are restored between human beings and nature. Healthy relations are mutual relations in which each entity is open to feeling the feelings of the other and recognizes that its good is increased by the increase of the other's good. Then the other is known, heard, seen, felt, and experienced as existing for itself and with its own unique perspective and experience and potential for contribution.

It is no accident that those who care about the socially marginalized and the environment are usually people who have spent time experiencing and developing positive relations with oppressed peoples or with the natural world. Intrinsic value cannot be simply asserted; it has to be discovered, and it can be discovered only through such positive experience of others.[7] Its discovery is healing, because isolated individuals rediscover their need for others and the fact that their own potentials can be fulfilled only through their contributions to others. Those who enter into solidarity with socially marginalized and oppressed people usually discover that the people they expected to help have as much or more to give them.

In the Genesis narrative, the meaning of human existence is found in the vocation to care for the garden in which the diversity and richness of life can flourish. According to Douglas John Hall, the affirmation that human beings are made in the image of God does not mean that they are thereby separated from and made better than the other creatures, partaking of a portion of divinity that other creatures lack. Instead, the *imago Dei* is a relational image, pointing to the vocation of humans to image the loving relations of God to the world.[8]

That human beings find the meaning of their existence through their relations with the natural world is reaffirmed by the image in Revelation. Healing for human persons and their communities is found through healthy relations between humans and nature. This does not mean that conflict and competition would be eliminated. On the contrary, relations that do not and cannot handle conflict are rarely healthy. And of course the natural world, like the human, is full of competition for resources. But healthy relations with the natural world would set competition within the framework of sustainable sufficiency, so that the context of a flourishing living planet would be protected.

HEALING WHEN THE CITY, NATURE, AND GOD ARE NO LONGER SEPARATED

That personality and community depend on each other and their natural environments is not so odd to the biblical traditions; it has only been missed by Western eyes. It has also been taken for granted in Eastern Orthodoxy, which affirms that human salvation is tied up with the salvation of the cosmos. Beginning with the affirmation of creaturely existence in the incarnation, through the acceptance of death on the cross, to the insistence on the unity of body and soul figured in the resurrection, to the further fulfillment of the person as a member of the body of Christ, to the promise that "the whole creation will obtain the glorious liberty of the children of God" (Rom. 8:21), the biblical witness affirms that salvation is a wholistic process in which body and soul, person and community, and community and cosmos are inseparable and mutually enhancing.

The vision of the new Jerusalem depicts an earth in which God, human communities, and nature are reunited. No longer are these dimensions of life split against each other and separated. There is no temple in the new city; there are no separate times or places for relating to God. God is freely accessible to all, and all of the earth is holy. Nor are worship and ordinary life separated.

Nature is also an integral part of the new city, and human beings have free access to the "fruits" of the tree and to its healing leaves. Human livelihood is thus no longer separated from nature and the land, as it has been in modern societies, where people are cut off from access to livelihood when they lose their land and are forced to move to cities, where livelihood then depends on the whims of the market.

This vision of God, human beings, and nature reunited gives us a different image of what to work toward as we seek to address the eco-justice crisis. When healing is understood to depend on healthy relations between human beings in intact communities and between those persons and communities and their intact ecosystems, it is easier to understand why the attempt to solve human problems through unlimited and unsustainable economic growth is not working.

The fact of mutual dependence means that the scale of human economies must respect the limits of natural resources and the consequences of waste production to the integrity of the land. Current economic wisdom asserts that economies that are not growing are in trouble. But economic wisdom for the long term would assert that economies that are damaging their natural environments, thus unsustainable, are in trouble, because they cannot continue for long. The question of how much growth, and of what kinds, must be tailored to respect the integrity of the environment, or the economy will fail.

Economic development that respects inherent relations and intrinsic value would proceed along different lines than the capitalist and Marxist attempts to industrialize rapidly.[9] It is not idealistic to envision a reuniting of God, people, and nature. Much of the world has not yet lost that sense of interconnection. Development that respects this would stop moving people off their land and into cities to work in factories; it would respect the integrity of communities and their land, instead of taking the fertile land for export agriculture. Development would mean the transformation of traditional communities along lines they themselves participate in choosing, toward greater richness of relations for all, rather than the destruction of communities and nature for the sake of greater riches for now disconnected individuals. Such development would increase the likelihood of voluntary family planning and restraint of population growth for creation's sake.

Nations that have already industrialized at the price of disconnection can begin to reverse the process by working to transform the cities in ways that reconnect persons and nature. One key to this is to reconceive the problem in terms of making sure people have access to livelihood.[10] The most obvious need is to stop pushing people out of farming who want to stay on the land. At the same time, urbanized people who do not want to go back to rural life still have a right to healthy neighborhoods, meaningful work, and cities designed to include and respect nature.

For example, many antipoverty programs have had the unintended effect of taking people out of their communities rather than changing the whole community. The result has been the "integration" of some into the "mainstream" while the rest are left in devastated ghettos. But healing of the whole person requires the transformation of the whole community. New initiatives for social transformation need to take this into account more carefully. For neighborhoods to be healthy they require that their residents have access to livelihood, or meaningful work, preferably in their own community and locally controlled, and access to some diversity of natural life.

THE IMAGE OF GOD IN THE VISION OF SHALOM

As we have seen, the image of God that results when relations are assumed to be only external is of a God who is self-enclosed and unaffected by the world, yet as Creator is free to act arbitrarily toward both human beings and the natural world. But this goes against both the human experience of God and the biblical witness. There are numerous movements seeking to image and worship the divine in ways that are inclusive, relational, and environmentally sensitive. Christians have much to learn from these movements, which can help to transform traditional liturgies in light of the recognition of inherent relations and intrinsic value.

Despite my largely critical descriptions, the image of God *has* changed in the past century or so in positive directions. Only the most rigid forms of fundamentalism still insist that God damns most human beings to eternal torment and look enthusiastically for the final destruction of the world. Many Protestants have gradually come to believe that there is something wrong with this image of God as arbitrary judge, and the image of God is being transformed into that of a loving parent who at least offers salvation to all. The Greek idea that God is impassible has almost completely given way to the more biblical image of God as one who suffers with those who suffer and bears the pain of all the world.

But most theologies still cling to the notion that God has both the right and the power to do what God pleases with God's creation, though God will not exercise that power destructively because God loves human beings and respects our freedom. This is what I call the "nuclear deterrence" doctrine of God's power. It is the divine analogue of the human stockpiling of nuclear weapons. It maintains that God must have the power of ultimate destruction, even though God would never never use it. Even though it rejects the doctrines of damnation and apocalypse, it still worships power conceived as the capacity to destroy.

This view of God's power and God's rights is inadequate for the biblical witness to God as known in Jesus Christ and for human experience, and it certainly cannot help human beings to learn to respect other human beings or the rest of creation. The threat of arbitrary destruction remains. We need to follow up on the widespread intuition that there is something wrong with the image of God as arbitrary judge who has the right to condemn the world because God created it and so "owns" it.

That God is inherently related to the world has been obscured by the assumption of external relations, but it is not alien to the biblical witness and some central Christian doctrines. That the Holy Spirit indwells the world, or that God in Christ suffers with God's people, is difficult to conceive when relations are external. But God who is inherently related to the world through the indwelling of the Spirit is able to empower and liberate the whole creation through God's loving influence in every entity. This God can take into God's self every facet of existence and redeem it.

Power conceived as externally imposed control is comparatively crude. It is also incapable of achieving the empowerment and liberation of others, because it tries to hold all power for itself. The idea that this is the kind of power God wields leads to images of God as either clumsy puppeteer who is responsible for all the evil in the world, or impotent bystander whose power is unable to achieve real change.

When read with the glasses of inherent relations and intrinsic value, the Bible shows us a God who recognizes that creation is good and who works to preserve, liberate, and empower all life, so the whole creation can flourish together. This God is not interested in holding all power, but in empowering all, so that all can contribute to each other, including God who delights in all and recognizes the intrinsic goodness of all. This relational God is fully involved in and with the world, as affirmed in the doctrines of Creation, Providence, Incarnation, Cross, Resurrection, and Pentecost. The world is not the passive object of God's activity, but a plurality of participating subjects, inherently related yet distinct, in communion with God and each other.

The power of God is revealed in this relational community through the persuasive and receptive presence of God that empowers the healing and enhancement of a flourishing diversity of creative life. Elizabeth Bettenhausen comments on the problem of imaging God in terms of characteristics of human agency, only without "flaw or finitude." It leads to thinking of God as an independent individual agent, so that "God is to the world as a potter is to the pot." But the world is not only passive, and God is not only agent. We need more adequate images of God:

> God is not absolute Cause but rather Love seeking community. A personal God is not a human writ large but God as love, which is never an individualistic but always a communal matter. To confess God as Creator is not to speak of a singular divine agent but to interpret the universe as directed toward Love and to respond with praise and justice.[11]

To image God as relational is not new. Such an image already exists in the doctrine of the Trinity and has functioned as a relational image in Eastern Orthodoxy. But Western Christianity, except for the largely ignored Celtic tradition, has misunderstood the Trinity and failed to realize its potential, precisely because its underlying images of the self and God have been based on external relations. Consequently the three Persons of the Trinity have usually been taken separately. In modern Protestantism, at least, Jesus has been separated from God the Father and functions independently. While the Father tends the public realm and masculine identity, Jesus has become the God of the private realm and serves to reinforce a sentimentalized feminine identity.

The Holy Spirit, in the meantime, has been viewed as wholly disconnected from either the Father or the Son, floating around to be co-opted by anyone who wants to make use of it. According to M. Douglas Meeks, the Holy Spirit without the incarnate Son is empty infinity, available for empowerment without finite identity and without suffering:

> The God who is sheer spirit and the corresponding human being who is sheer spirit support a society that focuses all of its economic problems on the spiraling increase in insatiable wants and the doctrine of growth which has become the secular religion of our society.[12]

This Spirit of easy grace and easy satisfaction of infinite desire is a favorite of middle-class charismatics.

Liberation theologian Leonardo Boff and Reformed theologian M. Douglas Meeks have both argued for the importance of recovering the doctrine of the Trinity. They believe that the fully relational God imaged by the Trinity is a key to a relational understanding of the self and society.[13]

Boff argues that God as Trinity images a God of "communion of the different Persons by which each is in the others, with the others, through the others and for the others." It is an "affirmation that the name of God means differences that include, not exclude, each other" and that is open to other differences, "so the created universe enters into communion with the divine."[14]

Boff believes insistence on a fully trinitarian image of God would undermine the claims of dictators because it images shared power, and it could provide the church with a model: "As a network of communities living in communion with their brothers/sisters and all participating in its benefits, the church can be built on the model of the Trinity and become its sacrament in history" because "God is not a solitary power, but an infinite love opening out to create other companions in love."[15] According to Boff, in both socialism and capitalism there is "no full realization of the social dimension, starting at the base, involving personal relationships, building a network of communities which in turn become the basis for the organization of civil society. . . ."[16] Meeks argues along similar lines.

CONCLUSION

When inherent relations and intrinsic value are recognized, Christian doctrines such as the Trinity can begin to function more fully, and perhaps achieve positive significance for postmodern Westerners. Beyond doctrine, the recognition of inherent relations and intrinsic value can help lead to a convergence of understandings. It is becoming increasingly clear that the forms of oppression that victimize women, members of U.S. minority groups, and Third World peoples are different but interlinked, and that land and nature are covictims of the same forces that oppress people.

At the heart of this linked victimization is the drive for dominance and control that is currently most fully seen in the global economy. Persons and their human and natural communities are systematically pulled apart in the name of economic "growth," usually with no consideration of their own wishes and no respect for their own generations-old knowledge of their local conditions (where that knowledge still exists).

When inherent relations and intrinsic value are recognized, it becomes clear that: (*a*) economic schemes must include respect for persons as communal and natural beings, and as participating subjects of their own lives; and (*b*) all other creatures have their own integrity and value for themselves and their ecosystems. So, (*c*) humans must learn how to share the planet with the rest of life, both for the sake of other creatures and for our own sake.

According to the vision of the new Jerusalem in the book of Revelation, the fullness of salvation will be achieved when the divisions between individuals and communities, between humans and nature, and between city, God, and nature are healed and healthy relations are restored. Whenever and wherever such healing of relations takes place, so that personal, community, and environmental integrity and their interactions are enhanced instead of splintered, there the reign of God is already effective.

10
NATURE'S HISTORY AS OUR HISTORY
A Proposal for Spirituality

Philip Hefner

There is a feeling the body gives the mind
of having missed something, a bedrock poverty, like falling

without the sense that you are passing through one world,
that you could reach another
anytime. Instead the real
is crossing you,

your body an arrival
you know is false but can't outrun. And somewhere in between
these geese forever entering and
these spiders turning back,

this astonishing delay, the everyday, takes place.
—Jorie Graham

*I*n her poem "The Geese," of which these lines are the conclusion, Jorie Graham describes her experience when one day as she was hanging out the wash she noted that the geese were flying overhead and the spiders were working in the yard around her spinning their webs.[1] She makes the key point that our minds have the capacity to deceive us, to miss something that is important about our very own human nature. What the mind misses, our body takes the occasion to remind us of: our lives are not so much a traveling through nature's space and time, as if we were making progress on a journey or conquering obstacles in our way toward a destination that is important to us, as

171

our lives are stations on a journey whose traveler is something that transcends us, and for whom we are an arrival point beyond which there lie still more stations. We are not so much moving through and over nature as we are natural creatures who represent a discrete station on nature's way. We are not sovereign over nature, but are rather an occasion within nature's sovereignty.

The poet is not offering a plan of how to live our lives, but she is making a proposal to us for the organization of our consciousness. The consciousness thus organized serves as the matrix in which we seek to understand our lives and determine how they ought to be lived. This phenomenon of the organization of consciousness deserves our most concentrated attention for at least two reasons: (1) it is an important component of any responses we make to the environment (or to any other challenge to human existence), and (2) it is particularly critical to the life of religious communities. One distinctive contribution these communities can make in responding to the environment is to midwife the visions and forms that are essential to the organization of consciousness which, in turn, inwardly shapes the people who make up our communities. What we call *spirituality* has to do with this constellation of factors—organization of consciousness, inward shaping, and formation of the matrix from which self-understanding and behavior proceed. Spirituality includes the images, symbols, stories, and rituals that sculpt the consciousness that forms the place of habitation for the hearts, minds, souls, and wills of our people as they confront the urgent and everyday challenge of praxis that relates to the environment.

I do not want to minimize in any way the responsibility we have for study, analysis, and influencing policy, but I do suggest that spirituality stands as an essential component of religious communities. Furthermore, analysis, action, and policy formation are inevitably influenced by the organization of consciousness; to leave that factor unattended would be to render our other efforts lamed.

Before moving to consider Jorie Graham's proposal in detail, I should make clear the conceptual framework that provides the foundation for my reflections, as well as for the implications that follow from them. This conceptual framework is heavily dependent upon (1) certain scientific theories concerning the evolution of life and of the human being, (2) the work of psychologist Mihaly Csikszentmihalyi, (3) the theological thought of Joseph Sittler and certain classical Christian biblical and theological traditions, as well as (4) the conclusions of historians of religion and philosophers who have engaged in studies of myth and ritual.

THE SIGNIFICANCE OF HUMAN EVOLUTION

We begin with a thoroughly evolutionary understanding of human being. *Homo sapiens* has emerged within a process that has its origins in the emergence of the universe itself, even though our attention is drawn chiefly to the later stages of that process, particularly the emergence and development of human life on planet Earth. Contemporary science provides many examples of how fully planet Earth and its living creatures are dependent upon the events of cosmic history since the so-called Big Bang. It is enough to say that the essential materials from which Earth and humans are formed were manufactured in the billions of years of galactic history that preceded the appearance of the Earth.

With the emergence of DNA and its evolution, the basis for human life was established. Just as the earth and its life are what they are because of the elements that were formed in earlier cosmic evolution, human life has been enabled by the processes and constituents that were provided by prehuman history on Earth. The unique breakthrough that marks *Homo sapiens* has to do with the emergence of a central nervous system and brain that are complex enough to allow reflexive consciousness and the appearance of culture.

Ralph Wendell Burhoe has suggested the human being may itself be a kind of symbiosis of two living systems, one comprised of genes, the other of culture.[2] The *genotype* is a term for the integrated system of gene-based information that links each of us to the prehuman history of the planet and beyond. This information is not enough to make us human, however. We are dependent upon and constituted by an extra-genetic system of information that is stored in our brains and in the products of those brains—folkways, systems of mores, libraries, computer banks, and the like. Burhoe calls this our *culturetype;* Teilhard de Chardin termed it the *noosphere.*[3] Genetic information is transmitted from generation to generation through sexual reproduction and inheritance from parents to offspring, whereas cultural information is transmitted by teaching and learning in many forms and knows no final barriers of biological kinship, as genetic transmission does. Although Charles Darwin and his successors have succeeded in mapping genetic evolution in exhaustive detail and theoretical grandeur, we are just beginning to comprehend the quite different processes that govern the evolution of culture.

The major crises that face human life today are for the most part rooted in the confusion that besets the cultural dimension of our nature.[4] Technology is the most breathtaking manifestation of that culture, and it exemplifies our confusion. We simply do not know how our learned cultural patterns should be shaped in order to adapt successfully to our world. Environmental collapse, overpopulation, poverty, war, depletion of resources, and hunger are all results of our confusion. The genetic dimension of our nature adapted through millions of years. But culture, characterized by quite different processes that move much faster and leap across the terrain with much more facility, is very nearly out of control and heading for its self-destruction. Human culture faces the monumental challenge of forming a guidance system constituted by its own cultural information, comparable in scope to the genetic guidance system and intimately interrelated with it, that can adequately direct human living and motivate behavior that makes for life rather than death.

LOCATING SPIRITUALITY

In gaining an understanding of this human being and its culture, I follow Mihaly Csikszentmihalyi in utilizing the research of the sociologist Pitirim Sorokin, who defined two alternating principles by which cultures organize their consciousness: *sensate* culture, in which people trust above all the empirical evidence of their senses, and *ideational* culture, in which people give precedence to truth that is grounded by faith or reason.[5] There may be a kind of dialectic at work, in which the Western modern culture, which includes science, secularity, and the like, emerged in the Renaissance as counterpoint to the organization of consciousness of the previous centuries that undervalued the empirical, material awareness of the senses. We may now be in a time when the dialectic is moving toward a higher valuation of that which is based on faith and reason that is not, as Csikszentmihalyi writes, "amenable to material representation." It is this dimension, which is not totally defined by the material representations, that forms the context for my use of the terms "spiritual" and "spirituality." This dimension of the spiritual is not aloof from the material world and what we know about it, nor does it seek to diminish the empirical realm, but it augments our representations of the world. Csikszentmihalyi reminds us that we are dealing with packets and traditions of information; genes are the unit of biologically formed information, which as a functioning whole form the genotype. The cultural information, which forms the culturetype, is carried in units that many scholars now call *memes*, in obvious parallelism to genes. Religions are information systems that promulgate memes, and spirituality is itself a kind of meme-system. I quote from Csikszentmihalyi:

> To trust only memes that refer to material entities, to the satisfaction of needs, to the evidence of the senses, blinds us to some of the aspects of reality that are most important for the survival of humankind and for its future evolution. To do so would imprison us in a present pragmatism from which it would be very difficult to move into the future. . . . [For this] we have to rely on memes that refer to entities not yet amenable to material representation. These include the various "spiritual" values that in the past have supported Sorokin's ideational civilizations, and that must again be recovered if they are to serve our future needs. Spiritual values are memes—ideas, symbols, beliefs, instructions for action which can be passed on from person to person—that bring us out of the present, out of ourselves. *The best of them take the material limitations of our genes into account, but at the same time point to possibilities to which our biological inheritance is not yet sensitive. The sensate deals with what is, the ideational— or spiritual—with what could be. . . . The essence of spirituality consists in an effort to pry consciousness loose from the thrall of genetic instructions.* (Emphasis added.)[6]

I attempt to define spirituality in these terms and concepts set forth by Csikszentmihalyi. It may be open to critique, but it has the merit of being rather precise and discussable: *Spirituality refers to the cultural information that directs us outward from one-dimensional descriptions and understandings of ourselves and the empirical world, toward the possibilities of that world.* (These possibilities are finally grounded only by faith and reason that are not fully explained by material representations.)

MYTH AND MORALITY/SPIRITUALITY AND PRAXIS

Scholars of the history of religions have suggested that all human actions, including what we call morality or ethics, and praxis, are grounded in myth.[7] That is, all our action is caught up in the effort to behave in a manner that is in conformity with the most fundamental nature of reality itself. The relationship between myth and morality recalls our earlier argument, that our action is shaped in the matrix that is configured by the way in which our consciousness is organized. Myth is a primordial way of organizing the consciousness. It has functioned since the origins of the human species as one of the most significant cultural inputs by which prehuman hominids were taught to live as creatures who are indeed genetically programmed, yet for whom that programming is not enough, requiring augmentation through additional, cultural, inputs.

Myth is one of the central cultural inputs that taught the creature to live under conditions that were genuinely human.

We mean to live in harmony with the "way things really are." We desire that the "oughts" that govern our lives be continuous with the "is" that constitutes the reality system in which we live. Myth provides such a picture of the way things really are, in the form of a narrative or story that sets forth the ultimate nature of our lives and the world we inhabit. This mythic picture provides the rationale for ritual, even when the rationale is not explicit in the awareness of those who perform the ritual. The ritual acts out the myth in symbolic action and relates it to the lives of the worshipers. The Christian myths of creation and of Jesus' redemptive death on the cross, for example, are acted out in the eucharistic liturgy in such rituals as the Kiss of Peace, which symbolically acts out a universal solidarity among individual persons, and the distribution, which acts out in a symbolic manner our taking the very body and blood of the crucified Jesus into ourselves and thereby becoming united with him in his action on the cross, as well as with the redemptive outcome of that action. We remind ourselves that this is what we are doing in such accompanying prayers as these:

> Pour out upon us the spirit of your love, O Lord, and unite the wills of those whom you have fed with one heavenly food.[8]

> Almighty God, you gave your Son, both as a sacrifice for sin and a model of the godly life. Enable us to receive him always with thanksgiving, and to conform our lives to his.[9]

The picture of how things really are is translated, through ritual, into the lives of real human beings in a real world, but only symbolically. My solidarity with the person next to me in the pew may dissolve with the ending of the Eucharist. The symbolic action of ritual is translated into the literal behavior of the worshipers outside the sanctuary after the liturgy, in day-to-day praxis. That we have praxis clearly in mind is expressed in an offertory prayer at the beginning of the Eucharist, such as this one:

> O Lord our God, maker of all things. Through your goodness you have blessed us with these gifts [of bread, wine, money offerings]. With them we offer ourselves to your service and dedicate our lives to the care and redemption of all that you have made; for the sake of him who gave himself for us.[10]

Spirituality, as I defined it above as cultural information that organizes our consciousness by directing it outwards from the empirical world toward that world's dynamic possibilities, finds its traditional substance grounded in myth and ritual. The narratives of myth, together with the symbolic actions of ritual, translate our experience into terms of ultimacy—ultimacy with respect to where we have come from, where we are going, and why we are here. Consequently they do by their very nature direct our gaze and our actions outward, not remaining in the material world of everyday, but rather projecting toward the possibilities that govern that world when it is perceived from the perspective of ultimacy.

Nothing could be more relevant for our attitudes and our actions toward our natural environment than spirituality and its core of myth and ritual, since it is precisely our thoughtless and arrogant refusal to view nature from the perspective of ultimacy that has obstructed good and wholesome behavior from humans and actually precipitated demonic manipulation and its companion, environmental collapse.

With this, I have come full circle, on the basis of contemporary scientific understandings, to reinforce my initial suggestions that spirituality is essential to a proper stance vis-à-vis nature, that it is a distinctive concern of religious communities, and that it is a requisite for adequate praxis toward nature. The criterion for our spirituality of creation or nature is that it weave together the information of Christian myth and ritual into a vision of the ultimate ground and possibilities of nature that (1) expresses the integrity of the myth and ritual, while at the same time (2) relating its information to the best of contemporary knowledge about nature and human life. (3) It should always convey the intrinsic necessity of praxis, without which the vision of nature is incomplete, and (4) it should motivate within the church communities both individual and group action that is continuous with the spiritual vision. Spirituality aims at organizing the consciousness on the basis of primordial Christian myth and ritual, under the impact of current knowledge, so as to nurture understanding and action that are life-enriching as Christians understand life within the will of God revealed in its myth and ritual.

HUMAN HISTORY AS NATURE'S HISTORY

We now bring this conceptual framework to Jorie Graham's proposal for organizing our consciousness and hence for our spirituality. She concludes that the history that belongs to us is caught up in nature's history. The trajectory of the geese told the poet that she was living beneath the geese "as if beneath the passage of time." The spiders, as they

bind and bind
the pins to the lines, the lines to the eaves, to the pincushion bush

reveal to her that

the world thickens with texture instead of history,
texture instead of place.

And she asks herself,

if these spiders had their way,
chainlink over the visible world,
would we be in or out?

There is more to a full-orbed spirituality than this, but this sense that we are integrally part of the natural world is certainly one of its central memes, and one that we as a human community are far from comfortable with. Graham asks the question, When we recognize that the world thickens with texture rather than with history or place, are we within that texture or outside it? Are we chainlinked in or out of the texture that is bounded by geese above and spiders below? The answer, she suggests, is to be found in the message that our bodies send to our minds: it is not so much the case that we are passing through time and space as

the real
is crossing [us],
[our] body an arrival
[we] know is false but can't outrun. And somewhere in between
these geese forever entering and
these spiders turning back,

this astonishing delay, the everyday, takes place.

The Lutheran theologian Joseph Sittler (1904–1987) believed that the challenge of our times comes in the necessity to understand human history as being in the context of the history of nature. His generation of theologians, as well as my own, was nurtured on the insistence that sacred history (we called it *Heilsgeschichte*) was more real than secular or natural history. Sittler urges us to recognize that natural history is the matrix in which sacred history transpires. Jorie Graham puts the point in her striking image that we are not passing over or through the world and its history, as the Vespuccis and the Pizarros and the Cabots triumphantly crossed the seas in their search for conquest and empire.

Reality, rather, is crossing us. We are not so much riding on Chicago's Jackson Park elevated train passing station after station on the way to O'Hare International Airport, where we will take wings for a flight into the wild blue yonder. Rather, we are a station through which the tracks run, through which the real passes. Our bodies are an arrival, which we know is "false," in the sense that it is neither permanent nor the whole, but it cannot be outrun. And the mind should know this, since it is pinned firmly to the body by the webs of biochemistry, limbic tissue, and neocortex.

Sittler understood these issues in christological terms. He wrote in 1977:

> The life-world that characterizes our time and to which an adequate christology must be proposed includes both the world as nature and the world as history. I would suggest that so does the biblical world. The biblical thinker goes from reflection on nature ("when I regard the heavens, the work of thy fingers, the moon and the stars which thou hast ordained") to a historical reflection ("what is man?"). Our time has a scope of reflection that includes both the world of nature and the world of history, but we know much more about nature than the psalmist did.[11]

Sittler stands in a tradition of theological reflection, cosmic Christology, that is now receiving considerable attention.[12] The tradition is rooted in the Prologue to the Gospel of John, Ephesians, and Colossians (Col. 1:16-17: "in [Christ] all things in heaven and on earth were created, things visible and invisible. . . . in him all things hold together"), but it also finds echoes in such early sources as the liturgical text found in 1 Cor. 8:6, "yet for us there is one God, the Father, from whom are all things and for whom we exist, and one Lord Jesus Christ, through whom are all things and through whom we exist."

There is a substantial biblical and theological foundation for considering the appearance and continuation of the human species as events of the same process as nature's history. Marie E. Isaacs and Eduard Schweizer have documented the fascinating history of Hebrew and early Christian understandings of the spirit of God (*ruach/pneuma*).[13] Pivotal in this history is the Septuagint translators' decision to render the Hebrew term, *ruach,* with the Greek *pneuma. Ruach* is clearly a term whose referent is the transcendent God, with particular reference to that God's presence and action in the total created order (embracing the act of creation in Genesis 1 and 2), and also in plants, animals, charismatic humans, prophets, kings, and even the entire chosen people. *Pneuma,* although it commonly referred to "wind," as the Hebrew *ruach* did, was a term that had a history of referring to the natural order. In the classical philosophers, *pneuma* was an element of natural science, and as such it was used, for example, by the physician Galen. By conjoining *ruach* and *pneuma*, the translators "introduced a new dimension into the usual Greek usage,"[14] in that they chose a term that ordinarily applied only to natural phenomena (wind, breath, life, principle of natural order) and introduced into it the presence of God. This usage exercised a heavy influence upon the New Testament and even subsequent pagan Greek usage.[15]

It is little wonder that theologies of the Holy Spirit have traditionally included theological reflection upon nature and upon the immanence of the transcendent God within the natural world. It would not be difficult to demonstrate, within a trinitarian perspective, that each of the three persons of the Trinity portrays the presence and action of God with respect to human beings in the context of the natural order and its history. In contrast to these substantial traditions, the trend of modern theology, particularly the "holy history" strand, has diminished or even countered the primordial sense of God's action in nature being at one with the divine action for humans.

Csikszentmihalyi has suggested that such reflections as these will give rise to a spirituality that replaces the "brotherhood of man" with the "beinghood of all nature."[16] The Christian will say that the beinghood of all nature is the creation of God and the theater of Christ's redemption, and in this nexus we find not only our identity and our destiny, but also our meaning under God.

One of our major responses to the challenges of the environment must be such probes into spirituality. Only then will the kinds of obstinacy and recalcitrance that have brought us to the brink of environmental disaster be transformed. It is through such spirituality as I have sketched above that the human consciousness will be organized in such a way as to regenerate the species that has become savage *Homo sapiens,* and this regenerated spirit can be the nurturing matrix for the praxis that serves life. These probes must refashion our images of God, of the world, and of ourselves. They must be the symbols and visions on which we can reflect in our quiet moments, to which we can pray, in whose presence we can sing hymns, into whose company we can be baptized, before whom we can eat bread and drink wine, and in whose image we can shape our lives.

THE POETS AS RESOURCES

The kind of analysis I have presented risks the danger of confusing talk *about* spirituality with spirituality itself. By placing the poetic images of Jorie Graham at the beginning of the discussion, I hope to remind the reader that the memes of spirituality that best serve to organize the human consciousness are the bold, dramatic images of myth and ritual. These images are crafted by artists, particularly poets. Artists will most likely give form to the symbols that will vivify our prayers, our songs, and our rituals. It is not the concepts of philosophy, theology, and psychology that will shape our inmost consciousness so much as the images of our ordinary life, as they open outward to nature's possibilities. This can happen in the common meal of the Eucharist, in the ordinary bath of Baptism, and in Jorie Graham's images of the common act of hanging out clothes in the company of geese and spiders.

The poetic images carry power, because they are unambiguously rooted in the earthy stuff of our experience, even while they do what Csikszentmihalyi suggests—open us up to the possibilities that reside in that experience of nature. Every bath we take is a reminder that natural persons like ourselves have the possibility for transformation. Every meal can recall to us the complex web of our kinship with all that God has created, in which we stand with Jesus, committed to the care and redemption of all nature, including human beings. The common act of seeing the birds fly overhead and the insects in the foliage that surrounds us bids us reflect upon the linkage between us, on how we can place ourselves destructively outside that linkage or in a wholesome solidarity with our natural links. This reflection in turn opens upon the question of what kind of solidarity humans really can enjoy with the rest of nature, as well as upon what praxis best expresses that solidarity. Such reflection has already organized the consciousness so as to be far along the road of environmental wholesomeness, even if it has not arrived at final answers to the questions raised by these images.

Two additional sets of images provide further examples of poetic resources for reflecting on the fundamental linkage of our human history to nature's history. These images are provided by the Jesuit poet Gerard Manley Hopkins (1844–1889) and by an ancient Hebrew poet.

In his sonnet, "Ribblesdale," Hopkins gives us the image of all nature as one body, of which we are part:

Earth, sweet Earth, sweet landscape, with leavès throng
and louchèd low grass, heaven that dost appeal
To, with no tongue to plead, no heart to feel;
That canst but only be, but dost that long—
Thou canst but be, but that thou well dost; strong
Thy plea with him who dealt, nay does now deal,

Thy lovely dale down thus and thus bids reel
Thy river, and o'er gives all to rack or wrong.

And what is Earth's eye, tongue, or heart else, where
Else, but in dear and dogged man? Ah, the heir
To his own selfbent so bound, so tied to his turn,
To thriftless reave both our rich round world bare
And none reck of world after, this bids wear
Earth brows of such care, care and dear concern.[17]

Graham asked, as if uncertain, or perhaps anxious, whether the spiders
would with their webs choose to count us in or leave us out. Hopkins
gives a vigorous response—we are fully inside nature's ambience; we
are earth's eye, tongue, and heart. So miserably have we failed to serve
earth well, however, that we cause its care and "dear concern." Graham
asks her question a century after Hopkins, when the failure of the human
tongue is so obvious that she might well fear that earth's concern has
turned into the anger that rejects the human element and chainlinks us
out.

In the eighth and ninth chapters of Genesis, four millennia before
Hopkins or Graham, is the story of the rainbow covenant that God
made with Noah. This ancient poet links humans and the rest of nature
in the covenant entity that God makes with all creatures.

Then Noah built an altar to the Lord. . . . And when the Lord smelled
the pleasing odor, the Lord said, "I will never again curse the ground
because of human beings, for the imagination of the human heart is evil
from their youth; neither will I ever again destroy every living creature
as I have done." . . . Then God said to Noah and to his sons with him,
"Behold, I establish my covenant with you and your descendants after
you, and with every living creature that is with you, the birds, the cattle,
and every beast of the earth with you, as many as came out of the ark.
I establish my covenant with you, that never again shall all flesh be cut
off by the waters of a flood, and never again shall there be a flood to
destroy the earth."
      And God said, "This is the sign of the covenant which I make between
me and you and every living creature that is with you, for all future
generations: I set my bow in the cloud, and it shall be a sign of the
covenant between me and the earth.

(Gen. 8:20—9:13)

This text occurs as the second reading within the ritual of the Easter
Vigil. As such, the rainbow covenant with Noah is connected to the
resurrection of Jesus Christ. The meaning is unavoidable: the resurrec-

tion of Jesus of Nazareth is an event within a continuum of events in which God has been active, and the continuum includes the history of nature. Here God affirms a covenant with every living thing and with the earth itself, in full recognition that in light of the evil that is in the human heart, this sets up a lover's triangle. In that triangle, consisting of God, humans, and all of the earth's other biological and physical systems, humans could find themselves outside the chainlink of the covenant with nature. God will never again permit that covenant to be breached in favor of humans at the expense of the earth. Hopkins pictured the human species as a kind of spokesperson or defense attorney for the rest of nature. The rainbow covenant predicates God as a higher advocate for nonhuman nature.

The proposals for organizing our consciousness contained in these packets of poetic, mythic information articulate themselves with forcefulness. They point outward in projecting possibilities for human involvement in community with the rest of nature that can make both for the wholeness of the Creator's covenant shalom and also for the terror that accompanies the destruction of that wholeness. Shalom comes when we consider that our calling to be: sibling to the geese and the spiders; eye, tongue, and heart to sweet earth; covenant partner with earth and its birds, cattle, and every beast. Terror lurks in the sense we have that earth's concern may lead to its excluding us from its company, as well as to the wrath of the God who has vowed never again to permit humans to be the curse of the earth.

If a spirituality can emerge among Christians from this vision of our history as nature's history, it will reorganize consciousness dramatically. Christians will have to retrieve our tradition anew, even as we reach out to new formulations of that tradition. Our images of ourselves, of God the Creator, of Christ the Redeemer, and of the quickening Spirit will also be reorganized in fresh images. Without such a reorganization, there can hardly be any certain foundation for wholesome praxis or credible proclamation of the gospel in our day.

The spirituality that is needed will be a spirituality of human solidarity with nature and of the possibilities inherent in that solidarity. The sense of solidarity will not in and of itself resolve the confusion that characterizes our situation today, nor will it provide easy answers for human culture as it attempts to form its human guidance system in symbiosis with its genetic guidance structures within its environmental context (see above). To organize our consciousness on this basis of solidarity with nature is indispensable, however, if we are to discover the nondestructive possibilities for human culture within the natural ambience in which it has emerged and in which it must chart its future.

NOTES

INTRODUCTION: ECO-JUSTICE THEOLOGY AFTER NATURE'S REVOLT
Dieter T. Hessel

1. Elizabeth Dodson Gray, "Watchman! Tell Us of the Night, What Its Signs of Promise Are," *The Churchman*, July 20–24, 1980.

2. Thomas Berry emphasizes that "when nature goes into deficit, then we go into deficit." See Berry's "Economics: Effect on the Life Systems of the World," in *Thomas Berry and the New Cosmology*, ed. Anne Lonergan and Caroline Richards (Mystic, Conn.: Twenty-Third Publications, 1990), 6.

3. Hans Jonas, *The Imperative of Responsibility: In Search of an Ethics for the Technological Age* (Chicago: University of Chicago Press, 1984), 139.

4. My overview of the environmental crisis briefly summarizes information presented in several publications: Presbyterian Eco-Justice Task Force, *Keeping and Healing the Creation* (Louisville: Committee on Social Witness Policy, 1989), chaps. 1–3; Global Tomorrow Coalition, *The Global Ecology Handbook* (Boston: Beacon, 1990); Worldwatch Institute, *State of the World* (annual vols.; New York: W. W. Norton, 1985–90); and Ruth Caplan, *Our Earth / Ourselves* (New York: Bantam, 1990).

5. Shantilal Bhagat, *Creation in Crisis* (Elgin, Ill.: Brethren, 1990), 91.

6. Daniel Yergin, *The Prize: The Epic Quest for Oil, Money and Power* (New York: Simon and Schuster, 1991).

7. Ibid., 769–70.

8. Earl Arnold ("The Solid Waste Crisis," *Church and Society* 80 [March–April 1990], 53ff.) provides a concise, realistic overview of the problem and sustainable solutions.

9. From the comprehensive report adopted by the Presbyterian General Assembly, *Restoring Creation for Ecology and Justice* (Louisville, Ky.: Office of

the General Assembly, 1990), 10. I was primary staff and Bill Gibson was primary consultant to the task force and committee that prepared this report. My numbered points in this profile of environmental peril follow its outline.

10. Bhagat, *Creation in Crisis*, 45.

11. Ibid., 100.

12. The bioregional movement takes geography, nature-culture, and socio-economic history seriously as the basis for an evolution of relatively self-reliant, ecologically sustainable communities. A bioregion is "defined naturally by mountain ranges, rivers, watershed, the climate, and the [animals and] people living there," suggests Susan Meeker-Lowry in *Economics as if the Earth Really Mattered* (Philadelphia: New Society Publishers, 1988), 232. Also see Jeremy Rifkin, *Biosphere Politics* (New York: Crown Publishers, 1991), chap. 38.

13. Two reflective books on the subject of sustainable development are J. Ronald Engel and Joan Gibb Engel, *Ethics of Environment and Development* (London: Belhaven, 1990); and Herman E. Daly and John B. Cobb, Jr., *For the Common Good: Redirecting the Economy Toward Community, the Environment, and a Sustainable Future* (Boston: Beacon, 1989). The June 1992 "Earth Summit in Brazil—the U.N. Conference on Environment and Development—also highlights the dilemmas of sustainable development.

14. William E. Gibson, "Eco-Justice: New Perspective for a Time of Turning," in *For Creation's Sake: Preaching Ecology and Justice*, ed. Dieter T. Hessel (Louisville, Ky.: Geneva, 1985), 25.

15. The term "positive ecology" is prominent in Jon Naar, *Design for a Livable Planet* (New York: Harper & Row, 1990), 313.

16. Roderick Frazier Nash (*The Rights of Nature: A History of Environmental Ethics* [Madison: University of Wisconsin Press, 1989]) traces the movement philosophically from natural rights for humans (slaves and women) to the rights of nature, which biocentric ethics seeks to institutionalize. It seeks to find a stronger base than voluntary "respect"—a discardable sentiment—for political economy that will observe ecological integrity and care for nonhuman creatures. The World Charter for Nature, adopted as a global code of conduct by the 1982 United Nations General Assembly, is reprinted in Bhagat, *Creation in Crisis*, Appendix A.

17. Lester Brown, "Outlining a Global Action Plan," *State of the World* (New York: W. W. Norton & Co., 1989), 192–94.

18. William Dryness, "Stewardship of the Earth in the Old Testament," in *Tending the Garden*, ed. Wes Ganberg-Michaelson (Grand Rapids: Wm. B. Eerdmans, 1987), 53–54.

19. See Christopher J. H. Wright, *God's People in God's Land: Family, Land, and Property in the Old Testament* (Grand Rapids: Wm. B. Eerdmans, 1990), chap. 5.

20. Walter Brueggemann, "Land: Fertility and Justice," in *Theology of the Land*, ed. Bernard Evans and Gregory Cusack (Collegeville, Minn.: Liturgical, 1987), 59–64.

21. Bill McKibben, *The End of Nature* (New York: Random House, 1989), 79.

22. Presbyterian Eco-Justice Task Force, *Keeping and Healing the Creation,* chap. 4, develops this theology.

23. Ibid., chap. 5, gives an overview of the four ethical norms of eco-justice. Chapter 6 by William E. Gibson in *After Nature's Revolt* explicates these norms as a framework for response to global warming.

24. J. Ronald Engel, "Ecology and Social Justice: The Search for a Public Environmental Ethic," in *Issues of Justice: Social Sources and Religious Meanings,* ed. Roger Hatch and Warren Copeland (Macon, Ga.: Mercer University Press, 1988), 261.

25. Wendell Berry, *Home Economics* (Berkeley: North Point, 1987), 16.

26. "Editorial: Who Needs Feminism?" *Theology* 93 (September–October 1990): 340–41. For a concise assessment of "The Structure and Limitations of Modern Thought," see Douglas C. Bowman, *Beyond the Modern Mind* (New York: Pilgrim, 1990), chap. 1.

27. For practical suggestions, see Dieter Hessel, ed., *Shalom Connections in Personal and Congregational Life* (Ellenwood, Ga.: Alternatives, 1986).

CHAPTER 1: POSTMODERN CHRISTIANITY IN QUEST OF ECO-JUSTICE
John B. Cobb, Jr.

1. John B. Cobb, Jr., *Is It Too Late? A Theology of Ecology* (Beverly Hills: Bruce Books, 1972).

2. Lynn White, Jr., "The Historical Roots of Our Ecological Crisis," *Science* (10 March 1967), 1205.

3. On the other hand, we also need a postpatriarchal Christianity, and that will have to be a new Christianity. A postmodern Christianity will move in that direction, incorporating many feminist insights. But to uproot patriarchal habits of feeling and perception is a far more radical task, one that must work against the Bible, however much inspiration it can still find there.

4. H. Richard Niebuhr, *The Meaning of Revelation* (New York: Macmillan, 1941).

5. Presbyterian Eco-Justice Task Force, *Keeping and Healing the Creation* (Louisville: Committee on Social Witness Policy, 1989).

6. Marjorie Spiegel, *The Dread Comparison: Human and Animal Slavery* (Philadelphia: New Society Publishers, 1988), 10.

7. Herman E. Daly and John B. Cobb, Jr., *For the Common Good: Redirecting the Economy Toward Community, the Environment, and a Sustainable Future* (Boston: Beacon, 1989).

CHAPTER 2: RETURNING TO OUR SENSES
Larry Rasmussen

1. Cited by James A. Nash in "Ecological Integrity and Christian Political Responsibility," *Theology & Public Policy* 1 (Fall 1989): 32, from Clarence J.

Glacken's *Traces on the Rhodian Shore* (Berkeley: University of California Press, 1967), 339, 322–38.

2. The subtitle of Paul Santmire's helpful volume, *The Travail of Nature* (Philadelphia: Fortress, 1985).

3. Kosuke Koyama, *Mount Fuji and Mount Sinai: A Critique of Idols* (Maryknoll, N.Y.: Orbis, 1985), ix.

4. James Cone, *For My People: Black Theology and the Black Church* (Maryknoll, N.Y.: Orbis, 1984), 182. The full paragraph reads: "Almost without exception, white American churches have interpreted religion as something exclusively spiritual with no political content useful in the struggles of the poor for freedom. By identifying the gospel of Jesus with a spirituality estranged from the struggle for justice, the church becomes an agent of injustice. We can observe this in the history of Lutheran churches with their emphasis on the two kingdoms, and also in their apparent failure to extend Luther's theology of the cross to society. Unfortunately all institutional white churches in America have sided with capitalist, rich, white, male elites, and against socialists, the poor, blacks, and women."

5. This section draws heavily from an article that elaborates the theology of the cross more extensively than is here the case. That article is "The Community of the Cross," *dialog* 30, no. 2 (Spring 1991): 150–62. In that article I reverse the order of (1) and (2) in this chapter. The change of order there is in keeping with Luther's own insistence that the revelation in Jesus Christ is primary and definitive. The order in this paper highlights creation.

6. Dietrich Bonhoeffer, "Aufträge der Bruderräte" (Dezember 1939), *Gesammelte Schriften* III (Munich: Chr. Kaiser Verlag, 1966), 388.

7. Santmire, in *Travail of Nature*, has cited this from Heinrich Bornkamm's *Luther's World of Thought* (St. Louis: Concordia, 1958), 189. The original quotation is published in the *Weimar Aufgabe* (hereafter WA), 32.134.34–32.136.36.

8. This phrase is, of course, a common figure of speech. But I have taken it from an essay by Mary Evelyn Jegen and used a form of it to title this chapter. The reference in Jegen's work can be found in her chapter, "The Church's Role in Healing the Earth," in *Tending the Garden: Essays on the Gospel and the Earth*, ed. Wesley Granberg-Michaelson (Grand Rapids, Mich.: Wm. B. Eerdmans, 1987), 96.

9. Santmire, *Travail of Nature*, 130, citing Martin Luther, *Lectures on Genesis* (chaps. 1–5), in *Luther's Works*, vol. 1, ed. Jaroslav Pelikan, (St. Louis: Concordia, 1955), 42.

10. This protest against human pretension to know what nonhuman experience of God might be like is not meant in any way to discourage identification with nonhuman life. On the contrary, this whole paper wants to help that happen. As we face a planetary environment in decline, we need far more of the worship materials like Ray McKeever's "Even the Stones Will Cry Out."

11. Alice Walker, *The Color Purple* (New York: Pocket Books, 1982), 178.

12. Santmire, *Travail of Nature,* 130, citing from Bornkamm, *Luther's World of Thought,* 189.

13. The discussion of *imago Dei* so necessary to eco-justice theology is helped along by Douglas John Hall's *Imaging God: Dominion as Stewardship* (Grand Rapids, Mich.: Wm. B. Eerdmans, 1986).

14. From the second draft of "Justice, Peace, and the Integrity of Creation," prepared for the World Convocation of the World Council of Churches in Seoul, Korea, 6–12 March 1990. I hasten to add that, in the document, the discussion is about the nature of humans' vocation in creation and not about the *imago Dei*. Connecting the two is my use of the quotation, not the authors'.

15. This is a paraphrase of Jürgen Moltmann's *The Crucified God: The Cross of Christ as the Foundation and Criticism of Christian Theology* (New York: Harper & Row, 1974), 205. I am grateful to Lisa Stoen Hazelwood for bringing this passage to my attention anew.

16. Though Luther's is, of course, a New Testament claim in this respect, the pattern is the Hebrew one. Just as the Hebrews moved from the experience of a redeeming God to the awesome realization that this very one was also the Creator of the universe and of life itself, so Luther moves from the redemptive presence of the transcendent God in the human Jesus to the awesome presence of this God in all things great and small. The universe is itself the primordial revelation of God, but the path to understanding God as Creator comes via the definitive, though not exclusive, revelation of God in Jesus. While I respect the experience of both Luther and the Hebrews, the fallout has often been to make the Second Article of the Creed the First, i.e., to obscure the fact that creation is primary and redemption is wholly the redemption *of* creation. God is first "maker of heaven and earth"; God is redeemer in order to save and serve creation's destiny.

17. H. H. the Dalai Lama, "Tissue of Compassion," *Cathedral* 5 (December 1989): 5.

18. Rorty as cited from Anthony Walton, "Awakening After Boston's Nightmare," *New York Times* (10 January 1990), A27.

19. The reference is to the line from Augustine that "hope has two lovely daughters, anger and courage; anger at the way things are, courage to set them right." For a profound treatment of this in Christian ethics, see Beverly Wildung Harrison, "The Power of Anger in the Work of Love: Christian Ethics for Women and Other Strangers," in *Making the Connections: Essays in Feminist Social Ethics,* ed. Carol S. Robb (Boston: Beacon, 1985), 3ff.

20. The reference is to the work of the Japanese theologian, Kazoh Kitamori, *The Theology of the Pain of God* (Richmond: John Knox Press, 1965).

21. The phrase is a reference to the excellent work of the Presbyterian Eco-Justice Task Force, *Keeping and Healing the Creation* (Louisville: Committee on Social Witness Policy, 1989). In my judgment, this is the best denominational statement on eco-justice to date.

22. I am keenly aware that moral discourse about suffering is fraught with danger. It is one of the chief reasons I question the Lutheran legacy for ethics.

Ethics talk about suffering is especially dangerous when the symbol is the cross, and always perilous when those who make history, rather than simply "take" it, have, like Constantine's progeny, discovered the cross as their sign of victory. W. H. Auden rightly says that "only the sated and well-fed enjoy Calvary, as a verbal event" and Koyama rightly worries about what happens when "the well-salaried and well-caloried" find this symbol at the center of their culture, rather than as a shocking sign from its periphery. Too, there is the perverse legacy of the cross among the poor and among many who are socialized to be self-denigrating. This is the deep strain of oppression and of sadomasochism in Christianity as expressed in pieties of crucifixion (in Roman Catholicism) and in cross theology as "worm theology" (in both Lutheranism and Calvinism). In Lutheranism this legacy of legitimized suffering has been reinforced with a patriarchal orders-of-creation theology that survived even Luther's anti-dualist and anti-hierarchical polemics against "the great chain of being." The dynamics of Luther's radical teaching on justification and his cross theology did not materialize in such a way as to recast his social theory. In social theory and social ethics he remained largely Constantinian, medieval, and patriarchal, thereby legitimizing suffering oppression rather than resisting it.

The morally perilous discussion of suffering constrains us to draw an important distinction. Some suffering, as Douglas Hall notes, belongs to finitude itself. This suffering may make life difficult but we cannot *live* without it. It belongs to our creaturely constitution to struggle in the process of becoming, to bump and grind and muddle our way through various stages of life, to know anxiety, temptation, and loneliness as pain, and to face limits of all kinds, including the ultimate limit of death itself. Such suffering is not, of itself, negative. That is, it is not destructive. It may in fact be integrative in that it furthers our development as mature and responsible beings. Even death, of itself, may not be negative suffering, though, needless to say, many deaths are and a great deal of dying is. But death in the sense of the cessation of all bodily functions belongs to life itself, and when it comes at the close of a life well and fully lived, it is not evil. Cross theology is bold here and a little unsettling. Death belongs to finitude and finitude per se is not evil. When shalom reigns in fullness, creatures will continue to die. When shalom reigns, creatures will in fact continue to experience suffering, but only suffering that is in the service of life itself, including that "good death" that comes as the final stage of a good life.

23. As Mary Evelyn Jegen notes, "to heal" is related to the Indo-European root *Kailo,* which means whole or uninjured, and to the Old English *halig,* meaning holy or sacred. See her "The Church's Role in Healing the Earth," in Granberg-Michaelson, ed., *Tending the Garden,* 97.

24. The cross as a symbol of suffering focuses as an ethic upon suffering and pain, not from a morbid interest in pain, "but because there *is* pain, because disintegrative pain is not part of what *should* be, and because there can be no healing that does not begin with the sober recognition of the reality of that

which needs to be healed" (Hall, *Thinking the Faith: Christian Theology in North American Context* (Minneapolis: Augsburg, 1989), 33.

25. See Dorothee Soelle, *Suffering* (Philadelphia: Fortress, 1975); Dietrich Bonhoeffer, *Letters and Papers from Prison* (New York: Macmillan, 1972); Kazoh Kitamori, *Theology of the Pain of God* (see n. 19 above); Kosuke Koyama, *Mount Fuji and Mount Sinai* (see n. 3 above); Jon Sobrino, S.J., *Christology at the Crossroads* (Maryknoll, N.Y.: Orbis, 1978). For a discussion of Bonhoeffer's themes, see my volume with Renate Bethge, *Dietrich Bonhoeffer: His Significance for North Americans* (Minneapolis: Fortress, 1989), chaps. 7 and 8.

26. Hall, *Imaging God*, 186.

27. See Hall's *Lighten Our Darkness: Toward an Indigenous Theology of the Cross* (Philadelphia: Westminster, 1976) and his *Thinking the Faith*.

28. A longer discussion would take up the matter of economic growth and sustainability. I am not opposed to economic growth. In fact, to say no to it, by choice or by virtue of systemic failures, would be to damn the lot of millions of already suffering peoples. I only insist that economic growth be, at the same time, sustainable development. But that requires a different economic system, together with different technologies and habits, from the ones we presently have. It also requires a different economic theory, one that does not consider costs to the environment as "externalities."

29. Francis Bacon's influence here is a powerful one. See his major works, *New Atlantis* and *Novum Majorum*, both available in several editions.

30. See Foucault's work in *Power/Knowledge: Selected Interviews and Other Writings, 1972–1977*, ed. Colin Gordon (New York: Pantheon, 1980).

31. Cited from Bill McKibben, *The End of Nature* (New York: Random House, 1989), 162. The page number and other bibliographical data are not given for *Future Man*.

32. Bonhoeffer, *Gesammelte Schriften* I, 145.

33. Martin Luther, "Exposition of Psalm 127, for the Christians at Rig in Livonia," in *Luther's Works*, vol. 45 (Philadelphia: Muhlenberg, 1962), 331.

34. Martin Luther, "To the Councilmen of All Cities in Germany That They Should Establish and Maintain Christian Schools," in ibid., 356. I am grateful to Elizabeth Bettenhausen for drawing the passages in nn. 30 and 31 to my attention.

CHAPTER 3: HEALING THE PROTESTANT MIND
H. Paul Santmire

1. For a thorough and up-to-date description of the extent of the environmental crisis, see *Keeping and Healing the Creation*, a resource paper prepared by the Presbyterian Eco-Justice Task Force (Louisville: Committee on Social Witness Policy, 1989), 1–38.

2. I have attempted to address such issues from a theological perspective for twenty-five years, both historically and constructively, beginning with my dissertation "Creation and Nature: A Study of the Doctrine of Nature with

Special Attention to Karl Barth's Doctrine of Creation" (Th.D. diss., Harvard University, 1966) and my programmatic essay, *Brother Earth: Nature, God, and Ecology in a Time of Crisis* (New York: Thomas Nelson, 1970). See also my historical study, *The Travail of Nature: The Ambiguous Ecological Promise of Christian Theology* (Philadelphia: Fortress, 1985). The most recent reviews of this work are: Peter W. Bakken, *Journal of Religion* 69, no. 4 (1989): 574–75; and Thomas Sieger Derr, *Princeton Seminary Bulletin* 10, no. 3 (1989). My constructive approach has been subjected to scrutiny, in comparison with the perspectives of John Cobb and Pierré Teilhard de Chardin, by Claude Y. Stewart, Jr., *Nature in Grace: A Study in the Theology of Nature* (Macon, Ga.: Mercer University Press, 1983). See also Roderick Frazier Nash, *The Rights of Nature: A History of Environmental Ethics* (Madison: University of Wisconsin Press, 1989), 103–8 and Thomas Sieger Derr, *Ecology and Human Need* (Philadelphia: Westminster, 1975), 36ff. My most recently published theological essay is "The Future of the Cosmos and the Renewal of the Church's Life with Nature," in *Cosmos as Creation*, ed. Ted Peters (Nashville: Abingdon, 1989), chap. 9. This can be read as a companion piece to the reflections in this chapter, as can my 1989 unpublished lecture at the Lutheran School of Theology in Chicago, "The Rhetoric of Grace and the Vision of Grace: Joseph Sittler's Theology of Nature as an Invitation to See as well as to Hear." As a "neo-Reformation" thinker (Stewart), I plead guilty to the description that I am also a "revisionist" (Derr). I address exegetical issues related to the theology of dominion in my essay "The Genesis Creation Narratives Revisited: Themes for a Global Age" in *Interpretation* 45, no. 4 (1991): 366–79.

3. See *Ecumenical Review* 41, no. 4 (1989). Most of the articles in this issue, introduced by Douglas John Hall, discuss "Justice, Peace, and the Integrity of Creation." The discussion was carried further at the Seventh Assembly of the WCC in 1991. See Michael Kinnamon, ed. *Signs of the Spirit: Official Report, Seventh Assembly* (Grand Rapids, Mich.: Wm. B. Eerdmans, 1991).

4. See also the discussion in *Keeping and Healing the Creation*.

5. See n. 3 above. In 1986, I reviewed and attempted to analyze the extensive, but then largely unnoticed, discussion of the theology of nature in the United States, from 1961 to 1986, in an essay, "Toward A New Theology of Nature," *dialog* 25, no. 1 (1986): 43–50. In that essay I observed that a detailed bibliography of works in this field was desperately needed. Thankfully, that kind of task has now been undertaken by J. Ronald Engel and Peter W. Bakken, *Ecology, Justice and Christian Faith: A Guide to the Literature, 1960–1990* (forthcoming).

6. For John Cobb, see especially *Is It Too Late? A Theology of Ecology* (Beverly Hills: Bruce Books, 1972) and the bibliography cited in Stewart, *Nature in Grace*. For Joseph Sittler, see especially *Essays on Nature and Grace* (Philadelphia: Fortress, 1972) and the references in the Engel and Bakken bibliography. Jürgen Moltmann's most creative contribution to this discussion is his Gifford Lectures, *God in Creation: A New Theology of Creation and the Spirit of God*, trans. Margaret Kohl (San Francisco: Harper & Row, 1985).

7. See, for example, Rosemary Radford Ruether, "Ecology and Human Liberation: A Conflict between the Theology of History and the Theology of Nature?" in *To Change the World: Christology and Cultural Criticism* (New York: Crossroad, 1981), chap. 5, and Karen L. Bloomquist, "Creation, Domination, and the Environment," *Bulletin of Gettysburg Seminary* 69, no. 3 (1989): 27–32; and inter alia, Vine Deloria, Jr., *God is Red* (New York: Grosset & Dunlap, 1973); and Harvey Sindima, "Community of Life," *Ecumenical Review* 41, no. 4 (1989): 537–51.

8. See Charles C. West, "Justice Within the Limits of the Created World," *Ecumenical Review* 27, no. 1 (1976): 57–64.

9. These church leaders should not be faulted for this because few biblical scholars during the last twenty years devoted any attention to the theology of nature. There are signs, however, that this disinterest among biblical scholars might be fading. See, for example, the thoughtful and thought-provoking essays by Terence E. Fretheim, "Nature's Praise of God in the Psalms," *Ex Auditu* 3, no. 1 (1988): 16–30; "The Reclamation of Creation: Redemption and Law in Exodus," in *Interpretation* 45, no. 4 (1991): 354–65; and the literature he cites.

10. An exception was the volume, *The Human Crisis in Ecology,* ed. Franklin C. Jensen and Cedric W. Tilberg (New York: Board of Social Ministry, Lutheran Church in America, 1972). Produced by a mainline Protestant denomination, this document nevertheless attempted to go beyond a singular reliance on the theology of dominion.

11. "Eco-justice" was first given currency by the Boston Industrial Mission in the late 1960s. This conceptuality is reflected in the essay by Norman J. Faramelli, "Ecological Responsibility and Economic Justice," in *Ecology: Crisis and New Vision,* ed. Richard E. Sherrell (Richmond: John Knox, n.d.), chap. 2.

12. See Derr, *Ecology and Human Need.*

13. Joseph Sittler, who helped to give the expression "care of the earth" currency, did *not* attach it as an appendix to the themes of distributive justice or environmental management. But Sittler remained more or less an isolated figure in this respect.

14. Lynn White, Jr., "The Historical Roots of Our Ecological Crisis," *Science,* 10 March 1967, 1203–7. See my essay also, "The Liberation of Nature: Lynn White's Challenge Anew," *Christian Century* 102, no. 18 (1985): 530–33.

15. See my *Travail of Nature,* 121–32 for the following discussion.

16. Ibid., 133–43.

17. Ibid.

18. Ibid., 145–55.

19. In a private conversation with Barth in Basel in 1965, relating to my interest in the theology of nature, he quoted verses from Psalm 8 to me, concerning the centrality of "the human" in the divine economy (cf. 8:5: "thou has made him a little less than God") and then admonished me not to get involved with "gnostic speculations about nature."

20. Cf. the following statement by Barth, recently called to our attention by Andrew Linzey and Tom Regan, eds., *Animals and Christianity: A Book of Readings* (New York: Crossroad, 1988), 122–23 [from *Church Dogmatics* III/4, *The Doctrine of Creation,* trans. A. T. Mackay et al. (Edinburgh: T. & T. Clark, 1978), 349–51], where Barth is discussing Albert Schweitzer's idea of "reverence for life." We can learn from Schweitzer, Barth says: "Our starting point must be that in this matter . . . , as a living being in co-existence with non-human life, man has to think and act responsibly. The responsibility is not the same as he has to his own life and that of his fellow-men. Only analogically can we bring it under the concept of respect for life. It can only follow the primary responsibility at a distance. If we try to bring animal and vegetable life too close to human, or even class them together, we can hardly avoid the danger of regarding and treating human life, even when we really want to help, from the aspect of the animal and vegetable, and therefore in a way which is not really apposite. But why should we not be faced here by a responsibility which, if not primary, is a serious secondary responsibility?"

But then Barth qualifies what he has just said, in his own characteristic the-anthropocentric way, in terms of a strong doctrine of human election and human dominion, which, by the time he concludes his discussion, seems to lead him to the point where he has finally taken back much of what he first said in favor of reverence for life. Plants and animals, he states, are indispensable, but they are the background for what is truly essential, the life of God with human beings. The nuance, moreover, as a matter of course shifts from the thought of reverence to the thought of control: "The special responsibility in this case rests primarily on this, that the world of animals and plants forms the indispensable living background to the living-space divinely allotted to man and placed under his control. As they live, so can he. He is not set up as lord over the earth, but as lord on the earth which is already furnished with these creatures. Animals and plants do not belong to him; they and the whole earth belong only to God. But he takes precedence of them. They are provided for his use. They are his 'means of life.' The meaning of the basis of this distinction consists in the fact that he is the animal creature to whom God reveals, entrusts and binds Himself within the rest of creation, with whom He makes common cause in the course of a particular history which is neither that of an animal nor a plant, and in whose life-activity he expects a conscious and deliberate recognition of His honour, mercy and power. Hence the higher necessity of his life, and his right to that lordship and control. He can exercise it only in the responsibility thus conferred on him."

21. See *Travail of Nature,* 84–96.

22. The authors of *Keeping and Healing the Creation* are typical in this respect; see pp. 44–45.

23. Cf. ibid., 56.

24. Douglas John Hall, *Imaging God: Dominion as Stewardship* (Grand Rapids, Mich.: Wm. B. Eerdmans, 1986), 201–2.

25. See below, pp. 73–75, "The Integrity of Nature."

26. I would say the same about my own theological labors in this field. See above, n. 3.

27. This discussion summarizes my reflections in *Travail of Nature*, 13–30.

28. I am also instructed here by the works of Jürgen Moltmann, beginning with his *Theology of Hope: On the Ground and the Implications of a Christian Eschatology*, trans. James W. Leitch (New York: Harper & Row, 1967). I regard Moltmann's works as a friendly amendment to Barth's *Church Dogmatics*.

29. This was already the conclusion of Robert Jenson in his early work *Alpha and Omega: A Study in the Theology of Karl Barth* (New York: Thomas Nelson, 1963).

30. See Jürgen Moltmann, *The Trinity and the Kingdom: The Doctrine of God*, trans. Margaret Kohl (San Francisco: Harper & Row, 1981).

31. See *Travail of Nature*, 97–105.

32. See Moltmann, *The Trinity*, 86–93.

33. Regarding the World Council of Churches discussion, see above, n. 4. I believe that I was the first to introduce this kind of terminology into the theological discussion. See my reflections about "the integrity of nature," *Brother Earth*, 92, 149, along with a discussion of the rights of nature.

34. Hall, *Imaging God*.

35. Ibid., 123ff.

36. Ibid., 127.

37. Ibid., 77.

38. Ibid., 112.

39. As I develop this thought, I am revising some of the materials I presented in *Brother Earth*, which, I now believe, accented the theme of human dominion too sharply.

40. Such as Derr, *Ecology and Human Need*.

41. The most forceful interpretations of the stewardship idea have been put forward by Douglas John Hall, *Imaging God; The Steward: A Biblical Symbol Come of Age* (New York: Friendship Press, 1982); and *The Stewardship of Life in the Kingdom of Death* (Grand Rapids, Mich.: Wm. B. Eerdmans, 1985). Here, it appears to me, a creative theologian who has a compelling message of his own to deliver is pouring new wine into old wineskins, with the result that these books are about to burst at the seams with the turn of every page.

42. One of the numerous virtues of the study by Bruce C. Birch and Larry L. Rasmussen, *The Predicament of the Prosperous* (Philadelphia: Westminster, 1978), is that they take shalom, rather than stewardship, to be the fundamental biblical construct.

43. See, further, my exploratory essay, "I–Thou, I–It, and I–Ens," *Journal of Religion* 48, no. 3 (1968): 260–73.

44. René Dubos, *Reason Awake: Science for Man* (New York: Columbia University Press, 1970), 126–27.

45. The issues we are touching on here are delicate and complex. How are we to balance homocentric and cosmocentric values? Some of the most thoughtful reflection on these issues has been done by Charles Birch and John Cobb in their study *The Liberation of Life: From Cell to the Community* (Cambridge: Cambridge University Press, 1981). See the helpful summary of their argument by Engel and Bakken (forthcoming bibliography).

46. On Irenaeus, see *Travail of Nature,* 35–44.

47. See Sittler, *Essays on Nature and Grace.*

48. See Moltmann, *God in Creation.*

49. The assumption, in this context, is that humanity alone has "sinned." *There is no cosmic fall.* See *Brother Earth,* 192–200.

50. On the vocation of Jesus Christ as the perfecter of the creation, that is, as one who is more than the Reconciler, see my discussion in *Brother Earth,* 162–78. Cf. also the comments of Jürgen Moltmann, *The Trinity,* 116: "According to Paul Christ was not merely 'delivered for our offences' but was also 'raised for our justification' (Rom. 4:25 AV). Reconciling sinners with God through his cross, he brings about the new righteousness, the new life, the new creature through his resurrection. . . . This surplus of grace over and above the forgiveness of sins and the reconciliation of sinners, represents the power of the new creation which consummates creation-in-the-beginning. It follows from this that the Son of God did not become man simply because of the sin of men and women, but rather for the sake of perfecting the creation."

51. See further my essay, "The Future of the Cosmos and the Renewal of the Church's Life with Nature" in *Cosmos and Creation.*

CHAPTER 4: ECO-JUSTICE AND LIBERATION THEOLOGY
Heidi Hadsell

1. Anthropocentrism is not new in Christian thought. For an example of Christian ethical reasoning in the area of eco-justice, that is human centered without being specifically liberationist, see Roger Shinn's "Eco-Justice Themes in Christian Ethics," in *For Creation's Sake,* ed. Dieter Hessel, (Philadelphia: Geneva, 1985).

2. Gustavo Gutierrez, *A Theology of Liberation* (Maryknoll, N.Y.: Orbis, 1973), 7.

3. Gustavo Gutierrez, *The Power of the Poor in History* (Maryknoll, N.Y.: Orbis, 1984), 13.

4. Gutierrez, *Theology of Liberation,* 10.

5. Enrique Dussel describes social relationships as follows: "Social moral relationships are actual, infrastructural, practical relationships among producers, within actual, historical modes of production. It is here that the drama of morality (and ethics) is played out" (Dussel, *Ethics and Community* [Maryknoll, N.Y.: Orbis, 1988]).

6. The Council of the Brazilian Catholic Bishops in its statement entitled "Preserve That Which Is for Everyone" reflects the position that thinking about nature is a luxury in situations in which human misery is widespread: "It does not make sense therefore to worry about the protection of the environment, without taking into account the imbalances in the human situation, caused or reinforced by the irrational production of superfluous goods and armaments, while part of humanity has no access to essential goods, and is being induced by planned consumerism to be in mental and political solidarity with consumer society, with its interests and its alienating ideology." Cited in João F. de Morais, *Os Bispos e a Política no Brasil* (São Paulo: Cortez/ Editora Autores Associados, 1982), 115. Translation by the author.

7. Dussel, *Ethics and Community,* 197.

8. This theme of justice, grounded in the Christian concept of love, is found in virtually all of liberation theology. One description is the following from Gustavo Gutierrez: "The only justice is the one that goes to the very root of all injustice, all breach with love, all sin. The only justice is the one that assaults all the consequences and expressions of this cleavage in friendship. The only justice is the definitive justice that builds, starting right now, in our conflict-filled history, a kingdom in which God's love will be present and exploitation abolished" (Gutierrez, *Power of the Poor in History,* 14).

9. For a full discussion of justice in liberation thought, see Ismael Garcia, *Justice in Latin American Theology of Liberation* (Atlanta: John Knox, 1987).

10. One of the strengths of liberation thought, and one of its potential contributions to thinking about the environment, is precisely in the location of ethical questions in their larger socioeconomic and political contexts. As Miguez Bonino observes: "The option for a historical, political language has, nevertheless, been radicalized in Latin America, by bringing it down, not merely to the language and categories of a 'general' analysis of historical existence, but to the concrete contents of our own social, cultural, political, and economic experience and to the categories that our own sociopolitical analysts have forged in order to grasp this experience" (José Míguez Bonino, *Doing Theology in a Revolutionary Situation* [Philadelphia: Fortress, 1975], 79).

11. The use of the term "fetish" recalls Karl Marx's use of this term. Here it indicates the way in which nature, fetishized, may be used to obfuscate the social relationships that are the true source of nature's destruction.

12. One can of course also find examples closer to home, such as the history of the westward expansion in North America. Here, too, land was valued far more than the people living on it.

13. Gutierrez brings together human history and human hopes for the kingdom as follows: "He is proclaiming a kingdom of justice and liberation, to be established in favor of the poor, the oppressed, and the marginalized of history" (Gutierrez, *Power of the Poor,* 14).

14. The phrase "the human project" is one that Míguez Bonino uses in one of his more recent books: José Míguez Bonino, *Toward a Christian Political Ethics* (Philadelphia: Fortress, 1983).

15. Hannah Arendt captures something of this difference between the human *telos* and the natural world in her discussion of the difference between human labor and human action. Labor, for Arendt, denotes that human activity that is directly tied to human survival, and as such is both necessary and in itself meaningless. Action, on the other hand, is that human activity that has escaped the cycle of the natural process and is expressive of the human capacity for meaning, played out in human political life. See Hannah Arendt, *The Human Condition* (Garden City, N.Y.: Doubleday and Co., 1985).

16. The sources available that describe the benefits of growth are, in this country, virtually unlimited. For a Christian apologetic for growth see any of the recent works by Michael Novak.

17. See, for example, Herman Daly, ed., *Towards a Steady-State Economy* (San Francisco: H. W. Freeman and Co., 1973).

18. A recent example of this kind of polemic between North and South is what took place in 1989 between President Sarney of Brazil and various Northern nations and international agencies over the protection of the Amazon rain forest. In 1989, Sarney was quoted as saying, "Persuasion is giving way to attempts at intimidation, to explicit and veiled threats that even question the principle of sovereignty of states." *New York Times*, 31 March 1989.

19. One of the major proponents of dependency theory is André Gundar Frank. He has written widely on the topic. A good place to begin is: James Cockcroft, Dale Johnson, and André Gundar Frank, eds., *Dependency and Underdevelopment, Latin America's Political Economy* (Garden City, N.Y.: Doubleday and Co., 1972).

20. See Samir Amin, *Accumulation on a World Scale*, vol. 1 (New York: Monthly Review Press, 1974).

21. Ibid.

22. A good description of rapid-growth policies in the Amazon may be found in the essay by Alcida Ramos, "Frontier Expansion and Indian Peoples in the Brazilian Amazon" in *Frontier Expansion in the Amazon*, ed. Marianne Schmink and Charles Wood (Gainesville: University of Florida Press, 1984).

23. This is a dominant theme in many international debates on economic and environmental issues. One recent example is the 1989 United Nations General Assembly discussion on a treaty between rich and poor countries to protect the atmosphere and encourage ecologically sound development. The poor countries are pushing for new international rules regarding transfers of technology and debt relief, as measures that will promote environmental protection, and also for changes in some of the international market rules and practices. "U.N. Takes Step Toward Global Climate Pact," *New York Times*, 3 January 1990.

24. I hasten to add that the critique of capitalism does not suggest that other forms of economic production are not also environmentally destructive. Examples abound in Eastern Europe and the Soviet Union of massive environmental destruction. Similar results however do not necessarily imply similar

causes. As Enrique Dussel has observed, both the capitalist and the socialist economic systems are oriented toward growth. The difference is that capitalism is oriented toward growth in the rate of profit, while socialism is oriented toward growth in the rate of production. See Dussel, *Ethics and Community*, 184–85.

25. Herman Daly and John Cobb, *For the Common Good: Redirecting the Economy Toward Community, the Environment, and a Sustainable Future* (Boston: Beacon, 1989).

26. See, for example, Leonardo Boff's description of the new church: "The actions of the humanity of Jesus Christ must remain as the critical norm for the Church built upon them. The concrete and consequent living out of this meaning of authority as service would certainly make the Church a place of liberty, fraternity, and open communication between all people, between those charged with the unity of the community and all of its members" (Boff, *Church, Charism, and Power* [New York: Crossroad, 1986], 61).

27. Gustavo Gutierrez writes: "What is to be done away with is the intellectualizing of the intellectual who has no ties with the life and struggle of the poor—the theology of the theologian who reflects upon the faith precisely from the point of view of those from whom the Father has hidden his revelation: the 'learned and clever' (Matt. 11:25)" (*Power of the Poor in History*, 103).

28. Jürgen Habermas, "Técnica e Ciência Enquanto 'Ideologia,' " in *Escola de Frankfurt, Os Pensadores XLVIII* (São Paulo: Abril Cultural, 1975).

29. Daniel Bell, *The End of Ideology, On the Exhaustion of Political Ideas of the Fifties* (New York: The Free Press, 1965).

30. See, for example, Sallie McFague, *Models of God: Theology for an Ecological, Nuclear Age* (Philadelphia: Fortress, 1987).

CHAPTER 5: THE NEW STORY
George H. Kehm

1. H. Paul Santmire, *The Travail of Nature: The Ambiguous Ecological Promise of Christian Theology* (Philadelphia: Fortress, 1985), 122–23. Santmire finds the term "the-anthropocentrism" useful to describe Luther and Calvin's thought. Karl Barth used the term "to refer to a theology that focusses on God and humanity as its chief subjects." The term fits much of Protestant orthodoxy and neo-Protestant theology, and while it makes a helpful distinction between secular and theistic forms of anthropocentrism, it is awkward. I will use "anthropocentrism" in this chapter and will focus on Protestant versions.

2. See Thomas Berry, *The Dream of the Earth* (San Francisco: Sierra Club Books, 1988), 123ff. Berry blames the Bible for promoting anthropocentrism in the Christian tradition. My view differs from both Berry's and Matthew Fox's. Both try to remedy the anthropocentrism of the Christian tradition (along with the dualism, hierarchialism, patriarchalism, and individualism Fox thinks necessarily accompanies it) by means of a creation-centered theology. Fox's criticism of Augustinian redemption-centered theology is so severe he seems to

think it necessary to develop creation theology independently from the idea of redemption.

3. The following samples from the Presbyterian Church (U.S.A.) *Book of Confessions* (Louisville: Office of the General Assembly), and a couple of the older, influential commentaries on two of the documents in the book may serve to illustrate the presence of the flawed story Berry describes.

The Heidelberg Catechism has been praised for its pronounced personalizing of the meaning of the doctrines of the Christian faith. Beginning with the answer to the first question, the leitmotif of the catechism is that "everything must fit his purpose for my salvation" (4.001). "His" refers to "my Father in heaven," whose favorable will toward the "me" in the document has been assured through "my faithful Savior, Jesus Christ." The meaning of the first article of the Apostle's Creed is explained in such a way that the believer is assured that God "will provide me with all things necessary for body and soul" and that "whatever evil he sends upon me he will turn to my good" (4.026). The idea of God's providence is further expanded in a way that makes everything in the created world ("heaven and earth together with all creatures") a means by which God directly rules whatever happens, leaving nothing to chance (4.027). Whatever "pastoral" benefit may be provided by such teaching, an individualistic or, at best, tribal view of salvation and an anthropocentric view of the world are what it communicates.

Zachary Ursinus, a coauthor of the catechism, gives a more detailed account of the theology behind it. He sets forth the standard Reformed doctrine that the "chief and ultimate end for which all things were created . . . is the glory and praise of God." (*Commentary on the Heidelberg Catechism*, trans. Rev. G. W. Willard [Grand Rapids, Mich.: Wm. B. Eerdmans, 1956], 146). To attain that end it was necessary for God to create a world that included "rational intelligences" capable of knowing and praising God and also "things destitute of reason" so that they "might furnish matter for praise" (ibid., 147). All that God does in creating and governing the world is for the purpose of gathering to Godself, "from the human race, an everlasting church, which might praise him as Creator" (ibid.). Thus, "God . . . created man for himself; and all other things for man, that they might serve him, and through him serve God" (ibid.).

The sharp dichotomy between the rational and nonrational creatures suggests that there may be a corresponding difference in their value for God. In his comments on the eschatological material in the catechism, Ursinus ignores the ultimate destiny of the nonrational creatures, concentrating all his attention on the rational ones. The elect portion of them (the everlasting church) is promoted to eternal blessedness and eternally praises God. The nonelect or those hardened in wickedness suffer eternal punishment (which in its own way is deemed to glorify God). The nonrational creatures do not appear in these descriptions of ultimate salvation in heaven. Is that because they had only temporary, instrumental value for God, as means for advancing the rational creatures to their eternal destinies but which may pass into oblivion once they are no longer needed for that? Perhaps that is what Ursinus meant when he wrote: "The means . . . by which the church is now gathered and preserved in the world, will then (i.e., in *eschaton*) no longer be required" (ibid., 634). Not only will prophecy, tongues, and knowledge pass away, but also sun and moon, he says. It seems logical to conclude that all the rest of those nonrational "ministers and instruments of God" would also be destined to pass away with these others. Apparently the ministries of nonrational creatures are not essential either to promoting the eternal praises of the elect nor to amplify the glory of God beyond what the elect could provide without them.

The doctrine of creation is given very brief treatment in *The Westminster Confession of Faith*. It is essentially the same as that of *The Heidelberg Catechism*. The creation of the world is the first act of God *ad extra* by which the necessary means for accomplishing God's eternal decree—the foreordination of "whatsoever comes to pass" (6.014)—are brought into existence. At the center of the created world was "man, male and female," distinguished from "the other creatures" by having "reasonable and immortal souls" (6.023). After the creation of the world, the Creator began the works of providence, upholding, directing, disposing, and governing all creatures to their appointed ends. The church is especially the object of God's care, and so God "disposeth all things to the good thereof" (6.030). The eschatology of this confession concentrates on the ultimate destinies of the elect and the nonelect, the two sets of rational creatures among humans (angels being a separate species). The ultimate destiny of the nonrational creatures is passed over in silence. This omission only tends to highlight the anthropocentric view of the world conveyed by the document.

In his commentary on *The Westminster Confession*, A. A. Hodge added something to the eschatology of the confession that could be the basis for a higher assessment of the value of nonhuman creatures. According to him, Scripture teaches that after the great conflagration of the earth accompanying the final judgment, "*this world* will be *reconstituted,* and as the 'new heaven and new earth' be gloriously adapted to be the permanent residence of Christ and his church." (*The Confession of Faith* [London: The Banner of Truth Trust, 1958], 393; emphasis mine.) This inclusion of the whole creation in the eternal kingdom of God is a welcome relief from the unmitigated anthropocentrism of the confession. Unfortunately, it is a wholly gratuitous comment without any support in the text whatever.

The Confession of 1967 continues the anthropocentric tendency of the Reformed doctrine of creation in viewing the created world as "the sphere of (God's) dealings with men" (9.16). The unique status of humankind as created for a "personal" relationship with God, and involving the endowment of "the capacities to make the world serve his needs and to enjoy its good things" (9.17) tends to promote an anthropocentric view of the world.

The strong statements on "Reconciliation in Society" include one on the appropriate use and protection of the "resources of nature" for the common welfare. Here, the confession moves toward the eco-justice position affirmed by the Presbyterian Church (U.S.A.) in 1990. However, its language is more compatible with an enlightened utilitarianism than it is with an ethic that would ascribe intrinsic value or rights to nonhuman creatures.

It is in the concluding section on "The Fulfillment of Reconciliation" (9.53ff.) that the confession breaks new ground. It explicitly states, as none of the other Presbyterian confessions does, that the redeeming work of God in Christ includes the whole of creation. "God's redeeming work in Jesus Christ embraces the whole of man's life. . . . It includes man's natural environment as exploited and despoiled by sin. It is the will of God that his purpose for human life shall be fulfilled under the rule of Christ and all evil be banished from his creation" (9.53; cf. 9.26).

To sum up, while we find here, at last, a view of God's redemptive work that has cosmic scope and appears to include all creatures, human and non-human, in ultimate salvation, the anthropocentric tendency of the earlier confessions is continued. The pronounced "personalism" of the view of "man" in the statements on creation obliterates the ontological bond between humankind and the extrahuman creation found in Scripture, as we shall see. The environmental ethic suggested in the confession provides little or no ground for the idea that all created beings have "intrinsic value" independent of their utility to humans; value that imposes obligations upon humans, including the obligation to preserve the presence and health of these others. The legacy of the Presbyterian confessional standards and of the Reformed tradition is as ambiguous as that of the Christian tradition generally on the issue of anthropocentrism and the participation of the extrahuman creation in ultimate salvation.

4. Thomas Berry, *The New Story: Comments on the Origin, Identification and Transmission of Values* (Chambersburg, Penn.: Anima Pubns., 1978), 3. Berry virtually abandons the effort to provide a biblical basis for his version of the new story, grounding it instead in his evolutionary view of the development of the earth community. My approach, however, does not exclude retellings of the biblical story that would correlate it with the processes of biological and cultural evolution on the planet earth. Any such retelling that would be justified in calling itself a version of the *Christian* story would have to show that it was normed by the *biblical* story.

5. Santmire, *Travail of Nature,* 217–18.

6. Ibid., 218.

7. Systematic theologian Michael Welker presented an interpretation of Genesis 1 and 2 at the meeting of the Society of Biblical Literature in New Orleans in November 1990. His exegetical effort brought out the essential interrelatedness of the human and extrahuman creatures in both biblical accounts of creation. Lively exchanges between Welker, Paul Hanson, and Phyllis Trible showed the openness of these biblical scholars to Welker's "ecological" reading of the creation narratives as well as Welker's openness to modifying or even abandoning his interpretive categories in the face of evidence that they did not fit certain elements in the text.

8. See Odil Steck, *World and Environment* (Nashville: Abingdon, 1980), 195–202.

9. I am committed to critical-historical study of the Bible (incl. form and redaction criticism and sociological and anthropological analysis) and to hermeneutical investigation of the biblical traditions, especially of the kind done by Paul Ricoeur and rhetorical criticism to augment the critical-historical approach, not displace it. Their results, however, while providing essential evidence, are ancillary to the questions of normativity and essentiality.

10. The material criterion or norm of Christian theology was traditionally called "Scripture," in Protestant circles. Some Reformed, Lutheran, and Roman Catholic theologians have preferred to name this norm "the gospel," whose original and most authoritative forms are given in the Bible. More recently, "the Christian story" has come into vogue as a new name for this material norm or "criterion of appropriateness," as David Tracy calls it. I see no essential difference between the material norms intended by these two expressions. The essence of the gospel is "the story of what God was doing in Jesus Christ for the reconciliation of the world." The essential content of this story—its main characters, their interactions, the plot, the climactic event, and its ultimate outcome—is what I take as the material norm of Christian theology and proclamation.

11. Arguments for the essentiality of a theological claim are not consistently employed by systematic theologians. This neglect is one reason for the relativism that has plagued recent Christian theology. Theologians have tried too hard to say something new or relevant that "speaks to the urgent issues of our time." True, part of the responsibility of theology is to attempt to correct church tradition and to "develop" it so it continues to make sense to contemporary people. It is also part of the responsibility of theology to show the ethical relevance of Christian claims to the personal and social issues of the day. What theologians claim as Christian will not be persuasive to any informed, critically thinking person so long as the theologians do not produce demonstrations of the essentiality of their claims to the Christian story. My position has much in common with Edward Farley's thought about "theological portraiture" in his *Ecclesial Reflection* (Philadelphia: Fortress, 1985).

12. Bernard Anderson, "Creation and Ecology," in *Creation in the Old Testament,* ed. Bernard Anderson (Philadelphia: Fortress, 1984), 167.

13. Ibid., 156.

14. Ibid.

15. Ibid., 157.

16. Ibid.

17. Ibid., 167.

18. Donald Gowan, *Genesis 1–11: From Eden to Babel* (Grand Rapids, Mich.: Wm. B. Eerdmans, 1988), 104.

19. Santmire, *Travail of Nature,* 146–55. See also Santmire's chapter 3 in this book that builds on his doctoral dissertation, "Creation and Nature: A

Study of the Doctrine of Nature with Special Attention to Karl Barth's Doctrine of Creation" (Th.D. diss., Harvard University, 1966).

20. Karl Barth, *Church Dogmatics* IV/1, trans. G. W. Bromiley (Edinburgh: T. & T. Clark, 1956), 26–27 and 34. In his most detailed discussion of the Noachic covenant here, Barth passes over Gen. 9:13, which contains the covenant with the earth. He identifies God's covenant partner in the Noachic covenant as "the whole of humanity after Noah" and also "all the living creatures," or, summarily, "man and . . . the creatures subordinate to him." In his volume on creation (*Church Dogmatics* III/1, p. 149), Barth does take note of the fact that this covenant is with the earth. However, he goes on to ask "What purpose does the earth serve?" His answer, "to be inhabited, specifically, by man." He goes on to say that "the most intimate connection" exists between man and the earth, according to Gen. 2:7. Earth is "home" for humankind: "the home where he lives and dies." Barth extols its goodness and construes it as the setting in which the fulfillment of God's covenant promises will take place. The meek shall inherit "the real earth." God's will shall be done "on earth" as it is done in heaven. Barth does not continue the discussion into the area of eschatology here, so the question of the ultimate destiny of the earth is left open. One is left with the impression that all earthly forms of fulfillment are provisional, penultimate realizations of salvation and not the ultimate form of salvation. As for the purely anthropocentric purpose of creation in Barth's theology, this quotation will suffice: "It is the divine will and accomplishment in relation to man—and nothing else—which really stands at the beginning of all things" (*Church Dogmatics*, III/1, p. 99, commenting on Gen. 1:1). There seems to be more than a merely methodological reason why Barth's doctrine of "the creature" is exclusively a theological anthropology. It is not just because he thinks Scripture presents little information about "heaven and earth" and the nonhuman inhabitants of the earth that he refrains from developing a theology of extrahuman creation. Rather, Barth's construal of creation as "the technical presupposition" of the covenant, and of the eternal covenant as concentrated in God's decision to unite humanity with himself in Jesus Christ, gives everything in creation an anthropological reason for being. Everything nonhuman has significance only as it serves the covenant history between God and human beings. It is difficult to find any basis for the intrinsic value of nonhuman creatures in such a scheme, despite the presence of passages in the *Church Dogmatics* where trees, plants, and animals are accorded value that is not reducible to any benefit to humans.

21. See Paul Van Buren, *A Theology of the Jewish-Christian Reality* (San Francisco: Harper & Row, 1987), 184ff. Van Buren follows Walter Brueggemann (*The Land* [Philadelphia: Fortress, 1977]) on this point, as does H. Paul Santmire, *Travail of Nature*, 190f.

22. Lev. 25:23; Ps. 24:1.

23. On the various circumstances that forced people to relinquish their property and the various provisions to provide equity for the new property

holders who had to allow the ancestral families to return to their land, see Martin Noth, *Leviticus* (Philadelphia: Westminster, 1965), 187ff.

24. Van Buren, *Theology of Jewish-Christian Reality*, 195.

25. The expression "land ethic" comes from Aldo Leopold's famous essay, "The Land Ethic," in his *A Sand County Almanac* (New York: Ballantine Books, 1970), 237–64. Leopold made a scientifically and philosophically persuasive case for the extension of ethical rights to the "land," by which he meant not only the soil but the animals and plants that live on it. He was aware that biblical prophets such as Ezekiel and Isaiah had already seen that "despoliation of the land is not only inexpedient but wrong." He went beyond them to affirm, as a matter of biotic right, the continuation of the biotic community rooted in the land regardless of the presence or absence of economic advantage to humans. His proposed standard for a land ethic was this: "A thing is right when it tends to preserve the integrity, stability, and beauty of the biotic community. It is wrong when it tends otherwise" ("The Land Ethic," 239). His ethic seems closer than he realized to the land ethic implied in Leviticus 25.

26. George S. Hendry, *Theology of Nature* (Philadelphia: Westminster, 1980), 117.

27. Donald Gowan, *Eschatology in the Old Testament* (Philadelphia: Fortress, 1986).

28. Ibid., 103–4.

29. Marvin Chaney has provided an illuminating account of the economic and agricultural practices alluded to by Amos and Isaiah in their denunciations of the oppression of the poor (the rural poor, the peasant farmers, in particular). See his article in *Economics and the Reformed Faith*, ed. Robert L. Stivers (Washington, D.C.: University Press of America, 1989).

30. See Claus Westermann, *Blessing* (Philadelphia: Fortress, 1978); and Patrick Miller, Jr., *Sin and Judgment in the Prophets* (Philadelphia: Fortress, 198) on the concepts of blessing and the act-consequence way of thinking.

31. So, Amos 9:14-15, a vision of rebuilt cities, fruitful fields, the people restored to their land and dwelling in security. Presumably they have learned the lesson that they must seek God in order to live, and that seeking God means doing justice (5:4, 14-15).

32. For God as Israel's Redeemer, Savior, and Creator, see Isa. 41:14; 43:1, 3, 14; 44:8; 45:17. On God as the Creator of the heavens and the earth, see Isa. 42:5; 44:24; 45:6-7, 18. Amos insists on this same identity, e.g., 5:8, 9:5.

33. Norman Perrin, *Jesus and the Language of the Kingdom* (Philadelphia: Fortress, 1976).

34. Two passages from First Isaiah, 61:1-2 and 58:8, have been brought together here. The reference to "a day of vengeance" in Isa. 61:2b has been omitted. Also, whereas the Isaiah text probably was talking about prisoners in real dungeons, the Lukan text probably was not. The Greek word behind release, *aphesis*, is prominent in Luke and most often means "forgiveness" (usually of sins), e.g., Luke 24:47. "Release" is probably a metaphor for forgiveness of

sins, although "captives" does include a wide range of victims whose affliction, while not the result of their personal sins, is rooted in the anticreational powers that are at work in the world according to this Gospel, e.g., oppression by "demons," diseases, poverty. For a judicious review of the exegetical problems related to this passage, see Patrick Miller's comments in *Interpretation* 29 (1975): 417–21.

John Howard Yoder has argued that in this passage Jesus indicated that the renewal of God's people he proclaimed would have "the form of the Jubilee" (*The Politics of Jesus* [Grand Rapids: Wm. B. Eerdmans, 1972], 38). There seem to be echoes of the Jubilee tradition in Isaiah 61, but Yoder tries to get more out of the allusions than the Lukan text will bear. Scholarly commentaries on Luke do not support his thesis. For a sympathetic but guarded treatment of the Jubilee thesis, see Marcus Borg, *Jesus: A New Vision* (San Francisco: Harper & Row, 1987), 185–86.

35. W. D. Davies, *The Gospel and the Land* (Berkeley and Los Angeles: University of California Press, 1974), 365.

36. Both the Hebrew and the Greek terms were used in wider and narrower senses in the biblical literature. The specific senses we are using for the texts in question seem to be required by the respective contexts in which they appear. The translations we have given are supported by the New Revised Standard Version.

37. On this consensus, see Marcus Borg, "A Renaissance in Jesus Studies," *Theology Today* 45 (October 1988): 280–92.

38. Sean Freyne, *Galilee, Jesus and the Gospels* (Philadelphia: Fortress, 1988), 245–46.

39. J. Christiaan Beker, *Paul the Apostle* (Philadelphia: Fortress, 1980), 181.

40. Ibid., 364.

41. Calvin's interpretation of Rom. 8:21 supports the line of argument developed above. He wrote on this verse: ". . . since all created things [are] in themselves blameless, both on earth and in the visible heaven . . . all creatures shall be renewed [along with the sons of God] in order to amplify it [i.e., the ultimate revelation of God's glory—my comment]." See John Calvin, *The Epistle of Paul the Apostle to the Romans* (Grand Rapids, Mich.: Wm. B. Eerdmans, 1948), 305. Note that Calvin suggests here that "sin," strictly speaking, is found only in humankind, and that the nonhuman parts of creation never rebelled against God although they were made to bear the sufferings that were consequent upon sin.

Augustine and Irenaeus held similar views of the world subsequent to the "fall." It is important to keep this distinction in mind and not speak glibly about the creation we live in as a "fallen world," as if it were so corrupted by evil as worthy of no better fate than abandonment and destruction. The goodness of the created world—that which God delights in, loves, and is bent on redeeming and bringing to ultimate salvation—persists in spite of the burdens sin-sick humanity has brought upon it.

42. Wisdom was not only a co-worker with God in creation (Prov. 8:27; Wisd. of Sol. 9:1f.) but also a mode of God's presence in the world instructing everyone receptive to her teaching in the ways of "righteousness" that make one wise.

43. The scene of the human and extrahuman creatures joined in praising God and the Savior of the world is just the sort of end one might imagine to portray the joy of creation finally released from its travail. The theme of the praise of God by the extrahuman creation, prominent in the Psalms, is an important one. It was omitted from this chapter because this chapter was concerned primarily with the inclusion of creation in redemption, not with the created world as such. The praise of God that constantly goes up from the extrahuman creation seems to be taken up by Revelation, maximized, and made an indispensable part of the situation of ultimate salvation. Here is another line of thought that supports my thesis. It is also a very important one for the claim that all created beings have an intrinsic right to exist and to flourish in their proper habitats since the praise of God they offer stems from their doing what is right for their being in relation to the being of others in the intricate ecological ordering built into the cosmos by the Creator.

44. Matthias Rissi, *The Future of the World* (Naperville, Ill.: Alec Allenson, Inc., 1966), 81.

45. Ibid., 81–82.

46. This is what Schubert Ogden tries to do in his *Faith and Freedom* (Nashville: Abingdon, 1979), 110–11. Ogden is correct in holding up what can be proven by the "biblical axioms" he defines, but he goes too far when he says that "the crucial reasons" against "homocentrism" and a dualism that separates history and nature "in no way depend on the exegesis of particular biblical passages" (p. 109). Theologies like his depend too much on the abstract universals of metaphysics and tend to avoid the arduous work of uncovering the more "determinate universals" in the biblical symbols and forms of discourse. (See Edward Farley, *Ecclesial Man* [Philadelphia: Fortress, 1970], 58–59 on the nature of "determinate universals" and their importance in theology.) Ogden's concern to avoid absolutizing individual biblical passages—a pitfall of what Farley calls "provincial hermeneutics"—is theologically sound. His definitions of Christian freedom as "freedom from" and "freedom for" all things and his argument that faithfulness to God requires loyalty to all to whom God is loyal are clear and convincing. Considerably less clear is his understanding of salvation and biblical eschatology. Metaphysical coherence is purchased at the price of insights only the particularities of the biblical symbols and forms of discourse make accessible.

47. John Calvin, *The Epistle of Paul the Apostle to the Romans* (Grand Rapids, Mich.: Wm. B. Eerdmans, 1948), 305.

48. Ibid.

49. Ibid.

CHAPTER 6: GLOBAL WARMING
William E. Gibson

1. Lester R. Brown et al., *State of the World 1989* (New York: W. W. Norton, 1989), 10.

2. "Policymakers' Summary of the Scientific Assessment of Climate Change," Report to the Intergovernmental Panel on Climate Change (IPCC) from Working Group 1, June 1990, 1.

3. Ibid., 2.

4. *Climate Alert* 3, no. 2 (October 1990): 4.

5. "Policymakers' Summary of the Potential Impacts of Climate Change," Report from Working Group 2 to IPCC, June 1990, 1.

6. Ibid., 12.

7. Ibid., 3.

8. Ibid.

9. Ibid., 4.

10. Ibid.

11. Ibid.

12. Ibid., 5.

13. *International Environment Reporter,* 7 November 1990, 455.

14. *International Environment Reporter,* 21 November 1990, 479, and *Science News,* 17 November 1990, 310.

15. For a fuller discussion of these norms see Presbyterian Eco-Justice Task Force, *Keeping and Healing the Creation* (Louisville: Committee on Social Witness Policy, 1989), chap. 5, and *Restoring Creation for Ecology and Justice,* A Report of the 202nd General Assembly (Louisville: Presbyterian Church [U.S.A.], 1990), 22–29.

16. Report from Working Group 2 to IPCC, 2.

17. Ibid., 4.

18. Ibid., 46.

19. "Policymakers' Summary of the Formulation of Response Strategies," Report Prepared for IPCC by Working Group 3, June 1990, iv.

20. Ibid.

21. Ibid., v.

22. Ibid.

23. Ibid., ii.

24. *Restoring Creation for Ecology and Justice,* 56–57.

25. World Convocation on Justice, Peace, and the Integrity of Creation, *Now Is the Time: Final Document and Other Texts* (Geneva: World Council of Churches, 1990), 29–32.

26. Report Prepared for IPCC by Working Group 3, iii.

27. *New York Times,* 7 November 1990, 16, and *International Environment Reporter,* 21 November 1990, 480.

28. *Global Initiative* 6 (23 August 1990): 2. This resource, no longer published, was a newsletter of the Global Environment Program, Center for Environmental Research, Cornell University, Ithaca, New York.

29. *New York Times*, 7 November 1990, 16.

30. *Global Initiative* 6 (23 August 1990): 2.

31. See World Commission on Environment and Development, *Our Common Future* (Oxford and New York: Oxford University Press, 1987). The theme of this important report is sustainable development. The critique that I make of the concept applies to its use by the World Commission.

32. This is already happening. See, e.g., Herman E. Daly and John B. Cobb, Jr., *For the Common Good: Redirecting the Economy Toward Community, the Environment and a Sustainable Future* (Boston: Beacon, 1989), and James Robertson, *Future Wealth: A New Economics for the 21st Century* (New York: The Bootstrap Press, 1990).

CHAPTER 7: WILDLIFE AND WILDLANDS
Holmes Rolston III

An earlier draft of this chapter appeared in *Church and Society* 80 (March–April 1990): 16–40.

1. *Wilderness Act of 1964*, sec. 2(c). Public Law 88–577. 78 Stat. 891.

2. William Cullen Bryant, "A Forest Hymn."

3. John Muir, *Our National Parks* (Boston: Houghton Mifflin, 1901), 331.

4. Linnie Marsh Wolfe, ed., *John of the Mountains: The Unpublished Journals of John Muir* (Boston: Houghton Mifflin, 1938), 313.

5. William Wordsworth, "Lines Composed a Few Miles above Tintern Abbey."

6. Aldo Leopold, "The Land Ethic," in *A Sand County Almanac* (New York: Oxford University Press, 1949, 1968), 224–25.

7. Ibid., viii–ix.

8. *Endangered Species Act of 1973*, Sec. 2(a)(3). Public Law 93–205. 87 Stat. 884.

9. *TVA v. Hill*, 437 U.S. 153 (1978) at 174, 184.

CHAPTER 8: CREATION AS KIN
George E. Tinker

This is a revision of an essay that was originally published as "Gerechtigkeit, Friede und die Integrität der Wienachtsbäume," *Ökumenische Rundschau* 38 (April 1989): 169–80.

1. World Convocation on Justice, Peace, and the Integrity of Creation, "Final Document: Entering into Covenant Solidarity for Justice, Peace, and the Integrity of Creation," in *Now Is the Time: Final Document and Other Texts* (Geneva: World Council of Churches, 1990).

2. So argues Robert A. Nisbet, *Social Change and History: Aspects of the Western Theory of Development* (Oxford: Oxford University Press, 1969). While Nisbet rightly sees temporality as important for understanding all Western culture, he finds this aspect to be wholly positive. I, of course, find it problematic.

3. Johannes Weis, *Die Predigt Jesu von Reich Gottes* (1892); Albert Schweitzer, *Das Abendmahl in Zusammenhang mit dem Leben Jesu and der Geschichte des Urchristentums* (1901) and *Von Reimarus zu Wrede. Eine Geschichte der Leben-Jesu-Forschung* (1906).

4. See Bruce Chilton, ed., *The Kingdom of God in the Teaching of Jesus* (Philadelphia: Fortress, 1984); and Wendell Willis, ed., *The Kingdom of God in 20th Century Interpretation* (Peabody, Mass.: Hendrickson, 1987).

5. Norman Perrin, *Rediscovering the Teaching of Jesus* (New York: Harper & Row, 1967), 55.

6. Werner Kelber, *The Kingdom in Mark: A New Place and a New Time* (Philadelphia: Fortress, 1974).

7. Norman Perrin, *Jesus and the Language of the Kingdom: Symbol and Metaphor in New Testament Interpretation* (Philadelphia: Fortress, 1976), 30. Also Philip Wheelwright, *Metaphor and Reality* (Bloomington: Indiana University Press, 1962), 92.

8. M. Eugene Boring, "The Kingdom of God in Mark," in Chilton, *The Kingdom of God in 20th Century Interpretation*, 140.

9. See Vine Deloria, Jr., *God Is Red* (New York: Dell, 1973); *The Metaphysics of Modern Existence* (New York: Harper & Row, 1979); George E. Tinker, "Native Americans and the Land: The End of Living and the Beginning of Survival," *Word and World* 6 (1986): 66–74; idem, "American Indians and the Arts of the Land," in *The Arts of the Land*, ed. John Charlot (Honolulu: University of Hawaii, forthcoming).

CHAPTER 9: ECONOMICS, ECO-JUSTICE, AND THE DOCTRINE OF GOD
Carol Johnston

1. John Calvin, *Institutes of the Christian Religion*, ed. John T. McNeill, trans. Ford Lewis Battles, Library of Christian Classics, vol. 20 (Philadelphia: Westminster, 1960), 70.

2. *Institutes*, I.xiv.22, p. 182.

3. *Institutes*, I.v.5, p. 56.

4. I refer to "voluntarism" meaning the philosophical tradition, not the social phenomenon of voluntary organizations.

5. See, e.g., Kenneth Arrow, *Collected Papers*, vol. 1, *Social Choice and Justice* (Cambridge, Mass.: Harvard University Press, 1983), 11, 97, 104.

6. For a much more complete discussion of these issues of value, see Jay B. McDaniel, *Of God and Pelicans* (Louisville: Westminster/John Knox, 1989); and Paul Custodio Bube, *Ethics in John Cobb's Process Theology* (Atlanta: Scholars Press, 1988).

7. See chapter 7 in this volume by Holmes Rolston, "Wildlife and Wild-lands," for a good example of the recognition of the intrinsic value of wildlife that comes from close observation and appreciation of animals in the wild.

8. Douglas John Hall, *Imaging God: Dominion As Stewardship* (Grand Rapids, Mich.: Wm. B. Eerdmans, 1986), chap. 3.

9. See John B. Cobb, Jr. and Herman E. Daly, *For the Common Good: Redirecting the Economy Toward Community, the Environment, and a Sustainable Future* (Boston: Beacon, 1989).

10. See M. Douglas Meeks, *God the Economist: The Doctrine of God and Political Economy* (Minneapolis: Fortress, 1989), 11–12.

11. Elizabeth Bettenhausen, "Abortion Catechisms: Creator and Cause," *Christianity and Crisis* 50 (19 February 1990): 31.

12. Meeks, *God the Economist*, 170.

13. Leonardo Boff, *Trinity and Society* (Maryknoll, N.Y.: Orbis, 1988) and Meeks, *God the Economist*.

14. Boff, *Trinity and Society*, 3.

15. Ibid., 22.

16. Ibid., 150.

CHAPTER 10: NATURE'S HISTORY AS OUR HISTORY
Philip Hefner

1. Jorie Graham, "The Geese," in *Hybrids of Plants and of Ghosts* (Princeton, N.J.: Princeton University Press, 1980), 38–39.

2. Ralph Wendell Burhoe, *Toward a Scientific Theology* (Belfast: Christian Journals Ltd., 1981), 151, 229.

3. Pierre Teilhard de Chardin, *Man's Place in Nature* (New York: Harper & Row, 1956), chaps. 4 and 5.

4. Philip Hefner, "Myth and Morality: The Love Command," *Zygon: Journal of Religion and Science* 26 (March 1991): 115–36, esp. 122–29. See also Hefner, "The Evolution of the Created Co-Creator," in *Cosmos as Creation*, ed. Ted Peters, (Nashville: Abingdon Press, 1989).

5. Mihaly Csikszentmihalyi, "Consciousness for the Twenty-First Century," *Zygon: Journal of Religion and Science* 26 (March 1991): 13–14.

6. Ibid., 17–18.

7. Hefner, "Myth and Morality," 127–29.

8. *Lutheran Book of Worship* (Minneapolis: Augsburg, 1978), 74.

9. Ibid., 74.

10. Ibid., 68.

11. Joseph Sittler, "Christology and Grace," *CSCM Yearbook 1977–78* (Valparaiso, Indiana: Center for the Study of Campus Ministry, Valparaiso University), 32–35. See also Sittler, *Essays on Nature and Grace* (Philadelphia: Fortress Press, 1972).

12. For sources of this tradition and complete bibliography, see Matthew Fox, *The Coming of the Cosmic Christ* (San Francisco: Harper & Row, 1988).

See also Sittler, "The Presence and Acts of the Triune God in Creation and History," in *The Gospel and Human Destiny,* ed. Vilmos Vajta (Minneapolis: Augsburg, 1971) as well as other essays in this volume.

13. Eduard Schweizer, "Pneuma, Pneumatikos," in *Theological Dictionary of the New Testament,* ed. G. Friedrich, trans. G. W. Bromily (Grand Rapids, Mich.: Wm. B. Eerdmans, 1968), VI, 389. Also, Marie Isaacs, *The Concept of Spirit* (London: Heythrop Monographs, 1976), esp. 10–18.

14. Isaacs, *The Concept of Spirit,* 17.

15. Ibid.

16. Csikszentmihalyi, "Consciousness for the Twenty-First Century," 22.

17. Gerard Manley Hopkins, "Ribblesdale," in *Poems and Prose of Gerard Manley Hopkins,* ed. W. H. Gardner (Baltimore, Md.: Penguin Books, 1953), 51–52.

ACKNOWLEDGMENTS

*T*his book grew out of a theology and ethics symposium on "Responses to the Environmental Challenges" held 1–3 March 1990 at the Lutheran School of Theology at Chicago. The idea for the symposium developed in late 1988 conversations with Karen Bloomquist, director of the Department of Studies, Commission for Church in Society, Evangelical Lutheran Church in America. I was then her counterpart as director of the Committee Social Witness Policy of the Presbyterian Church (U.S.A.).

Our idea was to conduct an ecumenical inquiry into the implications of the eco-justice crisis for the task of theology. The symposium core group was asked to concentrate on cutting-edge theological and ethical dimensions of Christian faith in response to "the combined oppression of people and nature, and the close links between environmental preservation and social justice." Assuming that participants would have a basic understanding of current ecology and justice problems, the symposium explored the implications of eco-injustice for the reconstruction of theology, as well as contributions to be made by theology in equipping Christians and others to engage faithfully in the work of "keeping and healing the creation."

The symposium was cosponsored by the Commission for Church in Society of the ELCA and the Committee on Social Witness Policy of the PCUSA. The symposium was a concluding step in the work of the Presbyterian Church's task force on eco-justice for which I was primary staff, and simultaneously it was the occasion to begin the Evangelical

Lutheran Church's new task force on the environment, health, and justice in a technological world.

To plan the symposium, Karen Bloomquist and I were joined by Robert Stivers, professor of religion and ethics at Pacific Lutheran University, Tacoma, Wash.; the Rev. Carol Johnston, then a visiting scholar with the Presbyterian Committee on Social Witness Policy, Louisville, Ky.; Heidi Hadsell, associate professor of social ethics at McCormick Seminary, Chicago; and Larry Jorgenson, who had just come to the ELCA staff from Alaska. I especially want to thank Carol Johnston and Karen Bloomquist, as well as Karen Clutz, conference registrar at LSTC, for the time and energy they invested in anticipating specific problems, recruiting respondents, and chasing details to achieve a successful symposium.

The event itself featured papers by seven Presbyterian and Lutheran theologians, following a keynote address by John B. Cobb, Jr., a United Methodist and pioneer in articulating ecologically sensitive theology and ethics. I am very grateful for the substantive contributions to this book of the presenters to the ecumenical symposium, and their openness to my editorial suggestions in preparation of this volume.

During the symposium sessions, each author briefly presented his or her paper, followed by a prepared respondent and open discussion involving interested conference registrants. Approximately eighty registrants—pastors, educators, lay leaders, and members of the Eco-Justice Working Group of the National Council of Churches—took part. One evening session featured a conversation with several scientists reflecting from the perspective of their profession on the theology and ethics papers. The event concluded with workshops led by NCC working group members on federal public policy advocacy, education in congregation and community, community organizing for environmental justice, corporate (investment) responsibility, and worship and liturgy for eco-justice.

In addition to those whose written reflections appear in this book, I would like to express appreciation to the following persons who offered prepared material and responses or led workshops at the symposium: Maria Paz Artasa, Karen Bloomquist, Carl Casebolt, J. Ronald Engel, Tom Gilbert, Laura Gross, David Hallman, Jaydee Hanson, Paul Lutz, Owen Owens, Winston Persaud, David Rhoads, William Somplatsky-Jarman, Robert Stivers, Carol Tabler, and Henry J. Young. Their contributions positively influenced the editor in completing this work. Ron Engel and Holmes Rolston, two scholars who have been keeping track of publications in eco-justice ethics and environmental philosophy, were additionally helpful in alerting me to some of the titles that are included in this volume's Select Bibliography.

Design of this collaborative work for maximum usability as a text in theology and ethics courses, as well as general reading, was shaped by J. Michael West, senior editor, Fortress Press. My completion of the book would not have been possible without his advice and attentiveness.

—Dieter T. Hessel

SELECT BIBLIOGRAPHY

Anderson, Bernard, ed. *Creation in the Old Testament*. Philadelphia: Fortress, 1984.

Attfield, Robin. *The Ethics of Environmental Concern*. New York: Columbia University Press, 1983.

Barbour, Ian G. *Technology, Environment, and Human Values*. New York: Praeger Publishers, 1980.

Bean, Michael J. *The Evolution of National Wildlife Law*. New York: Praeger Publishers, 1983.

Berry, Thomas. *The Dream of the Earth*. San Francisco: Sierra Club Books, 1988.

Berry, Wendell. *Home Economics*. Berkeley: North Point, 1987.

Bhagat, Shantilal. *Creation in Crisis: Responding to God's Covenant*. Elgin, Ill.: Brethren, 1990.

Birch, Charles and John Cobb. *The Liberation of Life: From Cell to the Community*. Cambridge: Cambridge University Press, 1981.

Bookchin, Murray. *Remaking Society: Pathways to a Green Future*. Boston: South End, 1990.

Borg, Marcus. *Jesus: A New Vision*. New York: Harper & Row, 1987.

This select bibliography lists current books that illumine eco-justice theology and ethics. A comprehensive, well-annotated bibliography of books and articles of theological-ethical reflection on issues of ecological integrity linked with aspects of social justice has been prepared by J. Ronald Engel and Peter W. Bakken. *Ecology, Justice and Christian Faith: A Guide to the Literature, 1960–1990*, forthcoming. (Information available from Prof. Engel at Meadville/Lombard Theological School, 5701 Woodlawn Ave., Chicago, IL 60637.)

Bowman, Douglas C. *Beyond the Modern Mind: Spiritual and Ethical Challenge of the Environmental Crisis*. New York: Pilgrim, 1990.

Brennan, Andrew. *Thinking about Nature: An Investigation of Nature, Value & Ecology*. Athens, Ga.: University of Georgia Press, 1988.

Brueggemann, Walter. *The Land: Place as Gift, Promise and Challenge in Biblical Faith*. Philadelphia: Fortress, 1977.

Burhoe, Ralph Wendell. *Toward a Scientific Theology*. Belfast: Christian Journals, Ltd., 1981.

Callicott, J. Baird. *In Defense of the Land Ethic*. Albany: State University of New York Press, 1989.

Caracas Report by the South Commission on Alternative Development. *Challenge to the South*. Oxford: Oxford University Press, 1990.

Chaney, Marvin. "Bitter Bounty: The Dynamics of Political Economy Critiqued by the Eighth-Century Prophets." In *Reformed Faith and Economics*, edited by Robert Stivers. Lanham, Md.: University Press of America, 1989.

Chilton, Bruce, ed. *The Kingdom of God in the Teaching of Jesus*. Philadelphia: Fortress, 1984.

Cobb, John B. and Herman E. Daly. *For the Common Good: Redirecting the Economy toward Community, the Environment, and a Sustainable Future*. Boston: Beacon, 1989.

Deloria, Vine, Jr. *God Is Red*. New York: Dell Books, 1973.

Dodson-Gray, Elizabeth. *Green Paradise Lost*. Wellesley, Mass.: Roundtable, 1981.

Engel, J. Ronald and Joan Gibb Engel. *Ethics of Environment and Development: Global Challenge, International Response*. London: Belhaven, 1990.

Evans, Bernard F. and Gregory D. Cusak, eds. *Theology of the Land*. Collegeville, Minn.: Liturgical, 1987.

Fox, Matthew. *Original Blessing: A Primer in Creation Spirituality*. Santa Fe: Bear and Company, 1983.

———. *The Coming of the Cosmic Christ*. San Francisco: Harper & Row, 1988.

Freudenberger, C. Dean. *Global Dust Bowl: Can We Stop the Destruction of the Land Before Its Too Late?* Minneapolis: Augsburg, 1990.

Garcia, Ismael. *Justice in Latin American Theology of Liberation*. Atlanta: John Knox, 1987.

Gibson, William E., consultant author for the Presbyterian Eco-Justice Task Force. *Keeping and Healing the Creation*. Louisville: Committee on Social Witness Policy, 1989.

Global Tomorrow Coalition. *The Global Ecology Handbook*. Boston: Beacon, 1990.

Gowan, Donald. *Genesis 1–11: From Eden to Babel*. Grand Rapids, Mich.: Wm. B. Eerdmans, 1988.

Granberg-Michaelson, Wesley, ed. *Tending the Garden: Essays on the Gospel and the Earth*. Grand Rapids, Mich.: Wm. B. Eerdmans, 1987.

Gustafson, James M. *Ethics from a Theocentric Perspective.* 2 vols. Chicago: University of Chicago Press, 1981, 1984.

Gutierrez, Gustavo. *The Power of the Poor in History.* Maryknoll, N.Y.: Orbis, 1984.

Hart, John. *The Spirit of the Earth: A Theology of the Land.* Mahwah, N.J.: Paulist, 1984.

Hall, Douglas John. *Imaging God: Dominion as Stewardship.* Grand Rapids, Mich.: Wm. B. Eerdmans, 1986.

———. *The Steward: A Biblical Symbol Come of Age.* Rev. ed. Grand Rapids, Mich.: Wm. B. Eerdmans, 1990.

Henderson, Hazel. *The Politics of the Solar Age: Alternatives to Economics.* Rev. ed. Indianapolis: Knowledge Systems, Inc., 1988.

Hessel, Dieter T., ed. *Energy Ethics: A Christian Response.* New York: Friendship Press, 1979.

———. *For Creation's Sake: Preaching, Ecology, and Justice.* Philadelphia: Westminster/Geneva, 1985.

Jonas, Hans. *The Imperative of Responsibility: In Search of an Ethics for the Technological Age.* Chicago: University of Chicago Press, 1984.

Joranson, Philip N. and Ken Butigan, eds. *Cry of the Environment: Rebuilding the Christian Creation Tradition.* Santa Fe: Bear and Co., 1984.

Kim, Yong Bock. "The Sustainable Society: An Asian Perspective." *Ecumenical Review* 31 (April 1979).

Koyama, Kosuke. *Mount Fuji and Mount Sinai: A Critique of Idols.* Maryknoll, N.Y.: Orbis, 1985.

Linzey, Andrew. *Christianity and the Rights of Animals.* New York: Crossroad, 1987.

McDaniel, Jay B. *Of God and Pelicans.* Louisville: Westminster/John Knox, 1989.

McFague, Sallie. *Models of God: Theology for an Ecological, Nuclear Age.* Philadelphia: Fortress, 1987.

McKibben, Bill. *The End of Nature.* New York: Random House, 1989.

Meeker-Lowry, Susan. *Economics as if the Earth Really Mattered.* Philadelphia: New Society Publishers, 1988.

Moltmann, Jürgen. *God in Creation: A New Theology of Creation and the Spirit of God.* Translated by Margaret Kohl. San Francisco: Harper & Row, 1985.

Nash, James A. *Loving Nature: Ecological Integrity and Christian Responsibility.* Nashville: Abingdon, 1991.

Nash, Roderick Frazier. *The Rights of Nature: A History of Environmental Ethics.* Madison: University of Wisconsin Press, 1989.

Peck, Jane Cary and Jeanne Gallo. "JPIC: A Critique from a Feminist Perspective." *The Ecumenical Review* 41, no. 4 (Oct. 1989).

Peters, Ted, ed. *Cosmos as Creation.* Nashville: Abingdon, 1989.

Plant, Judith, ed. *Healing the Wounds: The Promise of Eco-Feminism.* Philadelphia: New Society Publishers, 1989.

Plaskow, Judith and Carol P. Christ, eds. *Weaving the Visions: New Patterns in Feminist Spirituality.* San Francisco: Harper & Row, 1989.

Regan, Tom. *The Struggle for Animal Rights.* Clarks Summit, Pa.: International Society for Animal Rights, Inc., 1987.

Rifkin, Jeremy. *Biosphere Politics: A New Consciousness for a New Century.* New York: Crown Publishers, Inc., 1991.

Robb, Carol S. and Carl J. Casebolt, eds. *Covenant for a New Creation: Ethics, Religion, and Public Policy.* Maryknoll, N.Y.: Orbis, 1991.

Robertson, James. *Future Wealth: A New Economics for the 21st Century.* New York: Bootstrap Press, 1990.

Rolston, Holmes, III. *Environmental Ethics: Duties to and Values in the Natural World.* Philadelphia: Temple University Press, 1988.

———. *Philosophy Gone Wild.* Buffalo, N.Y.: Prometheus, 1986.

Ruether, Rosemary Radford. *To Change the World: Christology and Cultural Criticism.* New York: Crossroad, 1981.

Santmire, H. Paul. *The Travail of Nature: The Ambiguous Ecological Promise of Christian Theology.* Philadelphia: Fortress, 1985.

Scarce, Rik. *Eco-Warriors: Understanding the Radical Environmental Movement.* Chicago: Noble, 1990.

Schmink, Marianne and Charles Wood, eds. *Frontier Expansion in the Amazon.* Gainesville, Fla.: University of Florida Press, 1984.

Shinn, Roger. "Eco-Justice Themes in Christian Ethics Since the 1960's." In *For Creation's Sake,* edited by Dieter Hessel (listed above).

Sittler, Joseph. *Essays on Nature and Grace.* Philadelphia: Fortress, 1972.

Steck, Odil Hannes. *World and Environment.* Biblical Encounter Series. Nashville: Abingdon, 1978.

Stivers, Robert L. *Hunger, Technology & Limits to Growth: Christian Responsibility for Three Ethical Issues.* Minneapolis: Augsburg, 1984.

Taylor, Paul W. *Respect for Nature.* Princeton: Princeton University Press, 1986.

Trainer, F. E. *Abandon Affluence!* London: Zed Books, Ltd., 1985.

Walker, Alice. *The Color Purple.* New York: Pocket Books, 1982.

Wenz, Peter S. *Environmental Justice.* Albany: State University of New York Press, 1988.

Wilkinson, Loren, ed. *Earthkeeping: Christian Stewardship of Natural Resources.* Grand Rapids, Mich.: Wm. B. Eerdmans, 1980.

Winter, Gibson. *Liberating Creation: Foundations of Religious Social Ethics.* New York: Crossroad, 1981.

World Commission on Environment and Development. *Our Common Future.* Oxford: Oxford University Press, 1987.

World Convocation on Justice, Peace, and the Integrity of Creation. *Now Is the Time: Final Document and Other Texts.* Geneva: World Council of Churches, 1990.